Volume 23 Number 1

Michigan Journal
of
Community Service Learning

OCSL PRESS
The University of Michigan

Editor
Jeffrey Howard
DePaul University

Associate Editors

Dan Butin
Merrimack College

Patti Clayton
PHC Ventures

Sherril Gelmon
Portland State University

Susan Harris
University of South California

Barbara Holland
Independent Consultant

Arthur Keene
University of Massachusetts-Amherst

KerryAnn O'Meara
University of Maryland-College Park

Roger Reeb
University of Dayton

John Saltmarsh
University of Massachusetts-Boston

Randy Stoecker
University of Wisconsin

Kelly A. Ward
Washington State University

Book Review Editor
David Cooper
Michigan State University

Editorial Board

William R. Alexander	*University of Michigan*	Barbara A. Israel	*University of Michigan*
Richard Battistoni	*Providence College*	Novella Keith	*Temple University*
Robert Bringle	*Appalachian State University*	C. David Lisman	*University of Denver*
Tony Chambers	*University of Toronto*	Wilbert J. McKeachie	*University of Michigan*
Barry N. Checkoway	*University of Michigan*	Allen Menlo	*University of Michigan*
David D. Cooper	*Michigan State University*	Jerry M. Miller	*University of Michigan*
Deborah DeZure	*Michigan State University*	Barbara Moely	*Tulane University*
Thomas Erlich	*Stanford University*	David Moore	*New York University*
Sandra Enos	*Bryant University*	Keith Morton	*Providence College*
Janet Eyler	*Vanderbilt University*	KerryAnn O'Meara	*University of Maryland-College Park*
Helen Fox	*University of Michigan*		
Andrew Furco	*University of Minnesota*	Kenneth Reardon	*University of Memphis*
Dwight Giles	*University of Massachusetts-Boston*	Susan Root	*National Youth Leadership Council*
Michael D. Gordon	*University of Michigan*	David Schoem	*University of Michigan*
David Green	*Colorado State University*	Timothy K. Stanton	*Stanford University*
Lorraine Gutiérrez	*University of Michigan*	Sharon E. Sutton	*University of Washington*
Ira Harkavy	*University of Pennsylvania*	Kelly A. Ward	*Washington State University*
Gary Hesser	*Augsburg College*	Edward Zlotkowski	*Bentley University*

MICHIGAN JOURNAL OF COMMUNITY SERVICE LEARNING

VOLUME 23 NUMBER 1   FALL 2016

RESEARCH AND THEORY

Exploring Faculty Perspectives on Community Engaged Scholarship: The Case for Q Methodology 5
    Emily Morrison and **Wendy Wagner**

Cultivating Practitioners of Democratic Civic Engagement 15
    Novella Zett Keith

The Counter-Normative Effects of Service-Learning: Fostering Attitudes toward
Social Equality through Contact and Autonomy 37
    Margaret A. Brown, Jared D. Wymer, and **Cierra S. Cooper**

The *Social Justice Turn*: Cultivating "Critical Hope" in an Age of Despair 45
    Kari M. Grain and **Darren E. Lund**

Pathways to Adult Civic Engagement: Benefits of Reflection and Dialogue
across Difference in Higher Education Service-Learning Programs 60
    Dan Richard, Cheryl Keen, Julie A. Hatcher, and **Heather A. Pease**

SPECIAL SECTION: THE SLCE FUTURE DIRECTIONS PROJECT
Guest Co-Editors: **Patti H. Clayton, Sarah E. Stanlick, Edward Zlotkowski,** and **Lori E. Kniffin**

SLCE Future Directions Project: Sustaining a Dialogue, Challenging the Movement 75
    Sarah Stanlick and **Edward Zlotkowski**

Beyond Superheroes and Sidekicks: Empowerment, Efficacy, and Education
in Community Partnerships 80
    Sarah Stanlick and **Marla Sell**

Learning From and With Community Organizations to Navigate the Tensions
of Democratic Engagement 85
    Brandon Whitney, Stacey Muse, Barbara Harrison, Kathleen E. Edwards, and **Patti Clayton**

Winding Pathways to Engagement: Creating a Front Door 91
    Lori E. Kniffin, Timothy J. Shaffer, and **Mary H. Tolar**

Values-Engaged Assessment: Reimagining Assessment through the
Lens of Democratic Engagement 96
    Joe Bandy, Anna Bartel, Patti H. Clayton, Sylvia Gale, Heather Mack, Julia Metzker,
    Georgia Nigro, Mary Price, and **Sarah Stanlick**

Resisting the Siren Song: Charting a Course for Justice 102
    Joe Blosser

Teach the Partnership: Critical University Studies and the Future of Service-Learning 107
    David J. Fine

Responses to the Call for a National Strategic Plan 111
    Lori E. Kniffin and **Jeffrey Howard**

BOOK REVIEW ESSAYS

Publicly Engaged Scholars: Next-Generation Engagement and the Future of Higher Education 117
Margaret A. Post, Elaine Ward, Nicholas V. Longo, and John Saltmarsh (Eds.)
    Reviewed by Dick Cone and **Susan C. Harris**

Service-Learning and Social Entrepreneurship: A Pedagogy of Social Change 123
Sandra Enos
    Reviewed by Lane Graves Perry, III

Reviewers for Volume 23 128

Call for Papers 129

Paper Guidelines 130

Exploring Faculty Perspectives on Community Engaged Scholarship: The Case for Q Methodology

Emily Morrison and Wendy Wagner
The George Washington University

Over the past 25 years, community engaged scholarship has grown in popularity, practice, and scholarship. A review of the literature suggests that a wide range of personal, professional, institutional, and communal factors (Demb & Wade, 2012) interact in ways that shape faculty members' perspectives on, conceptualizations of, and means of conducting community engaged work. To make sense of the potential number of factor combinations and inform more customized support for community engaged faculty, the authors discuss the merits and utility of faculty typologies. Q Methodology offers a way to create a typology that is capable of not only managing the complexity of faculty engagement, but also providing rich descriptions of varied points of view that do not oversimplify the phenomenon. The techniques and foundational assumptions of Q Methodology are described, making the case for Q as a good fit for developing a typology of community engaged faculty that more fully reflects multiple points of view.

For America's colleges and universities to remain vital[,] a new vision of scholarship is required. What we are faced with, today, is the need to clarify campus missions and relate the work of the academy more directly to the realities of contemporary life. We need especially to ask how institutional diversity can be strengthened and how the rich array of faculty talent in our college and universities might be more effectively used and continuously renewed. We proceed with the conviction that if the nation's higher learning institutions are to meet today's urgent academic and social mandates, their missions must be carefully redefined and the meaning of scholarship creatively reconsidered. (Boyer, 1990, p. 13)

Recognizing the criticism that higher education was growing more disconnected from and irrelevant to society by no longer addressing the heart of the nation's work (Delve, Mintz, & Stewart, 1990; Newman, 1985), Boyer (1990) issued a clarion call to institutions of higher education to remember their missions and to reconsider how scholarship is conceptualized. Colleges and universities around the country began heeding this call to broaden their notions of scholarship and to take seriously their responsibility to serve their wider communities (Fitzgerald, Bruns, Sonka, Furco, & Swanson, 2016; Kezar, Chambers, & Burkhardt, 2005). These efforts entailed critically reflecting on the role of community involvement in their institutions, especially with regard to the nature of faculty work (Bringle, Hatcher, & Holland, 2007; Saltmarsh, 2011; Stanton, 2008; Zlotkowski, 2011), and sparked the growth of the scholarship of engagement (SOE) movement.

Since Boyer's landmark work, the scholarship *on* the scholarship of engagement has blossomed. Research on faculty engagement has focused on defining engagement (Boyer, 1990, 1996; Giles, 2008; O'Meara, 2002), examining dimensions of faculty life (Demb & Wade, 2012; O'Meara, 2008; Wade & Demb, 2009), exploring the impact of engagement on faculty (Rice, 2002; Rice, Sorcinelli, & Austin, 2000) and identifying activities that comprise faculty engagement (Glass, Doberneck, & Schweitzer, 2011; O'Meara, Sandmann, Saltmarsh, & Giles, 2010). Due to the range of engagement activities in which faculty and staff members participate, scholars have faced the challenge of determining which activities to emphasize (O'Meara et al., 2010), and how to ensure quality work (Glassick, Huber, & Maeroff, 1997) is made visible (Driscoll & Lynton, 1999). Expanding the scope of research from faculty to institutions, scholars have also examined the institutional context (Demb & Wade, 2012; Holland, 1997; O'Meara, 2005; Stanton, 2008; Wade & Demb, 2009), identified ways to integrate institutional research and learning within the broader context of their communities (Boyte & Hollander, 1996; Buzinski et al., 2013), and established key components to advance and institutionalize engagement efforts (Fitzgerald et al., 2016; Furco, 2010; Janke, Medlin, & Holland, 2015). Central to these research trajectories is the conscious effort to bring greater clarity and rigor to community engagement efforts (Barker, 2004; Glassick et al., 1997).

Given the range of research emerging from *Scholarship Reconsidered* (Boyer, 1990), it is not surprising that the SOE movement has evolved into a "multifaceted field of responses" (Sandmann, 2008, p. 91) that includes a range of community engaged practices such as service-learning, community-based participatory research, outreach, participatory action research, and public scholarship (Bringle, Games, & Malloy, 1999; Burawoy, 2005; Colbeck & Wharton-Michael, 2006; Fear & Sandmann, 1995; Glass et al., 2011; O'Meara & Rice, 2005; Sandmann, 2008; Strand, Marullo, Cutforth, Stoecker, & Donohue, 2003), as well as varying conceptualizations, terminology, and definitions (Barker, 2004; Bringle et al., 2007; Janke & Colbeck, 2008; O'Meara & Niehaus, 2009; Pearl, 2015; Sandmann, 2008; Wade & Demb, 2009). The study and practice of Community Engaged Scholarship (CES) is complicated further by different individual dimensions, academic disciplines, institutional types, and communal dimensions (Buzinski et al., 2013; Colbeck & Wharton-Michael, 2006; Demb & Wade, 2012; Holland, 1997; Townson, 2009; Wade & Demb, 2009).

Writ large, the wide-range of practices, conceptualizations, definitions, and influencing factors affecting CES among faculty warrant closer attention, especially as faculty and administrators strive to make informed decisions about how to invest time, talent, and resources in order to cultivate and sustain meaningful CES that is central to the academy (Fitzgerald et al., 2016). Hence, given what is known and not known about faculty involvement in CES, how can we make sense of it and articulate the complexity of CES among faculty without being unnecessarily reductionistic?

The creation and use of empirically-based classifications, such as typologies, are one way to balance complexity and simplicity by generating heuristics that offer parameters of understanding that then invite closer examination (Bailey, 1994). Within the CES literature, several classification systems exist (Barker, 2004; Pearl, 2015). Thus, the purpose of this article is twofold: (a) to review a conceptual framework and typologies of community engaged faculty with a critical eye toward reflecting on how the framework and typologies emerged and affect subsequent understanding, and (b) to describe Q Methodology – that offers a new way to extend and potentially challenge current understandings of community engaged faculty. To this end, we present the findings from a purposeful literature review that addresses a conceptual framework, typologies, and limitations to understanding CES among faculty; detail how Q Methodology may help refine that understanding; and, explore potential contributions from Q Methodology to understanding faculty engagement.

Conceptual Framework, Typologies, and Emerging Questions about Faculty CES

To thrive, 21st century higher education needs to ensure that community engagement is at the heart of its work (Fitzgerald et al., 2016), which means "anchor[ing] engagement firmly on the desk of our institutions and faculties as community-engaged scholarship" (Sandmann, 2009, p. 8). Given the critical role faculty play in this process, the literature on faculty engagement is extensive and examines a broad range of topics including, but not limited to, faculty motivations, supports and hindrances to engagement, disciplinary perspectives, and institutional context. Rather than discuss each of these streams in the literature, our focus is on reviewing the major conceptual framework and key typologies that have emerged from that literature and build on these collective scholarly efforts.

Conceptual Framework of Faculty Engagement

Several scholars have developed conceptual frameworks over the years to make sense of the myriad approaches, conceptualizations, and understandings of factors that affect faculty's scholarly engagement in and with the community. To synthesize the literature, Wade and Demb (2009) developed a comprehensive framework of faculty engagement based on theoretical and empirical evidence. Drawing heavily on Holland's (1997, 2005) matrix of ten organizational factors, the Kellogg Commission's (1999) seven-part test for engaged campuses, and Colbeck and Wharton-Michael's (2006) model of individual and organizational characteristics that influence faculty members' motivation and engagement in public scholarship, Wade and Demb proposed the "Faculty Engagement Model (FEM)," explicating the dimensions and factors at play and the relationship among those factors.

Initially, faculty engagement consisted of an interaction and degree of balance between personal, professional, and institutional dimensions (Wade & Demb, 2009). Personal dimensions include race/ethnicity, gender, personal values, motivation, epistemology, and previous experience. Professional dimensions include tenure status, faculty rank, length of time in academe, and professional orientation. Institutional dimensions include mission and priorities, institutional type, leadership, budget, prestige, engagement structure, institutional policies, faculty involvement, and community involvement.

(See Wade & Demb, 2009, for a full description of and evidence for each factor.) In 2012, Demb and Wade revised the framework, adding a communal dimension. The communal dimension (factors include socialization, department support, discipline support, and professional community support) can either affect faculty engagement directly or serve as a mediating effect of the institutional dimension on faculty engagement (see Figure 1).

Figure 1
Factors Influencing Faculty Engagement

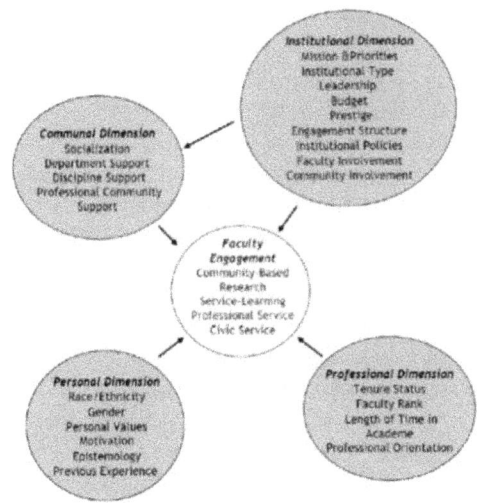

Note. "Revised Model Showing the Factors Influencing Faculty Engagement" from Demb and Wade (2012).

From "Reality Check: Faculty Involvement in Outreach and Engagement," by A. Demb and A. Wade, 2012, *The Journal of Higher Education*, 83(3), p. 361. Copyright 2012 by Ohio State University. Reprinted with permission.

Taken together, the four dimensions and 24 factors offer numerous combinations of factors influencing faculty engagement. While the original and revised FEM appear to have discrete factors and dimensions, the research to develop the model

> revealed a spectrum of definitions whose complexity could undermine further research until those definitions are made specific and explicit. The model further demonstrates the need for a far more multi-dimensional, dynamic and holistic description of the factors that affect faculty proclivities to value, or become active with, engagement-related activities. (Wade & Demb, 2009, p. 14)

Typologies of Faculty Engagement

To reduce complexity such as that encountered in FEM, classifying many cases into a few meaningful groups offers social scientists one of the most useful descriptive tools available for analysis, research, and theory-building (Bailey, 1994).

> Although we cannot focus upon all persons and all of their characteristics at once, by classifying persons according to salient underlying dimensions such as race, social class ... political party, religion, and so forth, we can simplify our complex reality sufficiently to allow us to analyze it. (Bailey, p. 12)

Classifications shed light on the similarities and differences within and across groups and surfaces the dimensions on which they are based. Consideration of the relationships among types, comparisons, and contrasts facilitates better understanding of the cases in each class and the issues that are most relevant to them. Typologies are one form of classification, which represent a conceptual framework (Bailey). Unlike other forms of classification, typologies do not create criteria for classifying a construct into a type, but rather provide a rich description of the attributes that distinguish groups from each other (Doty & Glick, 1994).

The CES literature includes several examples of the use of typologies for deepening understanding of engaged faculty. One such example is Pearl's (2015) typology, which used latent class analysis on a selection of items from the 2010 HERI Faculty Survey to identify five classes of faculty which he described as community engaged scholars, aspirational engagers, passive engagers, generational engagers, and traditional scholars. Little information is provided to explain how the labels and brief descriptions of each type were made; however, the survey items collected information about how faculty engage in the community and their beliefs about the role of colleges in their local communities and in shaping civic beliefs of their students.

Another classification structure is offered by Barker (2004), who reviewed the SOE academic literature, publications of civic engagement centers and higher education institutions, and interviewed SOE practitioners. From this inquiry, Barker created a classification system that describes five practices of engaged scholarship: public scholarship, participatory research, community partnership, public information networks, and civic literacy scholarship. Although the five practices appear distinct, they are not mutually exclusive. "Indeed, almost all of these practices overlap with one another, and indeed they are often practiced simultaneously by the same scholars and institutions" (p. 133).

Emerging Questions About Faculty Engagement

Since we know that each of the 24 factors and four dimensions presented in FEM (Demb & Wade, 2012) can affect faculty engagement, it is difficult to discern which factors have the most salience for individual scholars, the nature of the relationships between and among the factors and dimensions, and whether the more salient factors emerge in any sort of pattern within and across the dimensions. The possible number of factor combinations makes it difficult for scholars and practitioners to comprehend at once, let alone make informed, efficient decisions about the best way to allocate resources and support a diverse faculty. So, how can the complexity of faculty engagement be meaningfully classified?

Classifications such as those by Pearl (2015) and Barker (2004) offer ways to organize and simplify the complexity of approaches by providing distinct groups, noting their similarities and differences which allows for the generation of heuristics. While heuristics can expedite decision-making for scholars and practitioners, they may be misguided if the classifications are based on the researcher's conceptualization of the most salient issues or if they are unintentionally influenced by the researcher's (un)conscious assumptions (Morrison, 2015). In the case of Barker, SOE was conceptualized as forms of practice, while Pearl's typology was based on the researcher's selection of the salient issues from data already collected by the HERI 2010 Faculty Survey. Therefore, these classifications may be more representative of the researcher's view of community engaged faculty than the faculty's own views of CES.

Additionally, classifications are often developed based on demographic or other researcher-chosen variables (e.g., discipline, rank, time in academia). In some instances these variables may provide meaningful insight into a particular phenomenon; yet, there are other times when using these variables from the outset may limit, if not inadvertently minimize, subtle but important variations in the data. Rather than assume similarity within a particular variable (e.g., race, age, discipline) when examining a complex phenomenon, it is important to find ways to examine within groups as well as across groups. For example, a physicist, whose discipline is generally classified as a "pure hard" science (Becher, 1987), may have more in common with a social worker, whose discipline is generally classified as a "soft applied" science (Becher, 1987), than one might assume. Thus, it is important to avoid classifying responses and data prematurely. Research shows that there are some disciplinary differences; however, it may be presumptive to claim that a particular classification is the only one.

While there are distinct approaches, conceptualizations, and language regarding engagement, these specialized insights are not always apparent in practice. Despite research to inform the type of support campuses provide community engaged faculty, given limited staff time and resources, many campuses continue to have a "one size fits all" approach (Buzinski et al., 2013; Glass et al., 2011). However, as Pearl (2015) notes, having a typology may allow for customization that is simultaneously more individualized and more systemic.

The question then remains, if the goal is to more deeply understand how community engaged faculty make meaning of their work, how would the faculty themselves select the salient issues and frame them? What different typology might emerge if the classes were based on patterns of similarity and difference in the scholars' overall perspectives on the scholarship of engagement rather than on their reaction to the issues the researcher poses as salient? To achieve that goal, researchers need a way to classify faculty based on the study participants' own internal perceptions and their overall perspective rather than their responses to the researcher's specifically defined and operationalized variables.

Q Methodology

Q Methodology (Q) is a research approach that classifies research study participants into groups based on their shared overall viewpoints on a particular subject. Q was developed by psychologist William Stephenson in the early 1930s (Brown, 1980), and is described as *"qualiquantological"* (Watts & Stenner, 2005, p. 69) because it integrates qualitative and quantitative analyses (McKeown & Thomas, 1988), allowing it to address some of the weaknesses of each respective methodology (Peterson, Owens, & Martorana, 1999). As comfort with social constructivist and other non-positivist epistemologies has increased, interest in Q increased, and examples of Q studies are available across a wide variety of disciplines in the social sciences (Brown, 1986, 2006; Jay, 1969; McKeown & Thomas; Watts & Stenner).

Both Q and the more traditional approaches to classification reduce the complexity of a construct by identifying groups that share common meaning. Traditional classification methods classify variables into groups, reflecting some shared commonalities such as a latent variable. Q analysis classifies the study participants into groups, reflecting their shared perspectives or a common way of thinking about the construct under study (Brown, 1980; McKeown & Thomas, 1988).

Foundational Assumptions

Q Methodology is grounded in several important assumptions that influence the study design and interpretation of results. Each serves as an indicator of the usefulness of Q for understanding the complexity that exists in the variety of ways that community engaged faculty make meaning of their work. The first assumption of Q is the goal of *operant subjectivity*. In typical quantitative research, the researcher's aim is to be objective, so research instruments are designed to operationalize the variables so that each item will be interpreted by all participants in the same way (Brown, 1980). In Q, the goal is to capture the participants' subjective perspectives and their unique points of view instead of their responses to an objective definition that has been carefully operationalized in order to have one narrow, universal meaning. Rather than using objective measures that are based on operationalized variables, the researcher uses items interpreted by participants in their own way. The researcher does not qualitatively interpret the meaning of the items until after the data is collected. While it is frequently the case that the meaning of an item on the instrument is interpreted differently by participants who later fall into different classification groups, researchers are able to interpret the findings by examining how participants responded to other items and identifying patterns within the responses.

Q Methodology is a good fit for a construct like the SOE, which is difficult to define or for which the definition/operationalization of the construct is a subject of debate (Barker, 2004; Bringle et al., 2007; Sandmann, 2008). The path toward a shared definition for the field would be informed by the use of a research method that can collect participants' perspectives on their SOE without imposing a researcher's operationalized definition of it.

The second assumption of Q is that participants' perspectives are based on their own *internal frames of reference* (Brown, 1986, 1997). It is the study participants, not the researcher, who decide which items are meaningful, which issues are most significant, and which issues do not matter when conceptualizing the topic of study from their respective points of view, given their context (Watts & Stenner, 2005). The data reflects participants' own internal frameworks for understanding the construct, not their reaction to the researcher's framework. This aspect of Q makes it a particularly useful research method at this point in the field's understanding of SOE. The current attempts to address faculty needs through administrative supports or policies are based on external, observable categories such as academic discipline, institution type, and contract type (tenure track, term, adjunct, etc.). Some research, such as the Pearl (2015) or Barker (2004) studies described earlier, have resulted in more sophisticated typologies of faculty; however, they are also based on externally observed variables rather than emerging from the internal frameworks of the faculty themselves. It is the understanding of these internal perspectives – how faculty define and make meaning of CES for themselves – that is truly needed at this time in order to make sense of the complex list of factors influencing how faculty engage, their reasons for doing it, and how institutions can support them.

Brown (2006) described Q Methodology as a particularly useful approach to gather perspectives from marginalized populations, as the process allows the subjects to construct meaning from their own self-reference rather than simply responding to the meaning held by the majority or dominant group. On some campuses, community engaged faculty find that their perspectives on scholarly work and the aims of higher education may differ from those reinforced by the established processes of promotion and reward structures (Boyer, 1990; O'Meara, 2002; O'Meara, Sandmann, Saltmarsh, & Giles, 2010). Q Methodology may also result in giving voice to the perspectives of faculty who may otherwise not feel comfortable pushing against established frameworks that define scholarly productivity solely as research journal publications. This is a useful method, then, for gathering and including their points of view.

The third assumption is that the researcher's goal is to examine *a holistic viewpoint*. Rather than breaking a construct into component parts and designing the study with controls to hold other conditions or influences constant, Q Methodology is able to compare each participant's overall viewpoint to that of the other participants. The data analysis process does not examine the responses to any single item; it examines correlations in the overarching patterns that emerge (Brown, 1980). It is because of this aspect that Q Methodology studies tend to have high reliability. While participants' responses to specific items might shift from test one to test two, the pattern representing their overarching perspective does not typically change (Brown, 1980; D'Agostino, 1984; Thomas & Baas, 1993).

Data Collection to Maintain Subjective Self-reference

The foundational assumptions are met through each aspect of study design. Data collection involves three steps (McKeown & Thomas, 1988): (a) develop a set of statements that represent a diversity of perspectives on the subject being studied (Q Set); (b) identify participants whose points of view are representative of the contexts relevant to the study (Person Set); and (c) gather the data through a card-sort process in which the research participants sort the statements in the Q Set in a way that represents their overall perspective (Q Sort).

The Q Set. The Q Set is a series of statements that represent as wide a variety of perspectives on the topic under investigation as possible. The development of these statements is analogous to a process of population sampling. The "population" being the innumerable statements that could potentially relate to the topic of study, and "sampling" representing the selection of items from the population of potential statements. The primary objective of item selection is to provide enough breadth and variety of items in the sample that participants can convey their unique point of view without being constrained by the researcher's perspective or framework (Brown, 1980, 1986; McKeown & Thomas, 1988). For example, statements in the Q Set for the topic of faculty engagement might include, "My involvement in the community has influenced the direction of my research," "My teaching is more current and relevant because I am engaged in the community," or "Our students should work directly with community members, addressing their immediate needs."

The Person Set. The study participants who will be classified into groups are referred to as the Person Set. Participant selection in Q is analogous to the way traditional quantitative research selects variables to test. The Person Set is carefully selected to represent the perspectives the researcher is seeking to understand. The Person Set is neither a random sample nor a large number of participants. In Q, the items represent the sample and the subjects represent the measure, so it is typical to have more items than participants (Brown, 1980). The appropriate number of participants to include in the Person Set is a debated issue. Several Q Methodology researchers argue that too many participants can be problematic as complexity and subtle nuances can be missed (Brown, 1980; Watts & Stenner, 2005). Most Q Methodology researchers agree that the clearest indicator of the validity of the participant groups is having at least 5–6 participants in each resulting factor (Brown, 1980).

The Q Sort. To collect the data in Q Methodology, participants in the Person Set are presented a set of index cards with one statement from the Q Set printed on each card. The participants' task is to sort the statements into stacks along a continuum to represent their degree of agreement with each statement relative to the other statements. Each stack has a limited number of cards that are allowed, with more cards allowed in the stacks at the center of the continuum, creating a normal or bell-shaped curve. Each card has a unique, randomly assigned number used to record the finished sort and the results are recorded as illustrated in Figure 2. In this example, the study participant has indicated the statement on card #15 is the one for which she feels the strongest agreement. She agrees with statements on cards #4 and #17, but these statements are not as important as #15. The data analysis process, typically using Principle Components Analysis, can then identify

Figure 2
Sample Q Sort

Strongly Disagree	----		Neutral		----	Strongly Agree	
18	12	3	1	9	11	4	15
	16	7	10	6	2	17	
		15	5	8	14		
			13	19			

groupings of people based on the patterns in the Q Sorts that indicate the comparable ways the participants made sense of the Q Set items (Watts & Stenner, 2005).

Through the sorting process, participants are not assigning a discrete value to each statement in the Q Set; rather, they are assigning a level of agreement *in relation to* the other items. Participants sort the Q Set such that each item is ranked within the context of the other items (i.e., I agree with this item more than these items and less than those items). It is this feature that facilitates the data analysis process to correlate overall patterns and holistic perspectives rather than rely on responses to any one specific item.

The sorting process also facilitates an important dynamic described by Brown (1980) as "psychological significance" (p. 198). Participants not only indicate their agreement or disagreement, but also which items are most salient to forming their point of view. In theory, it is possible that a participant might agree with every statement in the Q Set, but the Q Sort process will still identify which issues play a larger role in representing the participant's overall point of view.

The sorting process addresses the assumption of internal self-reference by avoiding the insertion of the researcher's frames of reference as conventional standardized scales would. Through the sort, the participant (rather than the researcher) does the work of item reduction, with items sorted toward the middle being less important in the construction of participant's perspective. "It is one thing to 'put' something to a subject, as in the form of scale items; it is quite another to allow the subject to speak for himself" (Brown, pp. 44–45).

Limitations of Q Methodology

There are several aspects of Q that limit its usefulness for some research goals. Q studies, with small Person Sets compared to the number of Q Set statements, bear more resemblance to qualitative research when it comes to issues like generalization and prediction (Krathwohl, 2004). For example, if a Q study of community engaged faculty grouped the study participants into five types, it would be appropriate to generalize that those five points of view do exist in the general population, and that the faculty in those groups hold the subjective perspectives described by the study. However, it would not be appropriate to use the study results to generalize that a similar proportion of people in the population would classify into each group as did participants in the study (Brown, 1980; Thomas & Watson, 2002). As with most qualitative research, the purpose of Q Methodology is to provide rich descriptions that deepen understanding of the participants' perspectives (Stephenson, 1953).

Other classification methods, such as cluster analysis, ultimately result in a set of exhaustive categories where all participants classify into a group. The categories of classification are also distinct, meaning they have high within-group homogeneity and high between-group heterogeneity (Hair, Anderson, Tatham, & Black, 1998; Morf, Miller, & Syrotuik, 1976; Thomas & Watson, 2002). Q makes no claim to accomplish either exhaustive or distinct categories (Stephenson, 1953). Since Q Methodology classifications are based on participants' overall point of view rather than responses to specific variables, the resulting groups are more nuanced, allowing for the possibility that some participants might be moderately associated with more than one group (Morf et al.). As is true for most typologies, Q also does not result in a way to classify people in the population into the groups identified in the study (Bailey 1994; McKeown & Thomas, 1998; Stephenson, 1953). Instead, Q offers rich descriptions that synthesize the issues that shape the perspective of each type, such that the general population of faculty can identify the type that aligns with their views. Q findings can certainly inform the creation of measurement scales that can determine a person's type.

Potential Contributions from Q Methodology to Understanding Faculty Engagement

Given the list of factors and dimensions that affect faculty engagement (Demb & Wade, 2012), a classification system informed by Q Methodology based on engaged faculty's holistic, internal frameworks may offer new insights into engagement. Current literature relies on externally observed variables like discipline, contract type, or engaged practices; however, this may be unintentionally limiting understanding. For example, as with the physicist and social worker mentioned before, a tenured faculty member in sociology who conducts community based research and an adjunct faculty member in mathematics who uses service-learning pedagogy may, because of their shared epistemology, beliefs about student learning, and personal connections to the community, actually have much more in common with each other when it comes to how they connect their scholarly work with the community than they do with others in their respective departments.

If patterns emerge across the complex combination of influencing factors for faculty engagement (Demb & Wade, 2012), then it may help explain why it can be difficult to describe CES and why the field has struggled to find a common definition of engaged scholarship. It might also help prevent misunderstandings among colleagues who represent different perspectives, or create more open dialogue about not only what "counts" as engaged work but also why it counts. Moreover, a classification system based on shared patterns in an overall internal framework might make it possible for administrators and colleagues to more quickly understand differing points of view, offer more customized supports and policies for engaged work, and invest resources in ways that deliver the best return.

The potential benefit from building a supportive community of engaged faculty cannot be overstated. Calls for higher education faculty to be more collaborative, integrating knowledge across disciplines to address community concerns are consistent (Boyer, 1990; Fitzgerald et al., 2016; Pearl, 2015). Such a community is not accomplished by simply gathering scholars in a room, but by fostering understanding relationships and appreciation for each others' contributions. As Boyer (1990) noted, the scholarship of integration speaks to an entire process of collaboration throughout a particular project. A community engaged faculty typology with rich descriptions of the various points of view could help faculty from different fields become aware of the perspectives they share in common. It could also help faculty come to appreciate the benefits of working with people whose perspectives on the work are very different from their own, creating opportunities for complementarity, innovation, and true interdisciplinary work.

Conclusion

We began this article with Boyer's (1990) call to strengthen institutional diversity so that notions of faculty work can be redefined in ways that allow faculty to use their talents to meet the needs of society and uphold the purpose of higher education. Institutional diversity includes recognizing the variety of ways that faculty partner with the community and collaboratively generate new knowledge that informs our collective theories, practice, and research. Given the myriad combination of factors and dimensions that affect faculty engagement, as well as the strengths and limitations of existing typologies, it is helpful to reconsider how we can manage the complexities surrounding faculty engagement while still honoring unique faculty perspectives. Q Methodology offers a way to reconsider faculty engagement from faculty members' perspectives rather than from the perspectives of researchers interpreting the perspectives of faculty. This approach invites a new way to explore whether there are patterns of faculty engagement that may otherwise be missed with more traditional or reductive approaches. The results of such an inquiry may complement, refine, or even challenge existing conceptualizations of the factors that affect faculty engagement, which in turn can inform practice and higher education's ability to embody its civic aims.

References

Bailey, K. D. (1994). *Typologies and taxonomies: An introduction to classification techniques* (Sage University Paper series on Quantitative Applications in the Social Sciences, series no. 07–102). Thousand Oaks, CA: Sage. https://doi.org/10.4135/9781412986397

Barker, D. (2004). The scholarship of engagement: A taxonomy of five emerging practices. *Journal of Higher Education Outreach and Engagement, 9*(2), 123–137.

Becher, T. (1987). The disciplinary shaping of the profession. In B. R. Clark (Ed.), *The academic profession: National, disciplinary, and institutional settings* (pp. 271–303). Berkeley, CA: University of California Press.

Boyer, E. L. (1990). *Scholarship reconsidered: Priorities of the professoriate.* Stanford, CA: The Carnegie Foundation for the Advancement of Teaching.

Boyer, E. L. (1996). The scholarship of engagement. Bulletin of the American Academy of Arts Orchestrating Change at a Metropolitan University. *Metropolitan Universities, 18(3),* 57–74. https://doi.org/10.2307/3824459

Bringle, R. G., Games, R, & Malloy, E. A. (1999). *Colleges and universities as citizens.* Boston: Allyn & Bacon.

Brown, S. R. (1980). *Political subjectivity: Applications of Q Methodology in political science.* New Haven, CT: Yale University Press.

Brown, S. R. (1986). Q technique and method: Principles and procedures. In W. D. Berry & M. S. Lewis-Beck (Eds.), *New tools for social scientists: Advances and applications in research methods* (pp. 57–76). London, UK: Sage.

Brown, S. R. (1997). The history and principles of Q Methodology in psychology and the social sciences. Retrieved from http://facstaff.uww.edu/cottlec/QArchive/Bps.htm

Brown, S. R. (2006). A match made in heaven: A marginalized methodology for studying the marginalized. *Quality & Quantity, 40*(3), 361–382. http://doi.org/10.1007/s11135-005-8828-2

Burawoy, M. (2005). For public sociology. *American Sociological Review, 70*(1), 4–28. https://doi.org/10.1177/000312240507000102

Buzinski, S.G., Dean, P., Donofrio, T.A., Fox, A., Berger, A.T., Heighton, L.P., et al. (2013). Faculty and administrative partnerships: Disciplinary differences in perceptions of civic engagement and service-learning at a large, research-extensive university. *Partnerships: A Journal of Service-Learning & Civic Engagement, 4*(1), 45–75.

Colbeck, C. L., & Wharton-Michael, P. (2006). Individual and organizational influences on faculty members' engagement in public scholarship. *New Directions for Teaching and Learning, 105,* 17–26. https://doi.org/10.1002/tl.221

D'Agostino, B. (1984). Replicability of results with theoretical rotation. *Operant Subjectivity, 7,* 81–87.

Delve, C. I., Mintz, S. D., & Stewart, G. M. (1990). Promoting values development through community service: A design. In C. I. Delve, S. D. Mintz, & G. M. Stewart (Eds.), *Community service as values education.* New Directions for Student Services #50 (pp. 7–29). San Francisco: Jossey-Bass. https://doi.org/10.1002/ss.37119905003

Demb, A., & Wade, A. (2012). Reality check: Faculty involvement in outreach and engagement. *The Journal of Higher Education, 83*(3), 337–366. https://doi.org/10.1353/jhe.2012.0019

Doty, H. D. & Glick, W. H. (1994). Typologies as a unique form of theory building: Toward improved understanding and modeling. *Academy of Management Review, 19*(2), 230–251.

Driscoll, A., & Lynton, E. A. (1999). *Making outreach visible: A guide to documenting professional service and outreach.* Presented at the AAHE Forum on Faculty Roles and Rewards, Washington, D.C.: American Association for Higher Education.

Fear, F., & Sandmann, L. R. (1995). Unpacking the service category: Reconceptualizing university outreach for the 21st century. *Continuing Higher Education Review, 59*(3), 110–122.

Fitzgerald, H. E., Bruns, K., Sonka, S., Furco, A., & Swanson, L. (2016). The centrality of engagement in higher education. *Journal of Higher Education Outreach and Engagement, 20*(1), 223–243.

Furco, A. (2010). The engaged campus: Toward a comprehensive approach to public engagement. *British Journal of Educational Studies, 58*(4), 375–390. https://doi.org/10.1080/00071005.2010.527656

Giles, D. E. (2008). Understanding an emerging field of scholarship: Toward a research agenda for engaged, public scholarship. *Journal of Higher Education Outreach and Engagement, 12*(2), 97–106.

Glass, C., Doberneck, D., & Schweitzer, J. (2011). Unpacking faculty engagement: The types of activities faculty members report as publicly engaged scholarship during promotion and tenure. *Journal of Higher Education Outreach and Engagement, 15*(1), 7–30.

Glassick, C. E., Huber, M. T., & Maeroff, G. I. (1997). *Scholarship assessed: Evaluation of the professoriate.* San Francisco: Jossey-Bass.

Hair, J. F., Anderson, R. E., Tatham, R. L., & Black, W. C. (1998). *Multivariate data analysis* (5th ed.). Delhi, India: Pearson Education.

Janke, E. M., & Colbeck, C. L. (2008). An exploration of the influence of public scholarship on faculty work. *Journal of Higher Education Outreach and Engagement, 12*(1), 31–46.

Janke, E., Medlin, K., & Holland, B. (2015, November). *Collecting scattered institutional identities into a unified vision for community engagement and public service.* Paper presented at the meeting of the International Association for Research on Service-Learning and Community Engagement Conference, Boston.

Jay, R. L. (1969). Q technique factor analysis of the Rokeach dogmatism scale. *Educational and psychological measurement, 29*(1), 453–459. https://doi.org/10.1177/001316446902900223

Kellogg Commission. (1999). *Returning to our roots: The engaged institution.* Kellogg Commission on the Future of state and Land-Grant Universities, National Association of State Universities and Land-Grant Colleges.

Kezar, A. J, Chambers, A. C., & Burkhardt, J. C. (Eds.). (2005). *Higher education for the public good: Emerging voices from a national movement.* San Francisco: Jossey-Bass.

Krathwohl, D. R. (2004). *Methods of educational and social science research: An integrated approach.* Long Grove, IL: Waveland Press.

McKeown, B., & Thomas, D. (1988). *Q Methodology.* Newbury Park, CA: Sage. https://doi.org/10.4135/9781412985512

Morf, M. E., Miller, C. M., & Syrotuik, J. M. (1976). A comparison of cluster analysis and Q factor analysis. *Journal of Clinical Psychology, 32*(1), 59–64. https://doi.org/10.1002/1097–4679(197601)32:1<59::AID-JCLP2270320116>3.0.CO;2-L

Newman, F. (1985). *Higher education and the American resurgence.* Princeton, NJ: Carnegie Foundation for the Advancement of Teaching.

O'Meara, K. (2002). Uncovering the values in faculty evaluation of service as scholarship. *The Review of Higher Education, 26*(1), 57–80. https://doi.org/10.1353/rhe.2002.0028

O'Meara, K. (2005). Effects of encouraging multiple forms of scholarship nationwide and across institutional types. In K. O'Meara & R. E. Rice (Eds.), *Faculty priorities reconsidered: Rewarding multiple forms of scholarship* (pp. 255–289). San Francisco: Jossey-Bass.

O'Meara, K. (2008). Graduate education and community engagement. *New Directions for Teaching and Learning, 113*, 27–42.

O'Meara, K., & Niehaus, E. (2009). Service-learning is . . . How faculty explain their practice. *Michigan Journal of Community Service Learning, 16*(1), 17–32.

O'Meara, K., & Rice, R. E. (2005). *Faculty priorities reconsidered: Rewarding multiple forms of scholarship.* San Francisco: Jossey-Bass.

O'Meara, K., Sandmann, L.R., Saltmarsh, J., & Giles, D.E. (2010). Studying the professional lives and work of faculty involved in community engagement. *Innovative Higher Education, 36*, 83–96. https://doi.org/10.1007/s10755–010–9159–3

Peterson, R. S., Owens, P. D., & Martorana, P. F. (1999). The group dynamics Q sort in organizational research: A new method for studying familiar problems. *Organizational Research Methods, 2, 107–139.* https://doi.org/10.1177/109442819922001

Post, M. A., Ward, E., Longo, N. V., & Saltmarsh, J. A. (Eds.). (2016). *Publicly engaged scholars: Next generation engagement and the future of higher education.* Sterling, VA: Stylus Publishing.

Rice, R. E. (2002). Beyond scholarship reconsidered: Toward an enlarged vision of the scholarly work of faculty members. *New Directions for Teaching and Learning, 90 (summer),* 7–17

Rice, R. E., Sorcinelli, M. D., & Austin, A. E. (2000). *Heeding new voices: Academic careers for a new generation.* Washington, DC: American Association for Higher Education.

Saltmarsh, J. (2011). Engagement and epistemology. In J. Saltmarsh & E. Zlotkowski (Eds.), *Higher education and democracy: Essays on service-learning and civic engagement* (pp. 342–353). Philadelphia: Temple University Press.

Sandmann, L. R. (2008). Conceptualization of the scholarship of engagement in higher education: A strategic review, 1996–2006. *Journal of Higher Education Outreach and Engagement, 12*(1), 91–104.

Sandmann, L. R (2009). Placing scholarly engagement "on the desk." Research University Engaged Scholarship Toolkit. Boston: Campus Compact.

Stanton, T. K. (2008). New times demand new scholarship: Opportunities and challenges for civic engagement at research universities. *Education, Citizenship, and Social Justice, 3*(1), 19–42. https://doi.org/10.1177/1746197907086716

Stephenson, W. (1953). *The study of behavior: Q technique and its methodology.* Chicago: The University of Chicago Press.

Strand, K., Marullo, S., Cutforth, N., Stoecker, R., & Donohue, P. (2003). *Community based research and higher education: Principles and practices.* San Francisco: Jossey-Bass.

Thomas, D. B., & Baas, L. R. (1993). The issue of generalization in Q Methodology: "Reliable schematics" revisited. *Operant Subjectivity*, *16*(1/2), 18–36.

Thomas, D. M., & Watson, R. T. (2002). Q sorting and MIS Research: A primer. *Communications of the Association for Information Systems*, *8*(1), 141–156.

Townson, L. (2009). Engaged scholarship at land-grant institutions: Factors affecting faculty participation. (Doctoral dissertation). Retrieved from Dissertations and Theses database. (UMI No. 3363733)

Wade, A., & Demb, A. (2009). A conceptual model to explore faculty community engagement. *Michigan Journal of Community Service Learning*, *15*(2), 5–16.

Wade, A., & Demb, A. (2012). Reality check: Faculty involvement in outreach and engagement. *The Journal of Higher Education*, *83*(3), 337–366. https://doi.org/10.1353/jhe.2012.0019

Watts, S., & Stenner, P. (2005). Doing Q Methodology: Theory, method and interpretation. *Qualitative Research in Psychology*, *2*(1), 67–91. https://doi.org/10.1191/1478088705qp022oa

Zlotkowski, E. (2011). Social crises and the faculty response. In J. Saltmarsh & E. Zlotkowki (Eds.), *Higher education and democracy: Essays on service-learning and civic engagement* (pp. 13–27). Philadelphia: Temple University Press.

Authors

EMILY MORRISON (Emily_m@gwu.edu) is the director of the Human Services and Social Justice Program and an assistant professor of Sociology at The George Washington University in Washington, DC. Before becoming faculty, she directed volunteer and service-learning programs at both the undergraduate and graduate levels, as well as founded a 501(c)3 nonprofit organization focused on health education. Morrison received a B.S. in Psychology from Kansas State University, an M.A. in College Student Personnel from the University of Maryland, and her Ed.D. in Human and Organizational Learning from The George Washington University.

WENDY WAGNER (wagnerw@gwu.edu) is the Honey W. Nashman Faculty Fellow at the Honey W. Nashman Center for Civic Engagement and Public Service, as well as a visiting assistant professor in Human Services and Social Justice at The George Washington University in Washington, DC. Prior to her current roles, she was the Director of the Center for Leadership and Community Engagement at George Mason University. Wagner received a B.A. in Communication Studies from the University of Nebraska-Lincoln, an M.A. in College Student Personnel from Bowling Green State University, and her Ph.D. in College Student Development from the University of Maryland-College Park.

Cultivating Practitioners of Democratic Civic Engagement

Novella Zett Keith
Temple University

How can we support campus-based practitioners of civic and community engagement in moving from normalized engagement toward practices that engage others democratically and respectfully across borders created by social race, class, gender, status, and other markers of difference? The article presents a framework derived from practice theory, a social science perspective that has influenced professional and organizational studies. The framework, which is meant as an aid for practice, integrates Bourdieu's habitus, field, and capital with the theory of practical wisdom or phronesis. Bourdieu helps us understand how normal practice is constituted while phronesis provides the tools to consider practice that is ethical, democratic, border-crossing, and wise. Two mini-cases drawn from a graduate and an undergraduate course in urban education feature engaged practitioners in school settings and provide illustrations for the theory. The concluding section discusses implications of this way of framing the cultivation of community-engaged practitioners for the practice of reflection, course design, and research.

The question I am asking in this article is how to support campus-based practitioners (students, faculty, and staff) in moving from the *normalized* practice of engagement – still too often practiced as charity, spectatorship, activity and place, or outreach (Bheekie & van Huyssteen, 2015; Saltmarsh & Hartley, 2011) – toward the capacity to engage democratically and respectfully across borders created by race, class, gender, professional and educational status, and other markers of difference. Constituted by webs of unequal power, borders typically pose obstacles for campus-community partnerships and democratic engagement.[1]

To this end, the article presents a theoretical framework that I believe can help us consider what influences *normal* or habitual practice and its transformation. Theory here is intended as a heuristic to support understanding and practice rather than as an explanatory and predictive model: It provides thinking tools that can help us make new connections, construct differently what we know, and ask questions that lead to new knowledge and ways of seeing and doing. I sought theories that could advance community-engaged practitioners on a transformational path, where what was wanted was change in both person (mindset, dispositions, and so on) and service-learning/community engagement (SLCE) practice while also considering ethical practice.

Working with community-engaged practitioners (CEPs), among whom I include myself, has been an important focus of my professional life, and I have come to think of this work as a *cultivation* or an organic process that involves a collaboration with nature – here, the gifts and qualities of practitioners. Cultivation should be about providing fertile ground and good conditions for seeds to grow into the best possible versions of themselves. My involvement in social-justice oriented service-learning and what is now called civic and community engagement goes back about twenty-five years. Of late, I have been moved particularly by the call to action around *A Crucible Moment* (National Task Force on Civic Learning and Democratic Engagement, 2012) for higher education to commit more fully to preparing graduates for *democratic* civic engagement. I hope to make a contribution to an understudied area in the field by focusing on transformative *practice* (more than transformative *learning*), and those moments in practice that can become turning points toward more democratic, equitable, and ethical engagement. Understanding process and practice can complement outcomes-oriented work on the attributes of the community-engaged graduate and professional (e.g., see Clayton, Bringle, & Hatcher, 2013) and initiatives on the preparation of community engagement professionals (Dostilio & McReynolds, 2015; McReynolds & Shields, 2015; http://compact.org/initiatives/professional-development-training/).

The central idea of the article is to see SLCE through the lens of practice. Practice is commonly used either as a qualifier of specific domains (e.g. clinical practice) or as a reference to learning through repeated action. As used here, however, it references a family of theories or perspectives termed practice theory, comprised of different strands united in problematizing everyday (including professional) activities through insights from the fields of sociology, anthropology, and organizational studies (Nicolini, 2012). Whereas scholars informed by the cognitive and behavioral sciences generally take the individual as a starting point, practice theorists locate the practitioner and the practice at the intersection of socio-cultural-discursive, economic-material, and political arrangements that both enable and constrain the practice.

The focus, thus, is on practice- and the practitioner-in-context, where contextual factors may include language and forms of speaking, tools, and material objects (including bodies), as well as ways of relating and exercising power, solidarity, authority, and privilege. Kemmis and his colleagues (2014) refer to these, respectively, as *sayings, doings, and relatings*. Through this lens, the actions of practitioners emerge from the interrelatedness of all aspects – present and historical, experiential and structural, individual and group-based – that enter into a given *situation* in which they are involved. I used the term 'context' above because we are familiar with this language; the theories refer instead to the *practice site, situation,* or (in the version I use) *field*. Context can be seen as a container for the practice, whereas the site is about "a set of conditions that make the practice possible though they do not determine it" (Kemmis, Wilkinson, Edwards-Grove, Hardy, Grootenboer, & Bristol, 2014, p. 14).

For the practitioner, thus, it is not only a matter of being cognizant, say, of the historical origins, structural aspects, and current conditions impacting the community (see Dreese, Dutton, Neumeier, & Wilkey, 2008) but of how the material aspects of that setting enter into the practice site, or how a particular faculty, staff, or student participant responds, based on her/his prior experiences and history, and what actions are possible and are taken. Additionally, how one engages in this practice situation goes beyond positionality and identity – say, a white middle class college student entering this school and neighborhood motivated to become a community engaged professional – and involves the student's and community partners' prior embodied experiences, their orientations and desires, capacities, skills, and qualities as they interact in and with the situation.[2]

Thinking with practice means shifting the focus of course and program development, pedagogy, and research from the individual unit, including individual learning and development to a wider lens such as the activity and activity 'system'. Community service learning might thus be seen, as McMillan (2011a) suggests, as "two communities of practice interacting via one activity system and engaged in joint activities" (p. 557). Thus the unit of analysis for research is the 'boundary zone' where the service-learning project takes place and the practitioner is a 'boundary worker.' The practitioner still retains an important place in this perspective, especially in the versions of practice theory I use, but his or her *cultivation* must take this complex system into account. Through a practice theory lens, organizations can be seen as ecologies and architectures of interdependent practices, where social regularities are produced and reproduced through webs of mutually interactive and relational processes taking place in particular sites. This does not mean that the oppressive nature of some social relations is, suddenly, easy to change. However, interactions always leave room for unpredictability through creativity and innovation even within existing structures, and as such practice theories help us see reality as somewhat more fluid, opening up ways to rethink both persistence and change and consider how engaging in practices differently, in specific sites, might expand the limits of what is possible.

Practice-based approaches have received renewed attention in the last twenty years, even generating new terms such as the *practice turn*, practice-based studies (PBS) and practice-based education (PBE) (Darling-Hammond, Chung Wei, Andree, Richardson, & Orphanos, 2009; Gherardi, 2008, 2009; Kinsella & Pitman, 2012; Macintyre Latta, & Wunder, 2015; Perry, 2015; Shulman, 2007). Their meanings do vary and, as Boud and Drew (2013) remark, their use may at times constitute simply a new label. In the SLCE field, social practice theory is represented by approaches that use situated learning and community of practice (CoP). At times these are paired with complementary theories, including critical social theory and critical discourse analysis, which address tendencies in the CoP framework to overemphasize individual learning and undertheorize power. To cite a few examples, Nemeth and Winterbottom (2016) put "a socially situated theory of learning in conversation with [Butin's] poststructuralist service-learning" (p. 313). McMillan (2011b) bridges CoP and activity theory, which she presents as an extension of Vygotsky's (1978) work that "brings history and power into the picture . . . and provides a link between micro and macro perspectives and contexts" (p. 110). Carrington, Deppeler, and Moss (2011) draw from critical social theory and collaborative inquiry in CoPs to engage teachers (pre-service and in-service) in critical dialogue about professional learning; they demonstrate how their continuum of teacher learning led to changes in teachers' beliefs and knowledge that were reflected in new, contextually appropriate teaching practices. Other scholars and researchers approach the field in ways that are partly congruent with practice theory. I will return to the work of Butin (2007), Kiely (2005), and Mitchell (2014) in this regard. Together, these and other contributions suggest an ongoing search in the SLCE field for approaches that are broadly aligned with or friendly to practice theory.

The remainder of the article is organized as follows. I begin with two vignettes that anchor the theoretical presentation and return to them after that presentation. The vignettes center on two SLCE practices that will be familiar to readers: practitioner reflection on experience and course or program design. The framework provides a broad understanding of ethical practice that puts the practitioner-in-context at the center. It also provides new ways of thinking about reflection and design and the cultivation of ethical practitioners. The concluding sections consider the framework and vignettes in light of relevant SLCE literature and the implications of the framework for SLCE practice and research.

Two Vignettes

Both vignettes are drawn from courses taught using a capacities or assets stance vis-à-vis community partners and involved students in service-learning/partnership projects in impoverished urban neighborhoods. I was the instructor in one course and part of an instructional team in the other. Given space constraints, I hope readers will accept my assertion that the courses were designed to meet standards of good quality as broadly summarized by Felten and Clayton (2011) and, for reflection, Eyler (2002). In particular – and the importance of this will become clearer once the framework has been presented – considerable time was devoted to the students sharing their life experiences in relation to their community-based work.

The first vignette is drawn from a graduate course on campus-school-community partnerships taught in fall 2015. This class was partly co-designed with the students and was modeled on a CoP that included sharing stories and experiences, providing support through the inevitable challenges, and mutual learning. The second vignette offers a snapshot of a four-year partnership (1999–2003) between a university, high school, and coalition of neighborhood groups; the college course was part of the teacher education core and was designed so students would both experience service-learning and begin to learn how to use it in their future teaching. Each vignette includes an abbreviated sketch of the context and of a practice situation that constituted a critical incident and stimulated reflection and change.[3] I invite readers to think actively about the vignettes and issues they evoke while reading the theoretical framework, perhaps beginning to "find the theory" in the everyday.[4] The later discussion of the first vignette will focus mainly on Cynthia's *habitus, virtues*, and *sensemaking*. The discussion of the second vignette will also focus on *enacting the good*.[5]

A Civically-Engaged Practitioner Reflects on Her Habitus

The context. Cynthia is a VISTA working as a school-community coordinator in a middle school located in a high-poverty African American neighborhood. She is a middle class white woman in her mid-20s in her second year at the school and in a Master's program at Temple University, where she is enrolled in a course on campus-school-community partnerships. She considers herself a successful practitioner in this setting and offers in support for her self-evaluation that "only a few months into the [first] year, my principal begged me to come back for a second year." A major requirement of the course is a partnership project that typically takes place at the students' work site (schools and other youth- and education-oriented organizations). Students also complete an autobiographical narrative and two critical reflections on critical incidents in their partnerships.

Cynthia's project centers on developing greater parental engagement at her school, and as the semester progresses she begins to focus on her relationship with the parent coordinator, Gaby, a middle-aged Haitian woman who was recently hired for that position. It is important to Cynthia and the school that the two have a good working relationship; for Cynthia, this includes valuing Gaby's and the community's actual and potential resources or *capital*.

The critical incident. Cynthia's critical incident shows her struggling internally with her perception of Gaby, which had been quite positive but has started changing, potentially jeopardizing the relationship. Cynthia links this change to an interaction she had with her principal, during which the principal expressed her frustration with Gaby's conduct at a parent meeting. Principal Davis is an African-American woman whom Cynthia describes as an excellent principal and a "personal super-hero" of hers. Cynthia writes:

> Initially, both outwardly and internally, I defended Gaby to Principal Davis and shook off her remarks. My inner monologue went something like this: *Parents love Gaby's liveliness. Davis just has a lot going on right now and clearly hasn't had time to fully appreciate her*

energy. No big deal. The next time I saw Gaby, however, I started to notice that I acted differently towards her. I was slightly less receptive . . . I was short with my words and slightly more impatient. . . . I was irritated by behaviors that had, only weeks prior, inspired me. This caused me to reflect on my thoughts and actions . . . *What were the skills and attributes I liked about Gaby? Had they been an asset to [the school] or how could they be? Why was I refusing to recognize them all of a sudden?*

Changing Course Elements in a Campus-School-Community Service-Learning Partnership

The context. The partnership created teams of college and high school students working together on service-learning projects. The high school students were enrolled in the school's only college-bound small learning community and were in the leadership group for the school's Youth-Driven Community-Service Center. The school was in a hyper-segregated high-poverty neighborhood and its students were all African-American or Black. The college students were about 75% White and mostly of working- or middle-class background. All the students participated in a joint class, held at the high school, which brought together the two student groups for about ten weeks of the college semester. The joint group was supported by an instructional team that included community, high school, and university personnel. The projects that the student teams planned and implemented were in the neighborhood and were selected and planned in collaboration with the community-based organization. With regard to goals, the high school and community partners wanted to engage young people in empowering community-based work and the college partners were in agreement with this goal; the high school and college students had various motivations but they all needed to complete a service-learning project and other course requirements; and all the instructors wanted to apply the principles of sound service-learning practice and collaboration across social divides.

The critical incident. It is the end of the second year and the instructional team is meeting to evaluate the work accomplished. Team members take turns sharing their perception of what is going well and what needs attention. There are successes on the part of both the high school and college students. The service-learning project requires the teams to conduct research on community needs, which has really helped the high schools students become comfortable in an area that had constituted a huge stumbling block. The college students have been an invaluable resource in making college more real and accessible for the high school students, as they have taken their teammates to campus, their residences, and even their classes. The college students are enjoying being in a school and getting a first taste of their future profession. They have mostly overcome their initial fear of the neighborhood, have developed relationships, changed their views, and begun to come to grips with racial and class privilege. Memories of the final joint celebration on campus are still with us and fill us with excitement and pride that we were able to create this community across these borders.

Everything is not great and we have all noticed problems around collaboration in the student teams. Communication is often one-way, with college students directing and managing the work, and each of us has intervened at times to interrupt their taking control of group talk and making arbitrary decisions. For their part, some college students, reverting to the normalcy of seeing problematic behaviors simply as personal character deficits, have complained about their high school teammates 'fooling around' and not fulfilling their responsibilities. It is clear that we will need to put more effort into team building. We are almost ready to start considering solutions, when Sharon, one of the two high school teachers in the team stops the process and makes a simple and powerful statement: "My students are becoming passive."

Both critical incidents raise questions about cultivating democratic practitioners of civic engagement in border-crossing settings. Both involve seasoned, competent practitioners (Cynthia and her principal in the first vignette, the leadership team in the second vignette) and relatively novice ones (Gaby in the first vignette and the high school and college students in the second vignette) – all learning to practice as civically engaged partners in cross-border settings. I now take a detour into the theories. My primary focus is on campus-based practitioners. I hope readers will not take it as a sign that I am privileging this group: My position is that, in border crossings, the partners who come from more dominant social positions have a special responsibility and, quite frankly, more to learn.

Practice Knowledge and a Practice Theory Framework

Practice Knowledge: Epistemological Divides

In an article exploring faculty and service-learning community partners' theories of learning, Bacon (2002) hypothesizes "that members of different groups [or discourse communities] will differ . . . in how they use language and that differences in language use may reveal underlying differences in the group's values, goals, or beliefs" (p. 35). Analysis of focus groups revealed significant overlaps but also three main differences between the faculty and community partner groups. Faculty tended to (a) identify themselves more as knowers and experts than as learners; (b) examine students' words in evaluating successful learning; and (c) value group work but represent learning as an individual activity. Community members tended to (a) identify as learners and see learning as a continuous activity based in experience; (b) consider the ability to take action as evidence of successful learning; and (c) subordinate the individual learner to the group's collective development, talking "less about specific instances of interaction such as discussion and . . . more about relationships developing over time." (p. 41)

Those familiar with cognitivist and situated perspectives on learning will see here the signs of the two discursive communities: the faculty in the study were more cognitivist and community members were more situativist. Bacon (2002) suggests that these divides are slowly being dismantled and remarks that all participants were developing a more comprehensive view. She attributes these remaining differences "to where these people [faculty and community partners] spend their time and what sort of learning they habitually witness and experience" (p. 43).

Epistemological divides such as these are common in academic fields. Each of these theories of learning falls in a broader divide that Schwandt (2005) terms the scientific knowledge tradition and the practical knowledge tradition. The scientific knowledge tradition values analytical and scientific approaches that follow the precepts of the physical sciences and produce decontextualized and generalizable knowledge. Objectivity and certainty are important values here. The researcher is an expert who generates knowledge through rigorous methods that whenever possible approach those of the physical sciences; practitioners (here, the community partners) look to the university for knowledge that will help them in their practice. One example of this approach is *evidence-based practice* (Biesta, 2007) promoted, among others, through the Institute of Education Sciences' *What Works Clearinghouse* (http://ies.ed.gov/ncee/wwc/). The practical knowledge tradition is aligned with situated learning, communities of practice, and practice theory. Briefly, knowledge is generated in practice and thus is context-dependent; it is embodied rather than being situated in cognitive processes alone. Ambiguity and uncertainty are the norm.

In practitioner-oriented fields, the divide is most frequently discussed in terms of the legitimate sources of practitioner knowledge. But Bacon's findings point to a more subtle manifestation of it. She remarks on a *curious* absence in the community partners' conversation: "these participants spoke about faculty and graduate students in terms of their expertise, [but] they did not claim expertise for themselves (though all four had college degrees). Instead, they tended to represent their own knowledge as something arising naturally from their experience" (p. 39). We seem to be in the presence of an internalized self-marginalization: These practitioners' description of their own knowledge fits the tenets of the practical knowledge tradition, but they do not seem to accord value to it. The only site constructed as having legitimate knowledge (expertise) is the academy. Experiential knowledge is useful but suffers from a lack of recognition and has no language. Thus, they cannot be experts in their own right.

I believe that Bacon's *curious* absence is the sign of a border that the framework I propose can address. Introducing terms that are explained in the next section, the practice knowledge tradition is embodied in the habitus of the practitioners, but so is its devaluation as an asset. If education is a *field* and knowledge is one of its important resources, academics are winning the game. Cultivating practitioners would thus require the valorization of practitioner knowledge, not only through words, but through experiences of its value.

Before going further I should dispel a misperception this statement might create: I am not suggesting that, in a search for bridging the two knowledge communities, academics should abandon careful thought and rigorous scholarship and research but that our definitions of rigor and science should be expanded to include approaches that are relevant for practice (e.g., see Flyvbjerg, 2001; Nicolini, 2012). Nor am I suggesting that researchers cede the ground to practitioners' understanding of their practice in a reversal of the current relationship. Engagement calls for a serious rethinking of the relationship between research and practice, and practitioners and researchers – as recent activities in the field indicate.

Practice Theory: Thinking Tools for Cultivating SLCE Practitioners

The framework I propose brings together two strands of practice theory. The first is the construct of habitus-field-capital developed by Pierre Bourdieu, a French social theorist whose work has deeply influenced how we understand everyday practice. The second is modern-day or applied (neo-Aristotelian) phronesis or practical wisdom, which is about ethical and *wise* practice. This combination works well because the constructs are comprised of parts that are both similar and complementary. Together, they provide thinking tools that will help us delve into the movement of the practitioner from *normalized* to *wise* (and ethical) practice.

Two parts of Bourdieu's construct, habitus and capital (especially cultural capital), are well-known and have been used extensively in the sociology of education, contributing especially to our understanding of what is termed 'cultural reproduction' – how schooling actually generates (or *reproduces*) social inequality (see Bourdieu, 1977, 1989; Bourdieu & Passeron, 1990). Others have also used the framework in the service of equitable change, which is how I envision it here (e.g., see Horvat & Davis, 2011; Yosso, 2005). However, the three components of the construct (the final one is *field*) are less frequently understood and used as a single, interactive entity (Townley, 2014; Zembylas, 2007). One of the few instances I have found comes from SLCE. As Jagla, Lukenchuk, and Price (2010) explain, they have extended Bourdieu's tripartite construct and combined it with the relational ethics of Noddings and Levinas to develop the construct of a *service-learning habitus* (SLH). The approach is novel and potentially interesting, though I have not delved into it sufficiently to consider its relationship to my framework, because the purposes are different. In addition, my approach to Bourdieu remains closer to his original work, though I also combine it with the ethical thought of different scholars.

As I use it, Bourdieu's theory helps us grasp the relatedness between practitioners' dispositions, social environments, practice settings, and the motivation to strive for what is defined as excellence or high quality performance *in these settings*. I then integrate Bourdieu's theory and a phronetic understanding of the cultivation of *wise* practitioners and practice. The aim of phronesis is to infuse practice with an ethics centered on the promotion of human and community *flourishing* or lives worthy of human dignity (termed *the good*). This ethics is situational: It is not about an abstract and general common good but about what may contribute to flourishing, constructed (most often) dialogically, as achieving something of value in the situation at hand (Neher & Sandin, 2016). Classical phronesis was elitist, its definition of virtue grounded in the agreement of a *virtuous* community, and it did not address power relations. Current versions address power (see especially Flyvbjerg, 2001; Schram, 2012) and provide remedies that include dialogue and openness to multiple narratives and standpoints (Coulter & Wiens, 2002; Hursthouse, 1999). Together, both theories shed light on what shapes existing practices and create a path for envisioning possibilities for change.

An additional clarification is needed before moving on. In Bourdieu's framework, excellence in a given field is not equated with ethical action, as is the case in the phronetic framework. For example, institutions may achieve 'excellence' by manipulating quantitative performance indicators *(metrics)* that distort the true purposes of higher education. Similarly, a professor at a university may be rewarded for practicing engagement as outreach and even using the community as a laboratory, both of which are problematic for proponents of democratic engagement and usually for community partners.[6] The ethical dimension of Bourdieu's framework is in its exposure and critique of the power and privilege involved in these 'games.' Foucault's notion of discourse and its *normalizing* functions is a useful *critical* addition. Discourses are systems of thought and practices that circumscribe what can be said and thought. They support practices, many of which are oppressive, that we think of as normal, but are instead normalized through workings of power that are largely invisible (Foucault, 1977/1995). Disturbing and interrupting these normalcies, both in people and in social, material, and political arrangements, is necessary for changing practices. Let me now discuss each contribution in greater detail.

Bourdieu's Habitus-Field-Capital

Habitus. Think of *habitus* as a background matrix that is constituted in the course of our experiencing, as active agents, the everyday world, including its power relations – in actuality, vicariously, and through personal and group memories, narratives, and histories. These become part of who we are and our sense of 'how things work' not only insofar as we remember and actively refer to them, but as embodied dispositions and orientations that guide our perceptions, interpretations, and actions. The schema that generates these preferences is both personal and group-based and is generally outside our conscious awareness: we simply prefer certain foods, feel comfortable speaking in certain ways. If we are academics, analytical work may feel more natural than practitioner work; and if we are also teachers, thinking tools such as learning theories and pedagogies will likely feel more natural than practice theories. This is important with regard to SLCE: arguably, it is a practice field. What is left out when it is informed mainly by theories of teaching and learning – through the habitus of educators?

The best known definition of habitus has it as the "generative principle of regulated improvisation" (Bourdieu, 1977, p. 78). If you think about it, it becomes interesting and may even *feel* right. Our experience is that we are all unique individuals, who are different, seldom predictable, creative, and are certainly 'agents' constantly 'improvising' as we interact in the world. What we are less aware of is that we act individually, spontaneously, and creatively in the context of something – Bourdieu's 'matrix' is one way to put it – that regulates what is normal and possible for each of us. The source of this regulation is the social milieu and social relationships or, in Bourdieu's terms, the 'field'. Habitus and field thus account for the predictability-unpredictability of the everyday (also see Crossley, 2013).

Field. Bourdieu (1985) often uses terms without fully defining them and this is true of *fields*. He writes about them as relatively stable social spaces or networks of relationships in which people are distributed by virtue of the types of capital – economic, social, cultural and symbolic – that they possess and that have currency in each field. Some fields or social spaces intersect and are similar, which means that members of a social group and nearby groups have a similar habitus and feel more comfortable interacting with one another than with people whose 'coordinates' in the social space are far removed from theirs. This basic comfort is what keeps us in or close to our fields and what allows us to strive for and be our best in those fields.

Capital. This thinking tool refers to anything that has value in a given field and can be exchanged for *profit* – similar to an ace in a game of cards in which aces matter. People use the capitals available to them to compete for power and positional advantage and generally to 'play the game'; but symbolic capital is the most important because, like a wild card, it allows its holders to define what has value in the field (Bourdieu, 1985, 1989). Why is standard English 'better' than other ways of speaking? Bourdieu would say that thinking with symbolic capital, it is so because canonical writers, educated elites, and others who 'matter' possess the symbolic capital that allows them to set the standards. Some of us experience standard English as normal, while for others it is a border that only can be crossed by becoming assimilated or excellent at code switching.[7] Bourdieu's capital helps us see anew the social and material realms. As an example, it helps us to see clothing, tastes, ways of speaking, and gestures as sites of symbolic struggle through the use of cultural capital. These material differences matter: When crossing borders into the community, for instance, what counts as 'dinner'?[8]

Bourdieu incorporates here an important notion that is central to the critical/conflict traditions: fields are held together in tension, often through subtle forms of power/violence that operate at the conscious and unconscious levels. What constitutes capital in a field can be redefined through contestation. In this vein, constructs such as 'practitioner-scholar' (see McReynolds, 2015; McReynolds & Shields, 2015) can be seen as attempts to reposition the practitioner's knowledge as valuable capital. However, it takes symbolic capital to accomplish this; organizational leaders may not accept the revaluing and even deny rewards to would-be change agents. This also is true of proposals for a dialogical and multivocal SLCE epistemology (see Hoyt, 2010; Saltmarsh, Hartley, & Clayton, 2009) and for more inclusive criteria for faculty tenure and promotion (e.g. Glass, Doberneck, & Schweitzer, 2011). Through Bourdieu's lens, making traditional practices problematic in these ways signals a symbolic struggle being waged for recognition of community engagement as a field, which involves contesting what constitutes capital, changing rules of the game, and putting forth different models of exemplary academics.

Habitus-field-capital as a construct. In what is depicted sometimes as a formula, practice is created though the intersection of habitus with capital and field position. To clarify this interaction, Bourdieu uses a well-known metaphor: a game. The game is played by players who are differently positioned and skilled, have a 'feel for the game' (*sens pratique*), the motivation to play, and an interest in doing it well (Townley, 2014). Some may also decide that playing the game is not worth their while (this is one way to think about student disengagement). The game (*field*) has rules by which the players agree to play and resources, material and otherwise, that make it possible to play. Differential access to the field's valued resources (*capital*) creates disparities, which the more skilled or dominant players try to maintain; some players are more creative and innovative (the personal habitus) and become quite exemplary through the interaction of habitus, capital, and field. One of the dangers of metaphors, of course, is that they oversimplify what is a much more complex reality.[9]

Phronesis

Aristotle's Athens was dominated by technocratic and instrumental thinking, which he sought to correct by considering the purposes toward which knowledge is put (Gadamer, in McGee, 1998). He proposed three interconnected orientations to knowledge: episteme, techne, and phronesis. Episteme pertains to context-independent knowledge involved in the pursuits of science and logic, while both techne and phronesis are oriented to action in the world. Techne pertains to craft, technical knowledge, and skills, or know-how. Phronesis, as currently understood (e.g., 'applied phronesis') includes questions of values and power plays that are relevant to practice, as well as an "intimate familiarity with the contingencies and uncertainties of various forms of social practice embedded in complex social settings" (Caterino & Shram, 2006, p. 8). This sort of practical knowledge relies on judgment rather than techniques: Each situation is unique and the action that brought forth the good yesterday may not do so today. As educators know from experience, every group is different: their work is thus part of the practical knowledge tradition and requires cultivating practical judgment.[10] Noel (1999) brings together three distinct but interwoven aspects of phronesis adopted for this framework: embodying the virtues, sensemaking (making sense of the situation), and constructing and enacting the good.

Embodying the virtues. Phronesis posits an intimate connection between who we are, how we make sense of the world around us, and what we do.[11] Virtues are 'ways of being excellent' that are cultivated and practiced in communities and become embodied as our character and as capacities and motivations to act in ways that further *the good*. Virtue ethics, in turn, involves the aspiration and motivation to develop a virtuous character and act accordingly (Hursthouse, 1999; King, 2015). Three issues need clarification. First, virtues are not synonymous with moral qualities; in fact, a distinction is usually made between (overlapping) intellectual, moral, and civic virtues. Intellectual virtues, which support learning and sound thinking, include intellectual curiosity, courage, the disposition to consider issues carefully and thoroughly, and qualities Dewey considered necessary for reflection (see Rodgers, 2002): wholeheartedness, directness, open-mindedness, and responsibility. Moral virtues are akin to the qualities of a good neighbor, such as being trustworthy, kind, and compassionate. Civic virtues include the disposition to consider the well-being of others and work collaboratively toward the common good. Respect for freedom, openness to diversity, and all that goes under civic mindedness and social citizenship are also part of the mix (see Baehr, 2013; Bringle, Studer, Wilson, Clayton, & Steinberg, 2011; Hatcher, 2008; Kreber, 2016; Ladson-Billings, 2004; Musil, 2009).

Second, given that the overall purpose of phronetic action is to reach toward a situated and dialogically constructed good, what counts as a virtue is also situation-dependent. For instance, creativity and a sense of humor may be important when a situation is at an impasse. Research with community partners tells us that they value qualities such as respect, openness, mutuality, interest in the community's history, and the like (Dreese, Dutton, Neumeier, & Wilkey, 2008; Sandy & Holland, 2006; Stoeker, Tryon, & Hilgendorf, 2009). Again, however, it is not a matter of generic qualities but of the qualities that can help achieve a situated good.

Third, the expression of virtues needs to be balanced. This may mean treading a path between excess and deficit: For instance, an excess of respect could turn into subservience. Sternberg's (2003) 'balance theory of wisdom' calls for the relative weighting of various interests (intrapersonal, interpersonal, and extrapersonal) and the balancing of three possible courses of action: "adaptation of oneself or others to existing environments; shaping environments in order to render them more compatible with oneself or others; and selection of new environments" (p. 157). Judgment is important in weighing these aspects, as one is guided by the potential of various plausible alternatives for achieving some good in the situation at hand.

Sensemaking: Making sense of the situation. Sensemaking is an open-ended inquiry process that includes the body and multiple ways of knowing, such as *felt* sense and intuition, and integrates creativity, character and intellect, cognition and affect. Weick, Sutcliffe, and Obstfeld (2005) describe it as "being thrown into an ongoing, unknowable, unpredictable streaming of experience in search of answers to the question, 'What's the story?'" (p. 410). Or, better, what are the stories – what different ways of narrating this event are there? Whose voices are speaking and whose are silent, marginalized, or even elided from history? (Yalowitz, Malandra, & Keith, 2015). Sensemaking is thus about constructing meaning in ways that include one's personal beliefs and experiences so as to move toward actions consistent with these perceptions (Mitchell, 2014). Meaning construction is always a collective process, even if at the moment we are alone. Two central processes are situational perception (principally, discernment) and insight. The first refers to "finely tuned habits of salient focusing" (Dunne & Pendlebury, 2003, p. 207), while insight has to do with the ability to grasp seemingly obscure cues. Both are cultivated through experience with and reflecting or intuiting from a multiplicity of cases (see Flyvbjerg, 2001).

Weick, Sutcliffe, and Obstfeld (2005) studied sensemaking as a process and practice in organizations. Like Bourdieu's habitus-field-capital, this construct and research capture and describe the world as it is. It may include directing our attention to what we want to see and not seeing what we "passionately desire to ignore" (Argyris, 1991; Felman, 1982). Phronetic sensemaking involves constructing meaning through personal qualities, beliefs, values, and an orientation that guide a search for the possibilities for the 'good' that a situation might hold. When the Citizen Scholars in Mitchell's (2014) study make sense of their lived experiences through a social justice lens, they are not putting into action a code of ethics: They are enacting who they are and are striving to be. According to virtue ethics, it is one's character and the community in which it is cultivated that provide guidance: A *wise* (or virtuous) practitioner is motivated to make sense of situations by considering how to resolve them in ways that advance human flourishing for all concerned. Ethics thus enters the very process of understanding the practice situation and our engagement in it. Mitchell explains that "service-learning invokes a number of cues to facilitate sensemaking regarding social justice" (par. 2). The anchors here are one's virtues – a passion for social justice, to be sure, a willingness to doubt oneself, tolerance for ambiguity and uncertainty, humility, and the capacity to express them in the particular 'streaming of experience' in which we are immersed. Perhaps it is by "listening eloquently" or (my favorite) "negotiat[ing] traffic at the intersection where worlds collide" (Musil, 2009).

Constructing and enacting the good. The process here is about resolving on a line of action. Shotter (2012) describes it as "moving around within a landscape of possibilities . . . being spontaneously responsive to the consequences of each move, and judging which one (or combination of moves) seems best in resolving the initial tension aroused in one's initial confusion" (p. 253). While the fluidity and openness of this process may seem daunting, especially to the novice practitioner, thinking about it as practical reasoning and the somewhat more structured *deliberation* may help. Mathews (2004) defines deliberation as weighing "the possible consequences of various approaches to a problem against all that we consider truly valuable" (p. 8) (also see Pruitt & Thomas, 2007).

According to Toulmin (2003) practical reasoning is substantive, appropriate to the demands of the situation, and marked by a search for a plausible solution rather than a right answer. In Freire's terms, this might mean assessing the limits and possibilities of a situation: what is real (the status quo), what is desired (the ought), and what is possible (the situated good). Again, we sense the presence of power as the practitioner operates on the tension line between limits and possibilities (Boyte & Fretz, 2010). Applied phronesis offers four specific questions for sensemaking and deliberation that put power and values at the center. Action (or the last question, "what should be done,") must be preceded by practitioners' mindful search for the workings of power in the practice situation ("where are we going?" and "who wins and who loses, by which mechanisms of power?") and ethical and value considerations ("is it desirable?") (p. 162). As Barker et al. (2011) remark, the process is not meant to be expert-driven; it is "locally situated, self-regulating, and community-defined" (p. 20).

At this point readers should have a sense of how Aristotelian and current approaches to phronesis view the process leading to action that furthers the good. This ethical stance is aligned with the ambiguity, uncertainty, and undecidability that characterize the practical knowledge tradition mentioned above (Bacon, 2002; Schwandt, 2005). In the SLCE field, Butin's (2007) work shares some of its tenets, especially in his poststructural and antifoundational model of justice-learning. The practical judgments we make are not *objective* in the sense that modernist approaches (the scientific knowledge tradition) make of the term, but this does not mean that they are relativistic, self-serving, and irrational. When such judgments are enacted in the context of a cultivated practical wisdom, they are based on dialogical processes that bring in historical examples and experiences and on a reasoning that is substantive and attuned to the contingencies of an emergent situation. And we do it with others for whom those enactments matter.

The cultivation of practitioners follows on a path from *normal* to *wise* practice. Table 1 provides a bird's eye view of the process as the framework conceives it. Columns I and III present a summary comparison of the Bourdieusian and phronetic lenses. Column II, appropriately located between normal and wise practice, is about the spaces for and approaches to the desired transformation. Some of these have already been mentioned while others are presented below and in the concluding sections. The double reverse arrows serve as a reminder that the process is iterative and ongoing rather than linear.

Bourdieu's construct of habitus helps us consider people and their practices in terms of qualities and dispositions garnered through experiences in social settings or spaces they occupy more or less comfortably. Field and capital remind us of the settings and experiences that formed the person's habitus, the qualities and practices that emerge from it, and how changing aspects of the setting – field and capital – might support a transformation of the habitus. Phronesis provides the ethical lens, through the combined focus on virtues, situational ethics, and a much greater understanding of the process of

Table 1
Habitus-Field-Capital, Phronesis, and Cultivating Practitioners in the Third Space

	I WORLD AS IT IS *Normal* Practice	II *Third* Space for Cultivating Practitioners → ←	III POSSIBLE WORLD *Wise* Practice
Self-in-Context	Dispositions & orientations to practice (habitus) embodied through: • experiences, • in social settings (fields), • using the resources (capitals) of those settings.	Create multiple spaces for ongoing cross-border sensemaking, relationships, and dialogue, that: • Challenge AND support, • Use inclusive reflective/ sensemaking practices: movement, art, games, storytelling, emotions, lifestories, • Welcome discomfort & tensions, • Search for and interrupt oppressive normalcies, • Change the rules of the game and what counts as capital, • Reframe experiences/ situations to seek cues for human flourishing, • Provide repeated experiences that strengthen new meanings/ways of seeing, and related virtues, • Evaluate micro and macro practices to enact what is "truly valuable."	Character qualities (virtues): • cultivated in virtuous communities, • that motivate us to enact human flourishing (the good). Who we are=What we see=What we do
Sensemaking	Felt (embodied) sense – *feel* for the game: What are the rules of the game? What is my position in the game, given the resources I can access? Is this game worth playing?		Perception and Deliberation: • What are the stories? • What is this situation about, ethically/ morally/justly? Who gains, who loses, through what kind of power? How can we move toward 'flourishing' for all involved?
Practices	Strive for 'excellence' according to the rules of the game		Respond to the situation based on wise judgment (personal & collective).

sensemaking and constructing the good than we get from Bourdieu.[12] Sensemaking helps us understand how meanings are constructed and thus suggests that transformation can be fostered by directing the practitioner's attention to cues that can support different meaning constructions and wiser ways to respond in a practice situation.

The whole is a collective process that requires supportive social spaces or communities. Column II represents these spaces where new meanings, relationships and practices are cultivated, the habitus is potentially transformed, and the transformation is sustained. What is required here are perhaps not typical communities of practice but in-between spaces where we can show ourselves as vulnerable, less-than-perfect, uncertain beings who are motivated to engage in cross-border work. I call this a *third space*, which is a more fluid notion than community of practice and can take various forms, physical and symbolic, that support collaboration across borders and building communities of difference. Well-known examples include Jane Addams' Hull House (see Harkavy & Puckett, 1994) and Belenky, Bond, and Weinstock's (1997) public homeplaces.

Applying the Framework to the Vignettes

Rather than continuing with an abstract discussion, let me return to the vignettes to illustrate the framework and its implications for teaching and learning practices and research. I use the first case primarily to illustrate habitus and normal and phronetic sensemaking. The second case mainly will illustrate sensemaking and enacting the good.

Reflections of a Civically-Engaged Practitioner: Cynthia's Case

The main learning tools used in this course were a partnership project, an autobiographical narrative, written critical incident reflections, the classroom as learning community, and a text (Keith 2015), which presents contexts, theory, and several cases (see Jacoby, 2015). The first assignment asked students to draw from their biography and identify one personal and one work-related experience, both positive and negative, that shaped their understanding of 'partnership' and the orientation, values, qualities, capacities (resources), and motivations they were taking to the partnership project they were considering doing. Students also were asked to explain their choice of project and its focus, in light of this narrative. This assignment was designed to encourage students to begin to think of themselves and their projects along the lines of habitus-field-capital and phronetic character, without mentioning those terms.

Cynthia's autobiographical narrative revealed a highly reflective practitioner with considerable interest and experience in community work and strong values in the areas of youth empowerment, family engagement, and the ethics of collaboration. Instruments such as the Self-Assessment Matrix (SAM) would show her already on the 'expert' skill level (see Cress, Collier, & Reitenauer, 2013). The students were encouraged to share their narratives in class and online, thus beginning to build spaces for dialogue, empathy, sensemaking, support, and change. The critical incident reflections were related to their partnership projects; students were reminded that anything that had "stayed with them" was not too small or insignificant to be considered a critical incident. The point was to have them focus on micropractices, everyday moments in which actions are taken or not taken, where what is normal and habitual might be challenged and new insights and practices might emerge. Three such moments are described in Keith (2010). At this point, the class had become fairly familiar with the framework presented above and students selectively used its thinking tools to make sense of their incidents.[13]

In her critical incident reflection, Cynthia revealed that her immediate reaction to the principal's comment about Gaby was emotional and visceral: "Instantly, I felt powerless. My heart sunk." Using the framework, these were important signs of a disturbance to the habitus, which is embodied. In this situation, Cynthia was interested in understanding how to act in response to this incident so as to remain aligned with her goals. She was also concerned about acting wisely, especially by being respectful of all involved and fostering capacities. She perceived a good fit between the thinking tools and her interest and so she began by focusing on her habitus and the logics of fields in which she was situated, personally and professionally.

Habitus. Starting with the habitus means that the practitioner considers who she is in the present situation in light of dispositions and orientations acquired through past and present experiences, both personal and professional. These include what she considers her qualities and capabilities, and also how her resources (capital) compare to those of others in the field and how they can help her achieve her goals. Moving toward a phronetic perspective would mean looking at the qualities (virtues) that came to the surface in the situation and deciding to cultivate and express, in supportive third spaces, those that would help her grow into the person she wanted to be. Recall that the phronetic practitioner's practice is an enactment of who she/he is and is motivated to become. For Cynthia, it meant being and enacting a thoughtful, empathetic, and competent professional capable of collaborating in creating a space for a genuine partnership between school and parents. There is no need to analyze why the principal's statement was so disturbing to Cynthia. The framework suggested she look at her past experiences, and she directed her attention to relations in her family (a field, with logics, capitals, and field positions from which practices are constructed) that seemed to be still influencing, through her habitus, her emotional reactions and her construction of the present situation.

Sensemaking. Recall that after the principal expressed her frustration with Gaby, Cynthia started to be bothered by things about Gaby that she had previously seen as assets. Cynthia made sense of her changed perception of Gaby by referencing both her family field (practices resulting from her mother being "caring but slightly invalidating" of her) and the education field of which the school is a part. The questions Cynthia asked could have led her to use sensemaking explicitly as a thinking tool but she did not go in that direction. We can extrapolate that there were tensions in her sensemaking that had to do with her personal and professional habitus: before Principal Davis' comment, Cynthia (as she asserts) had looked for cues that valorized Gaby's assets (gestures, language, clothing, and so on) as community cultural capital (Yosso, 2005). This was in line with the experiences in community organizing that made Cynthia valuable in her present work (i.e., positioned her well in this field). After the principal's comment, Cynthia was looking for cues that invalidated what she had previously constructed as capital, demoting it instead to expressions and behaviors that were, simply, 'inappropriate'. This was clearly a move from an assets to a deficit approach, which Cynthia was able to catch 'in the making,' by focusing on micropractices. The education field, of which the school is a subfield, along with capitals associated with the field, fosters a professional habitus that would influence in undetermined ways the principal's leadership practices and possibly her assessment of Gaby. This could happen at the same time that the principal was heartily committed to parental engagement, which included giving Cynthia the responsibility of creating a 'third space' for parent engagement. This in-between, border space joining school and community needed to have logics and capitals that might be different from the school's. But what would it be like?

Cynthia understood that going along with the principal's perception of deficit or her original perception of Gaby's assets had implications for her practice in the larger sense of the entire project. At this point, she became aware that her personal habitus was "clouding her vision." The "personal superhero" principal was not her "caring but slightly invalidating mother" and this relational dynamic need not negatively influence her perception of and actions toward Gaby. Continuing with phronesis, we see Cynthia begin to make sense of the situation in light of her own 'virtues', or qualities. As she saw it, her dilemma involved an excess of one virtue and a (temporary) deficit of another: *respect* for the principal had clouded her *open-mindedness*. Although she now "generally had a good handle ... on her validation-seeking attribute," it had temporarily caused her to be overly influenced by Principal Davis's assessment of Gaby, which then negatively impacted her understanding of and actions toward Gaby in the current situation.

Cynthia identified a tension between normalized expectations and discourses concerning professional behavior and her own desire to respect the qualities Gaby embodied and change the field's rules by valorizing Gaby's 'community capital'. The discourse of professionalism was an oppressive normalcy needing to be disturbed because it ran counter to an important *good*, culturally relevant practice. The community-oriented discourse resonated not only with Cynthia's values, but also with her extensive experiences and successes. Thus came a second troubling question: why was the principal she so admired partaking in this oppressive discourse?

Cynthia returned to the lens provided by her habitus and also to her other experiences at the school. She saw that Principal Davis was more complex than the binary construct she had initially projected onto her through the incident: "she does a good job of balancing seriousness with lightheartedness"; she was, at any rate, not perfect and Cynthia did not have to rely unduly on her for her own self-validation. Her respect for the principal was now balanced by a renewed and more nuanced understanding and commitment to community values and voice. She was a stronger and wiser practitioner because of the unsettling and turmoil caused by the incident and the sensemaking that ensued and was becoming a more trustworthy, respectful, competent CEP.

Changing Course Elements in a Campus-School-Community Service-Learning Partnership

The framework presented here was not used in designing the course, which was developed in 1998–1999. So in considering this vignette, the framework is used as an analytical tool rather than a thinking tool for mid-course correction in practice – which is how it could also be used. The course, which had at least seven sections each semester (though only one was involved in this partnership), was designed by a team that included experienced K-12 teachers in urban schools (where all the service experiences would take place) and College of Education faculty. This team bridged several divides in addition to campus-school, especially those of race, class, and culture, and became a wonderful cross-border CoP that lasted the entire seven years the core requirement was in place. Initially, course design was based on shared knowledge from three sources: (a) principles of good practice in service-learning, including how to use service-learning to achieve K-12 curriculum objectives; (b) practice-based knowledge and theory on collaborations in the urban setting, which we described as "working with" rather than "doing to"; (c) interrupting seemingly normal behaviors that were actually oppressive ("interrupting oppressive normalcies"); and (d) active learning and student engagement.

Given that this was likely to be the first service-learning course for most of the college students, expectations and assignments were clearly spelled out. A handout described the service-learning process for both groups of students. It included collaborating with community partners to identify possible projects; doing community-needs research; planning and implementing the project; reflecting in each phase; and presenting it to peers, teachers, and community partners. For the college students, each step in the service-learning process had corresponding assignments and their weights in the final grade. The main readings for the college students were a service-learning text edited by Wade (1997) and articles on urban education, structured social inequality, and African Americans in cities. Other short readings and handouts were collected and kept on the ready, to be distributed when 'hot' issues arose in class, in the teams, or at the sites.

Sensemaking. Sharon's emotional revelation that her students were becoming passive had an immediate effect on the team. She shared her feeling that many of the college students needed to change their attitudes and behaviors toward her students. It was true that they fooled around at times, but it was usually because they didn't understand something or felt they were not being listened to and their contributions were not taken seriously. There was also the fear of not being liked and judged negatively by strangers coming into their neighborhood. Not enough care was being taken to draw them into the teams and the process.

The college instructors trusted her judgment, recognized in themselves the felt-sense she had put into words, and accepted her evaluation. They were motivated to enact a good that had been on the table from the beginning – student engagement – expressing shock that they had actually participated in the enactment of its opposite. The coming summer was used to consider the issue further and devise changes to address the problem. We decided that we needed to understand how the students made sense of the curriculum, including the service-learning experience in the school and neighborhood, and so revisited their reflections looking for cues about needed changes and the levers of change at our disposal.

Habitus-field-capital and sensemaking. The reflections told us a story that can now be seen through the lens of habitus-field-capital. The college students were taking their academic habitus into the borderland where the service-learning project was symbolically located and we had not done enough to change the logics and capitals that would define a new field and thus potentially change the students' practices. What were normalcies in the education field had become oppressive in the service-learning field. To obviate this known possibility, instructors had stressed the importance of team collaboration during all phases of the project; but collaboration was not sufficiently valorized by what counts most in coursework: graded assignments. Many of the students (not all, because some were motivated to act collaboratively by their habitus) were making sense of the course in terms of completing tasks that counted toward the final grade (which also meant being a good student) and they had interpreted "service-learning project" to mean completion of a physical project. The instructors, on their part, thought they communicated that all the tasks counted because they were all part of the "service-learning process." But words and exhortations had only gone so far.

In the terms of the framework, there was great anxiety and a disturbance to the students' habitus caused by the new field and their not quite having a *feel* for the new game. Interestingly, even those who were most anxious about completing assignments and so had left their high school teammates in the dust, expressed regret in their final reflections about that aspect of their experience, and their desire for good relationships. That desire was a common theme and suggested strongly an opportunity to enact ethical practice: the desired relationships of caring, respect, and collaboration were the situational manifestation of human flourishing in this site. The college students did not want to act in disrespectful and uncaring ways, just as the high school students did not want to disengage and be passive. We needed to create spaces that would allow them all to move toward becoming *virtuous* practitioners.

Constructing and enacting the good. Once we read the cues, the resolution of the dilemma was close at hand: We would do more to cultivate students' qualities that supported engagement and communicate what this 'field' was about, through our ways of speaking and changes in handouts about assignments and grading rubrics. A new collaboration rubric showed that team building and collaboration had value and defined what competent enactment meant. We dialogued with the students about their position in the *field*, considering meanings and identities for the students in that in-between state – neither teachers nor students vis-à-vis their high-school partners. We invited them to reflect on their roles and use the experience to develop a greater understanding and empathy for those who would be their future students. We were thus inviting them symbolically to use this third space to cross from *normal* to *wise* practice. New reflection prompts also drew the students' attention to cues that would alert them to the presence or absence of student engagement.

By the next fall, a restructured service-learning process was in place that succeeded in positively changing student practices over the next two years. One change that resulted from the team's collective intelligence was having SLCE projects that would last a whole year: one year-long class of high school students would work with two different groups of college students (one in the fall and another one in the spring) on the same project. This contributed to a reversal of relationships, as the high school students took ownership of the projects and became guides for their college teammates, especially in the spring term. This change gave them new positions and capital in the field and the motivation to play the game. We also decided, and community partners agreed and continued to participate in, conducting all the projects within the school. Navigating this field in new ways also created more capital for the high-school students and changed many teachers' perceptions of them.

Contributions of the Framework

Before briefly summarizing below what the framework suggests concerning teaching and research, I will start by highlighting some of what I see as its broad advantages. First, the framework is about practice. If this sounds too simple, we can recall that Bacon's community partners considered learning as competent practice while faculty considered learning as best expressed in words. An argument could be made that moving toward practice theory constitutes a move toward bridging the campus-community divide, as this perspective is potentially close to the questions and interests of community partners.

A second advantage is that the framework constitutes a comprehensive approach to ethical action. The more conventional approach is to identify principles and codes of ethics that are typically stated in terms of rights and responsibilities (or obligations) of the parties involved. A service-learning ethics code developed by Chapdelaine, Ruiz, Warchal, and Wells (2005) describes a common obligation termed competence. As an example, a competent faculty member plans the service-learning experience according to named quality standards. The book includes hypothetical dilemmas and decision-making guides that can be used in professional development sessions. The practitioner is then tasked with considering those rights and responsibilities that are relevant and applicable in any given situation. For a practitioner at this stage, it is a good start.

Phronesis as ethical practice provides a more holistic way of being ethical and engaging in ethical action. It includes, as we have seen, the whole area of perception, whereby one looks at a situation to see cues about possibilities it holds for human flourishing. As Kreber (2016) maintains, self-cultivation is also essential, as it is the inner aspect of civic mindedness. There should be conversations about what constitutes flourishing in the situation, of course, but the idea suggests a wider arena that encompasses more subtle aspects of practice, is more positively constituted than rights and responsibilities, and is possibly more attuned to issues of power. The essence of ethics in this approach is that its source is the character, habitus, heart of the practitioner-in-context, meaning that there need to be experiences and communities for support and further cultivation. Organizations will still need ethical codes such as the one mentioned above, but we also need to see ethics as the cultivation of empathy, the heart, and other qualities to be expressed through one's practices. And so we need other types of community spaces.

A third contribution is in the area of sensemaking, particularly those aspects that have to do with making meanings. Imagination, stories, and creativity are all involved in constructing plausible, multilayered, inclusive narratives about practice situations and the possibilities for human flourishing they hold and how they can be actualized through practical wisdom. Meaning making is a collective process; it must involve others because we need collective intelligence to create meanings but also because we cannot sustain meanings alone. This is a different way of understanding what happens when a group comes together and talks, with facilitation from a colleague, teacher, staff or other person. Again, invoking Bacon's community partners, in the academy we are used to interpreting the activity (and using the language) as a group discussion through which each participant may learn something. As these community partners' comments suggest, more valuable than a *discussion* and individual learning is seeing and engaging the process as a collective practice of meaning making leading to collective learning and action (*praxis*) and relationship building. As Cantrell and Sharpe (2015) use the process, the group can be guided to make meanings that include broader and more ethical understandings that are not deficit based, are more complex, include more perspectives, and broaden meaning horizons. Thinking of a service-learning group in this way opens up more modalities for participation, especially storytelling.

Implications for Teaching and Research

The vignettes have already presented some of the main implications of the framework for both and may have suggested, along with the above, some fruitful research agendas. This means, I hope, that the sketches provided below are sufficient for the time being.

Reflection

Following on the work of Boler (1999) and Zembylas (2007) on emotions, power and education, and pedagogies of discomfort, a fairly recent strand in the SLCE literature looks at emotions in teaching and learning, asking how they should enter the reflection process. Felten, Gilchrist, and Darby (2006) suggest a redefinition of service-learning reflection to include "the interplay of emotion and cognition" (p. 42). This redefinition provides a rationale for inclusive reflective practices (many in use by educators, especially in K-12 settings) that make room for insights and learning that involve emotions, as they emerge through the body (dance, movement, Theater of the Oppressed), art, poetry, storytelling, narratives, and even games (see Noyes, Darby, & Leupold, 2015). Active reflection practices used in intergroup dialogues provide additional insights and examples for teaching practice that specifically address multiple categories of diversity (Gurin, Nagda, & Zúñiga, 2013).

This research is relevant because, as we saw especially from the first vignette, disturbances of the habitus are visceral and emotional experiences. Not every emotional expression is the result of this kind of disturbance, but attention to the emotions, how they can be enmeshed in games of power, and how they can lead back to the dispositions and orientations of the habitus are good starting places for this sort of reflection. Given that the habitus is constituted through experiences, it can also be shifted through a reframing of those experiences and additional experiences that support the shift.[14] Reframing experiences can be supported by sharing them with a group, through various modalities as appropriate to the group: a narrative, artwork, movement, as well as writing, including creative writing, a story circle. This exercise is not about *explaining* how one's habitus is linked to one's prior experiences; it is a way of building connections and relationships through the sharing of experiences and the group 'talk back' that follows.

Course and Program Design

Understanding the relatedness of practice, practitioner, and practice situation means that changes in practices can result in changes in the practitioner. This is also true of other elements, which are interconnected. Looking at a course through the lens of habitus-field-capital and phronesis suggests ways to support desired practices and challenge undesirable ones. The issue, broadly, is what counts as resources and rewards and how they are used to excel in a setting that is conceived of as a *game*. Generally, assignments and their assessment are the main tools available for this purpose. There is no reason to revisit how change in collaboration practices was created in the second vignette and so let me comment on two additional points. First, we should take special steps to consider how students and participants will make sense of the assessments. Normal ways of making sense of pedagogical tools in the traditional field (the campus) will carry over into a border, in-between field (the school); thus more feedback, dialogue, and confirming experiences than usual are needed to enshrine new meanings.

The second point is to ensure that assessments that matter are also aligned with course goals in all important areas – academic, developmental, and partnership relations. It is often difficult, given the logic of the academic field, to include nonacademic learning in one's assignments as part of a grading schema – and what is not graded does not count for much unless the students' intrinsic motivation is engaged. The habitus of students as well as administrators and faculty is affected by this logic, as students' dispositions are to accept (and use their capital to succeed in) being graded on academic contents, but not in the other areas mentioned. This point supports the importance of program planning at the campus level, connecting academic, student development, and other areas (Bringle et al., 2011).

The second vignette revealed a strong desire for connection and relationships among the students. Recalling that habitus (and virtuous character) is formed in communities, through experiences with others, strong relationships are important for crossing borders and being invited into different fields where transformations can begin and be sustained. This suggests that learning and changing can happen without the intervention of structured reflection, simply by being for an extended time, and not just as a spectator, in the company of Others. According to practice fields and phronesis, knowledge is a dynamic achievement that occurs as people interact with their environments. As Kassam (2010) puts it, "it lies not in the heads of professors but in the world that they point out to students" (p. 209). This realization calls for a sense of humility on the part of campus-based practitioners. Kiely's (2005) research also points to what he terms *connecting*, and the potential transformation that comes not through rational reflection but through concrete experiences interacting with concrete human beings who were Other prior to the experience. This is an important finding, as such emotional and visceral human *learning* may play a role in keeping high-dissonance experiences alive in us, to continue their transformative work long after they happened.

Research

It should be clear by now, based on the proposed framework, that my value preference is for research that examines and changes practices in ways that support our capacity to pursue ethical goals, as defined phronetically. That this is not the only legitimate goal for research goes without saying; but it is one that should be of considerable importance for researchers who are committed to democratic engagement in a field that is practice-based. Research based on practice theory, as presented here, lends itself to the detailed examination of micropractices and processes that can result in 'small' positive changes in one's practices (as in Cynthia's case) or 'larger' changes in the ways practices are organized (e.g., a course, an organization, a 'system'). Of course, if we agree that these practices are all connected, then the notion of 'small' and 'larger' make less sense. Nonetheless, the point of entry into the research matters.

If I read them correctly, Giles and Eyler (2013) point to a gap and a need for research in SLCE that could be addressed through approaches informed by practice theory. They do this from the foundation of their extensive historical knowledge of the field and in the context of more recent contributions (the article is a book review essay of two-volumes on service-learning research edited by Clayton, Bringle and Hatcher, 2013). Giles and Eyler remark that an important way to strengthen research, given the state of the field, is to assess how key elements of service-learning practice are implemented. A starting point should be the "deconstruction of the service-learning experience itself . . . [to] provide descriptions of some of the varied ways these experience are developed, students are prepared, the sites are managed and monitored, and the reflective processes are designed" (p. 56). Among the research questions they offer are,

> How often and how does the service-learning class actually incorporate a process that genuinely creates a project that is mutually beneficial for the students and community members?" What does a placement that is mutually designed and beneficial . . . look like?" (pp. 55–56)

Given my own orientation, research should go further than descriptions, although this is an essential starting point. The problem is that, as I see it, it is not possible to offer impartial and objective descriptions of practice. Thus, if one is interested in 'mutuality,' issues that relate to power and power sharing should make more than a cursory appearance: One would have to describe the practice at least by including that lens. Who is participating in framing the questions, and later, interpreting the data? Whose voices are at the table? And, returning to the topic of this article, how is the capacity of the practitioners to *see* and surface these issues, through collaboration and dialogue, being cultivated? These, for me, are essential questions – although I do not know that Giles and Eyler and authors mentioned and included in the collection are not also equally concerned about them.

This brings me to the next possible contribution, which comes from the field of planning, originally, and more generally, the policy field. My interest in *phronetic* practice theory began when reading a book by Flyvbjerg (2001), *Making Social Science Matter*. Developing the theoretical supports and coining the notion of applied phronesis, he argued for understanding the *virtuoso* practitioner as a different sort of knower, one whose decisions are based not on the application of generalizable scientific data but on lived (and perhaps, to an extent, vicarious) experience in and with a multiplicity of concrete cases and the ability to use them *wisely* to grasp what mattered in the situation at hand. Flyvbjerg made a cogent argument that the social sciences had a vital contribution to make in this regard and that it would be best made by producing knowledge in support of wise practice. This meant taking a new look at a rather maligned method: the case study. Applied phronesis would provide the tools for the researcher-practitioner to enact an ethical practice that "challenges power relations and brings about positive social change" (Flyvbjerg, Landman, & Schram, 2016, p. 3).

Since that time, researchers in this vein have conducted extensive research at times involving very large case studies. Examination of these cases led them to identify an approach that supports critical policy analysis and the ability to induce significant change. It centers on identifying *tension points*, or "power relations that are particularly susceptible to *problematization* and thus *change*, because they are fraught with *dubious practices*, *contestable knowledge* and potential *conflict*" (Flyvbjerg, Landman, & Schram, 2016, p. 3, emphasis in original).

My point in writing this is twofold. The first is to note that case studies do not have to remain in splendid isolation. We can develop ways to examine them collectively, so as to uncover critical and actionable information such as indicated above. I have not thought about this sufficiently to produce answers or even interesting questions out of my thinking hat, but it strikes me that it is an avenue worth pursuing. Practice theory, as presented here by others and me, clearly provides conceptual frameworks that can be used to research and improve practice. The second point is that our goal could be larger and, perhaps, more *virtuous*: examining qualitative studies collectively might unearth tension points or their equivalent for SLCE, pointing to power relations and ways to initiate systemic changes in the field.

The field of practice theory and related research is still evolving and so are its methods. Phronetic practice researchers can, however, make use of established traditions such as sociological phenomenology (especially standpoint theories), critical ethnography, and participatory action research, with equally well-established methods and research agendas. Participatory action research, especially of the *critical* variety, involves participants in empowering research and action on issues that matter to them. The method is used by critical urban researchers and community organizers, among others (see Cammarota & Fine, 2008; Kemmis,

2009; Torre, Fine, Stoudt, & Fox, 2012). Among many interesting example is Fuentes' (2011) work with the VOCES Latinas (Latina/o Voices) Project in a Northern California city. Using critical ethnography along with critical participatory action research, Fuentes provides a detailed account of a process she terms *practicing citizenship* that built community voice and knowledge among Latino immigrant parents involved in their children's high school and led to transformation in public and personal practices.

Sociological phenomenology focuses on the everyday world and is concerned with the social construction of meanings, particularly the shared understandings that we tend to take for granted. Standpoint theories are especially interesting for us because they focus on the shared meanings and knowledge that emerge from the positionality of a given oppressed and disadvantaged group. For Hill Collins (2000), the search for the silenced voices and meanings of African American women necessarily straddles social, narrative, and historical fields. Using this lens for the standpoint of women, Smith (1987, 2005) developed notions such as 'relations of ruling' and a method she terms institutional ethnography. These are only a few of the methods that are well-developed and have yielded strong and interesting research.

Final Self-Reflection

I conclude with a brief reflection about my own process in writing this article. Writing and revising and trying to pay attention to language, thought, bodily sensing, and so on, and to 'getting it right' (or not) has made me quite conscious of the radical departure practice theory constitutes. Nicolini (2012) calls it a Copernican revolution and I now feel he may well be correct. If I accept that practices are inscribed in the body and that my own habitus as an academic was nurtured and cultivated in the context of ecologies and architectures of practices (and academic communities) that value the analytical, rational, and individual, I must also accept that my presentation here can only be partial at best, that a practice approach needs to be inscribed in my body through much more experience, more dialogue, and collective intelligence. As I reviewed my writing, I constantly had to remind myself of the counternormative nature of practice theory and of my own embeddedness, my critical mind notwithstanding, in the scientific/analytical tradition that kept creeping back unnoticed. Changing embodied practices is a work in progress. I thought I had taken a significant step forward when I imagined and felt myself standing in the classic river, conscious that, like experience, like practice, the river is ever-flowing, never the same. Then I realized that the metaphor applied to me as well: The river is different each time, and so am I. That's much harder to grasp.

Notes

[1] I am deeply grateful for conversations and thoughtful reading and suggestions made by Nora Pillard Reynolds, Martha Carey, Cynthia Jones, and Eric Hartman. To the anonymous reviewers of earlier versions of my writing, my humble thanks for your exemplary qualities in critical peer review.

[2] Additional features include embodiment, material mediation, relationality, situatedness, emergence, and co-construction. For a brief summary and explanation, see Boud, 2012.

[3] This is a shortened definition of critical incident I provide my students: It is "an experience in which you were involved, centrally or marginally, that stayed with you. The experience may bring up emotions and issues that are not easy to resolve. It may involve unease and uncertainty – about what to feel, how to act, and so on. It made you 'stop and think'. Because it stayed with you, it has the potential to cause a shift – small or large – about who you are, where you are going, and how you see and act in the world."

[4] The full cases are presented in Keith & Jones, 2015 (Cynthia's case) and Keith, Hafiz, & Peterson, 2015 (urban partnership case). In my teaching, I encourage students to "find the theory," starting by considering their experiences and the concepts (or thinking tools) in light of each other.

[5] These are components of the framework, which is represented in Table 1.

[6] Reynolds' (2014) research shows that situational ethics is important even in this realm: The community members in her study explained that being a 'laboratory' for a particular practice was not problematic *per se*; what was problematic was the absence of information and dialogue around the use of practices that were experimental.

[7] This is the import of the well-known work on language by anthropologist William Labov (2001), and writings on the culture of power in schooling by education researcher Lisa Delpit (1995). Keith (1997/2013) discusses these issues with specific reference to service learning.

[8] This point was made by Suad Islam with reference to a campus-community case in which she was a community representative. The (well-meaning) campus partners would bring *crudités* such as raw broccoli, celery, with dips to evening meetings. For community partners who came straight from work,

this was frustratingly "not dinner" (cited in Keith et al, 2003).

[9] For more studies, both theoretical and empirical, involving Bourdieu's habitus and *interrupting* habitus, see Crossley (2013), Horvat & Davis (2011), Malandra (2007), and Reay (2004). For cultural capital, see Lareau & Calarco (2012). For the intersection of field and habitus, see Leander (2009).

[10] Following the work of Dreyfus and Dreyfus, Flyvbjerg (2001) points out that novice practitioners do indeed need rules, which become less useful as they move toward becoming competent and expert performers. Performance by experts involves an embodied felt-sense of what to do that comes from experience with manifold concrete cases.

[11] What Nicolini (2012) says about habitus applies here as well: Agency in practice theory is primarily about ways of being (and felt-sense) and acting, not ways of thinking.

[12] Habitus does include schemes of perception that organize reality and experiences and the meanings persons attribute to experiences. For instance, in *Distinction*, Bourdieu (1984) considers class-based constructions of a photograph of an old woman's hands. Working-class respondents comment on her arthritis and the pain she must feel, whereas more privileged and thus more socially distant respondents comment on the hands as symbolic of work and the deforming effects of poverty. Both views are appropriate in the respective fields but through symbolic capital the latter may be constructed as more enlightened! Bourdieu locates such comments in the context of cultural capital rather than considering the process of perception as such.

[13] There is always a question about whether the thinking tools presented in a community-based course will be appropriate to the emerging issues and interests of the students and there was no requirement that the students use this particular framework. Most students did, however, possibly because they saw it constituting capital in the course. I conveyed the message in several ways, but "saying it isn't so" is not enough! The syllabus for the course is available on the Philadelphia Higher Education Network for Neighborhood Development (PHENND) website. See http://phennd.org/resources/syllabi/

[14] Mitchell et al's (2015) research on the lasting effects of undergraduate service-learning experiences strongly suggests that a design involving repeated experiences over time (e.g., one course a semester over several years) is more likely to produce such effects than shorter experiences. Putting this information through the lens of the framework supports the notion that the habitus-transformation process needs to be extended. A similar point can be made through a reframing of Warren, Park and Tieken (2016) along these lines.

References

Argyris, C. (1991, May-June). Teaching smart people how to learn. *Harvard Business Review*, 99–109.

Bacon, N. (2002). Differences in faculty and community partners' theories of learning. *Michigan Journal of Community Service Learning, 9*(1), 34–44.

Baehr, J. (2013, January 2). *Educating for intellectual character.* Retrieved from Harvard Education Publishing Group: http://hepg.org/blog/educating-for-intellectual-character

Barker, D. W., Allen, A. D., Robinson, A., Sulimani, F., VanderVeen, Z., & Walker, D. M. (2011). Research on civic capacity: An analysis of Kettering literature and related scholarship. Kettering Foundation Working Paper 2011–1. Retrieved from http://kettering.org/wp-content/uploads/Barker-Civic-Capacity-Final-KF-WP-2011-011.pdf.

Belenky, M.F., Bond, L.A., & Weinstock, J.S. (1997). *A tradition that has no name: Nurturing the development of people, families, and communities.* New York: Basic.

Bheekie, A., & van Huyssteen, M. (2015). Teaching, learning, and becoming mindful of discomfort. *International Journal of Research on Service-Learning and Civic Engagement, 3*(1). Retrieved from http://journals.sfu.ca/iarslce

Biesta, G. (2007). Why 'what works' won't work: Evidence-based practice and the democratic deficit in educational research. *Educational Theory, 57*(1), 1–22. https://doi.org/10.1111/j.1741-5446.2006.00241.x

Boler, M. (1999). *Feeling power: Emotions and education.* New York: Routledge.

Boud, D. (2012). Problematising practice-based education. In J. Higgs, R. Barnett, S. Billett, M. Hutchings, & F. Trede (Eds.), *Practice-based education: Perspectives and strategies* (pp. 55–69). Rotterdam: Sense Publishers. https://doi.org/10.1007/978-94-6209-128-3_5

Boud, D., & Brew, A. (2013). Reconceptualising academic work as professional practice: Implications for academic development. *International Journal for Academic Development, 18*(3), 208–221. doi:10.1080/1360144X.2012.671771.

Bourdieu, P. (1977). *Outline of a theory of practice.* (R. Nice, Trans.) Cambridge, UK: Cambridge University Press. https://doi.org/10.1017/CBO9780511812507

Bourdieu, P. (1984). *Distinction.* Cambridge, MA: Harvard University Press. https://doi.org/10.1007/BF00174048

Bourdieu, P. (1985). The social space and the genesis of groups. *Theory and Society, 14*(6), 723–744. https://doi.org/10.2307/202060

Bourdieu, P. (1989). Social space and symbolic power. *Sociological Theory, 7*(1), 14–25.

Bourdieu, P., & Passeron, J.-C. (1990). *Reproduction in education, society, and culture.* Thousand Oaks, CA: Sage.

Boyte, H. C., & Fretz, E. (2010). Civic professionalism. *Journal of Higher Education Outreach and Engagement, 14*(2), 67–90.

Bringle, R. G., Studer, M., Wilson, J., Clayton, P. H., & Steinberg, K. S. (2011). Designing programs with a purpose: To promote civic engagement for life. *Journal of Academic Ethics, 9*, 149–164. https://doi.org/10.1007/s10805-011-9135-2

Butin, D. W. (2007). Justice-learning: Service-learning as justice-oriented education. *Equity & Excellence in Education, 40*, 177–183. doi:10.1080/10665680701246492.

Cammarota, J., & Fine, M. (Eds.). (2008). *Revolutionizing education: Youth participatory action research in motion.* New York: Routledge.

Cantrell, D., & Sharpe, K. (2015). *Practicing practical wisdom.* Social Science Research Network. Retrieved from http://ssrn.com/abstract=2575945. https://doi.org/10.2139/ssrn.2575945

Carrington, S. B., Deppeler, J., & Moss, J. (2010). Cultivating teachers' beliefs, knowledge and skills for leading change in schools. *Australian Journal of Teacher Education, 35*(1), 1–13. Retrieved from http://eprints.qut.edu.au/32963/1/c32963.pdf. https://doi.org/10.14221/ajte.2010v35n1.1

Caterino, B., & Schram, S. F. (2006). Introduction: Reframing the debate. In S. Schram & B. Caterino (Eds.), *Making political science matter: Debating knowledge, research, and method* (pp. 1–13). New York: New York University Press.

Chapdelaine, A., Ruiz, A., Warchal, J., & Wells, C. (2005). *Service learning code of ethics.* Bolton, MA: Anker.

Clayton, P. H., Bringle, R. G., & Hatcher, J. A. (Eds.). (2013). *Research on service learning: Conceptual frameworks and assessment* (Vol. 2A & 2B). Sterling, VA: Stylus.

Collins, P. H. (2000). *Black feminist thought: Knowledge, consciousness and the politics of empowerment* (2nd ed.). New York: Routledge.

Coulter, D., & Wiens, J. R. (2002). Educational judgment: Linking the actor and the spectator. *Educational Researcher, 31*(4), 15–25. https://doi.org/10.3102/0013189X031004015

Cress, C. M., Collier, P. J., Reitenauer, V. L., & Associates. (2013). *Learning through serving: A student guidebook for service-learning and civic engagement across academic disciplines and cultural communities* (2nd ed.). Sterling, VA: Stylus.

Crossley, N. (2013). Pierre Bourdieu's habitus. In T. Sparrow & A. Hutchinson (Eds.), *A history of habit: From Aristotle to Bourdieu* (pp. 291–307). Lanham, MD: Lexington.

Darling-Hammond, L., Chung Wei, R., Andree, A., Richardson, N., & Orphanos, S. (2009). *Professional learning in the learning profession: A status report on teacher development in the United States and abroad.* Dallas, TX: National Staff Development Council and School Redesign Network.

Delpit, L. (1995). *Other people's children: Cultural conflict in the classroom.* New York: New Press.

Dostilio, L. D., & McReynolds, M. (2015). Community engagement professionals in the circle of service-learning and the greater civic enterprise. *Michigan Journal of Community Service Learning, 22*(1), 113–116. Retrieved from https://slce-fdp.org/essays/thought-pieces/dostilio-mcreynolds/dostilio-mcreynolds-full-text/

Dreese, D., Dutton, T. A., Neumeier, B., & Wilkey, C. (2008). A people's history: Teaching an urban neighborhood as a place of social empowerment. *transFORMATIONS, 19*(1), 138–158.

Dunne, J., & Pendlebury, S. (2003). Practical reason. In N. Blake, P. Smeyers, R. Smith, & P. Standish (Eds.), *Blackwell guide to the philosophy of education* (pp. 194–212). Malden, MA: Blackwell. https://doi.org/10.1002/9780470996294.ch12

Eyler, J. (2002). Reflection: Linking service and learning – Linking students and communities. *Journal of Social Issues, 58*(3), 517–534. https://doi.org/10.1111/1540-4560.00274

Fahey, G. M. (2002, June 1). The idea of the good in John Dewey and Aristotle. *Essays in Philosophy, 3*(2), Article 10.

Farnsworth, V. (2010). Concpetualizing identity, learning and social justice in community-based learning. *Teaching and Teacher Education, 26*, 1481–1489. doi:10.1016/j.tate.2010.06.006

Felman, S. (1982). Psychoanalysis and education: Teaching terminable and interminable. *Yale French Studies, 63*, 21–44. https://doi.org/10.2307/2929829

Felten, P., & Clayton, P. H. (2011). Service Learning. *New Directions for Teaching and Learning, 128*, 75–84. doi: 10.1002/tl.470

Felten, P., Gilchrist, L. Z., & Darby, A. (2006). Emotions and earning: Feeling our way toward a new theory of reflection in service-learning. *Michigan Journal of Community Service Learning, 12*(2), 38–46.

Finley, A. (2011). *Civic learning and democratic engagement: A review of the literature on civic engagement in post-secondary education.* Association of American Colleges and Universities. Retrieved from http://www.uwec.edu/Usenate/SenateCommittees/APC/1213/121030LiteratureReviewCivicEngagement.pdf

Flyvbjerg, B. (2001). *Making social science matter: Why social inquiry fails and how it can succeed again.* Cambridge, UK: Cambridge University Press. https://doi.org/10.1017/CBO9780511810503

Flyvbjerg, B., Landman, T., & Schram, S. F. (2016, forthcoming). Tension points: Learning to make social science matter. *Critical Policy Studies.* Available at Social Science Research Network, http://ssrn.com/abstract=2721321

Follman, J. (2015). An overlooked lens: Applying structuration theory, actor-network theory, and theories of space to service-learning. *International Journal of*

Research on Service-Learning and Community Engagement, 3(1). Retrieved from http://journals.sfu.ca/iarslce

Foucault, M. (1977/1995). *Discipline and punish: The birth of the prison.* (A. Sheridan, Trans.). New York: Vintage.

Fuentes, E. H. (2011). Practicing citizenship: Latino parents broadening notions of citizenship through participatory research. *Latino Studies, 9*(4), 396–414. https://doi.org/10.1057/lst.2011.48

Gherardi, S. (2008). Situated knowledge and situated action: What do practice-based studies promise? In D. Barry & H. Hansen (Eds.), *The SAGE handbook of new approaches in management and organization* (pp. 516–525). Thousand Oaks, CA: Sage. https://doi.org/10.4135/9781849200394.n89

Gherardi, S. (2009). Introduction: The critical power of the 'practice lens'. *Management Studies, 40*(2), 115–128. https://doi.org/10.1177/1350507608101225

Giles, D. E., & Eyler, J. (2013). Review essay: The endless quest for scholarly respectability in service-learning research. *Michigan Journal of Community Service Learning, 20*(1), 53–64.

Glass, C. R., Doberneck, D. M., & Schweitzer, J. H. (2011). Unpacking faculty engagement: The types of activities faculty members report as publicly engaged scholarship during promotion and tenure. *Journal of Higher Education Outreach and Engagement, 15*(1), 7–30.

Gurin, P., Nagda, B. A., & Zúñiga, X. (2013). *Dialogues across difference: Practice, theory, and research on intergroup dialogue.* New York: Russell Sage Foundation.

Harkavy, I. & Puckett, J. (1994). Lessons from Hull House for the contemporary urban university. *Social Service Review,* 299–321. https://doi.org/10.1086/604061

Hatcher, J. A. (2008). *The public role of professionals: Developing and evaluating the civic-minded professional scale.* Ph.D. Dissertation, Indiana University. Retrieved from https://scholarworks.iupui.edu/handle/1805/1703

Horvat, E. M., & Davis, J. E. (2011). Schools as sites for transformation: Exploring the contribution of habitus. *Youth & Society, 43*(1), 142–170. https://doi.org/10.1177/0044118X09358846

Hoyt, L. (2010). A city-campus engagement theory from, and for, practice. *Michigan Journal of Community Service Learning, 17*(1), 75–88.

Hursthouse, R. (1999). *On virtue ethics.* Oxford, UK: Oxford University Press.

Jacoby, B. (2015). Taking campus-community partnerships to the next level through border crossing and democratic engagement. *Michigan Journal of Community Service Learning, 22*(1), 140–146.

Jagla, V. M., Lukenchuk, A., & Price, T. A. (2010). *Imagining a better world: Service-learning as benefit to teacher Eeducation.* National Louis University Digital Commons. Retrieved from National Louis University Digital Commons, Faculty Publications: http://digitalcommons.nl.edu/faculty_publications/72

Kassam, K.-A. (2010). Practical wisdom and ethical awareness through student experiences of development. *Development in Practice, 20*(2), 205–218. https://doi.org/10.1080/09614520903564207

Keith, N. Z. (1997/2013). Doing service projects in urban settings. In A. S. Waterman (Ed.), *Service learning: Applications from the research* (pp. 127–149). New York: Psychology Press.

Keith, N. Z. (2010). Getting beyond anaemic love: From the pedagogy of cordial relations to a pedagogy for difference. *Journal of Curriculum Studies,* 1–34 (First published on 07 December 2009). https://doi.org/10.1080/00220270903296518

Keith, N. Z. (2015). *Engaging in social partnerships: Democratic practices for campus-community partnerships.* New York: Routledge.

Keith, N. Z., Cavanaugh, C., Islam, S., Hafiz, F., Mather, K., & Soler, J. (2003, March 1). Partnerships as new ground; Between private enterprise and democratic possibilities. *Practitioner Keynote, Ethnography in Education Research Forum, University of Pennsylvania.* Philadelphia, PA.

Keith, N. Z., Hafiz, F., & Peterson, J. (2015). From normal to wiser practice in a high school, community and university service-learning partnership. In N. Z. Keith, *Engaging in social partnerships: Democratic practices for campus-community partnerships* (pp. 133–160). New York: Routledge.

Keith, N., & Jones, C. (2015, November 17). Becoming practitioners of democratic civic engagement. Boston: International Association for Research on Service Learning and Civic Engagement. Retrieved from https://www.academia.edu/18665457/Becoming_Practitioners_of_Democratic_Civic_Engagement

Kemmis, S. (2009). Action research as a practice-changing practice. *Educational Action Research, 17*(3), 463–474. https://doi.org/10.1080/09650790903093284

Kemmis, S., Wilkinson, J., Edwards-Groves, C., Hardy, I., Grootenboer, P., & Bristol, L. (2014). *Changing practices, changing education: .* Singapore: Springer Science+Business Media. https://doi.org/10.1007/978-981-4560-47-4

Kiely, R. (2005). A transformative learning model for service-learning: A longitudinal case study. *Michigan Journal of Community Service Learning, 12*(5), 5–22.

King, R. (2015). Virtue ethics: Foundation for civic engagement and service-learning. In O. Delano-Oriaran, M. W. Penick-Parks, & S. Fondrie (Eds.), *SAGE sourcebook of service-learning and civic engagement* (pp. 17–22). Los Angeles: Sage. https://doi.org/10.4135/9781483346625.n9

Kinsella, E. A., & Pitman, A. (Eds.). (2012). *Phronesis as professional knowledge: Practical wisdom in the professions.* Rotterdam & Boston: Sense. https://doi.org/10.1007/978-94-6091-731-8

Kreber, C. (2016). *Educating for civic-mindedness: Nurturing authentic professional identities through transformative higher education.* New York: Routledge.

Labov, W. (2001). The anatomy of style-shifting. In P.

Eckert & J. R. Rickford (Eds.), *Style and sociolinguistic variation* (pp. 85–108). Cambridge: Cambridge University Press.

Ladson-Billings, G. (2004). Culture versus citizenship: The challenge of racialized citizenship in the United States. In J. Banks (Ed.), *Diversity and citizenship education: Global perspectives* (pp. 99–126). San Francisco: Jossey-Bass.

Lareau, A., & Calarco, J. M. (2012). Class, cultural capital, and institutions: The case of families and schools. In S. T. Fiske & H. R. Markus (Eds.), *Facing social class: How societal rank influences interaction* (pp. 61–86). New York: Russell Sage.

Leander, A. (2009, November 30). Habitus and field. *Working paper*. Copenhagen Business School: Department of Intercultural Communication and Management. Retrieved from http://openarchive.cbs.dk/handle/10398/7966

Lee, A., Dunston, R., & Fowler, C. (2012). Seeing is believing: An embodied pedagogy of 'doing partnership' in child and family health. In P. Hager, A. Lee, & A. Reich (Eds.), *Practice, learning and change: Practice-theory perspectives* (pp. 267–276). Dordrecht: Springer Science+Business Media.

Lukenchuk, A., Jagla, V. M., & Price, T. A. (2013). Critical discourse analysis of service-learning perspectives and models: Transforming teacher education. In V. A. Jagla, J. A. Erickson, & A. S. Tinkler (Eds.), *Transforming teacher education through service-learning* (pp. 51–69). Charlotte, NC: Information Age.

Macintyre Latta, M., & Wunder, S. (Eds.). (2012). *Placing practitioner knowledge at the center of teacher education: Rethinking the policies and practices of the education doctorate*. Charlotte, NC: Information Age.

Malandra, K. (2007). Interrupting habitus and community-based arts: Pedagogical efficacy in a university/community collaboration. (Order No. 3268170, Temple University). ProQuest Dissertations and Theses, 287. Retrieved from http://search.proquest.com/docview/304827516?accountid=14270 (304827516)

Mathews, D. (2004, April 7). *Six democratic practices. Kettering Foundation working paper draft*. Retrieved from http://www.publicpolicycenter.hawaii.edu/documents/PPC2Keynote_001.pdf

McGee, M. C. (1998). Phronesis in the Gadamer versus Habermas debates. In J. M. Sloop & J. P. McDaniel (Eds.), *Judgment calls: Rhetoric, politics, and indeterminacy* (pp. 13–41). Boulder, CO: Westview.

McMillan, J. (2011a). What happens when the university meets the community? Service learning, boundary work, and boundary workers. *Teaching in Higher Education, 16*(5), 553–564. doi:10.1080/13562517.2011.580839.

McMillan, J. (2011b). Boundary workers and their importance to community-university partnerships. *Metropolitan Universities, 22*(2), 106–120. Retrieved from https://journals.iupui.edu/index.php/muj/article/viewFile/20476/20076.

McReynolds, M. R. (2015). Developing practitioner-scholars for the future of community engagement. In O. Delano-Oriaran, M. Penick-Parks, & S. Fondrie (Eds.), *The SAGE sourcebook of service learning and civic engagement* (pp. 3–9). Thousand Oaks, CA: Sage. https://doi.org/10.4135/9781483346625.n7

McReynolds, M., & Shields, E. (Eds.). (2015). *Diving deep in community engagement: A model for professional development*. Des Moines, IA: Iowa Campus Compact.

Mitchell, T. (2014). How service learning enacts social justice sensemaking. *Journal of Critical Thought and Praxis, 2*(2), Article 6.

Mitchell, T., Richard, F. I., Battistoni, R. M., Rost-Banik, C., Netz, R., & Zakoske, C. (2015). Reflective practice that persists: Connections between reflection in service learning programs and in current life. *Michigan Journal of Community Service Learning, 21*(2), 49–63.

Musil, C. M. (2009). Educating students for personal and social responsibility: The civic learning spiral. In B. Jacoby (Ed.), *Civic engagement in higher education: Concepts and practices* (pp. 49–68). San Francisco: Jossey-Bass.

National Task Force on Civic Learning and Democratic Engagement. (2012). *A crucible moment: College learning and democracy's future*. Washington, DC: American Association of Colleges and Universities. Retrieved from http://www.aacu.org/crucible

Neher, W. W., & Sandin, P. J. (2016). *Communicating ethically: Character, duties, consequences and relationships*. New York: Routledge.

Nemeth, E. A., & Winterbottom, C. (2016). Communities of practice: Youth and social justice service-learning. In A. S. Tinkler, B. E. Tinkler, V. S. Jagla, & J. R. Strait (Eds.), *Service-learning to advance social justice in a time of radical enequality* (pp. 298–317). Charlotte, NC: Information Age.

Nicolini, D. (2012). *Practice theory, work, and organization*. Oxford, UK: Oxford University Press.

Noel, J. (1999). On the varieties of phronesis. *Educational Philosophy and Theory, 31*(3), 273–289. https://doi.org/10.1111/j.1469-5812.1999.tb00466.x

Noyes, E., Darby, A., & Leupold, C. (2015). Students' emotions in academic service-learning. *Journal of Higher Education Outreach and Engagement, 19*(4), 63–84.

Perry, J. A. (2015). The Carnegie project on the education doctorate. *Change: The Magazine of Higher Learning, 47*(3), 56–61. https://doi.org/10.1080/00091383.2015.1040712

Pruitt, B., & Thomas, P. (2007). *Democratic dialogue – A handbook for practitioners*. Washington, DC and New York: CIDA, GS/OAS, International IDEA, UNDP. Retrieved from http://www.idea.int/publications/democratic_dialogue/index.cfm.

Reay, D. (2004). 'It's all becoming a habitus': Beyond the habitual use of habitus in educational research. *British Journal of Sociology of Education, 25*(4), 431–444. https://doi.org/10.1080/0142569042000236934

Reynolds, N. P. (2014). What counts as outcomes? Community perspectives of an engineering partnership. *Michigan Journal of Community Service Learning, 21*(1), 79–90.

Rodgers, C. (2002). Defining reflection: Another look at John Dewey and reflective thinking. *Teachers College Record, 102*(4), 842–866. https://doi.org/10.1111/1467-9620.00181

Saltmarsh, J., & Hartley, M. (2011). "To serve a larger purpose". In J. Saltmarsh & M. Hartley (Eds.), *To serve a larger purpose: Engagement for democracy and the transformation of higher education* (pp. 1–12). Philadelphia: Temple University Press.

Saltmarsh, J., Hartley, M., & Clayton, P. (2009). *Democratic engagement white paper.* Boston: New England Resource Center for Higher Education.

Sandy, M., & Holland, B. A. (2006). Different worlds and common ground: Community partner perspectives on campus-community partnerships. *Michigan Journal of Community Service Learning, 13*(1), 30–43.

Schram, S. (2012). Phronetic social science: An idea whose time has come. In B. Flyvbjerg, T. Landman, & S. Schram (Eds.), *Real social science: Applied phronesis* (pp. 15–26). New York: Cambridge University Press. https://doi.org/10.1017/CBO9780511719912.003

Schwandt, T. A. (2005). Modeling our understanding of the practice fields. *Pedagogy, Culture and Society, 13*(3), 313–332. https://doi.org/10.1080/14681360500200231

Shotter, J. (2012). Knowledge in transition: The role of prospective, descriptive concepts in a practice-situated, hermeneutical-phronetic social science. *Management Learning, 43*(3), 245–260. https://doi.org/10.1177/1350507612437679

Shulman, L. S. (2007). Response to comments: Practical wisdom in the service of professional practice. *Educational Researcher, 36*(9), 560–563. https://doi.org/10.3102/0013189X07313150

Smith, D. E. (1987). *The everyday world as problematic: A feminist sociology.* Toronto: University of Toronto Press.

Smith, D. E. (2005). *Institutional ethnography: A sociology for people.* Lanham, MD: AltaMira.

Sternberg, R. J. (2003). *Wisdom, intelligence, and creativity synthesized.* New York: Cambridge University Press. https://doi.org/10.1017/CBO9780511509612

Stoecker, R., Tryon, E. A., & Hilgendorf, A. (Eds.). (2009). *The unheard voices: Community organizations and service learning.* Philadelphia: Temple University Press.

Torre, M. E., Fine, M., Stoudt, B. G., & Fox, M. (2012). Critical participatory action research as public science. In P. Camic & H. Cooper (Eds.), *Handbook of research methods in Psychology* (pp. 171–184). Washington, DC: American Psychological Association. https://doi.org/10.1037/13620-011

Toulmin, S. (2003). *Return to reason.* Cambridge, MA: Harvard University Press.

Townley, B. (2014). Bourdieu and organizational theory: A ghostly apparition? In P. S. Adler, P. Du Gay, G. Morgan, & M. Reed (Eds.), *Oxford handbook of sociology, social theory and organization studies: Contemporary currents* (pp. 39–63). Oxford, UK: Oxford University Press.

Vygotsky, L. S. (1978). *Mind in society: The development of higher psychological processes.* Cambridge, MA: Harvard University Press.

Wade, R. (Ed.). (1997). *Community service-learning: A guide to including service in the public school curriculum.* Albany, NY: SUNY Press.

Warren, M. R., Park, S. O., & Tieken, M. C. (2016). The formation of community-engaged scholars: A collaborative approach to doctoral training in education research. *Harvard Education Review, 86*(2), 233–260. https://doi.org/10.17763/0017-8055.86.2.233

Weick, K. E., Sutcliffe, K. M., & Obstfeld, D. (2005). Organizing and the process of sensemaking. *Organization Science, 16*(4), 409–421. https://doi.org/10.1287/orsc.1050.0133

Yalowitz, B., Malandra, K., & Keith, N. (2015). Building trust, sharing power, crossing borders: The art sanctuary-Temple/Tyler Partnership. In N. Z. Keith, *Engaging in social partnerships: Democratic practices for campus-community partnerships* (pp. 161–189). New York: Routledge.

Yosso, T. J. (2005). Whose culture has capital? A critical race theory discussion of community cultural wealth. *Race, Ethnicity and Education, 8*(1), 69–91. https://doi.org/10.1080/1361332052000341006

Zembylas, M. (2007). Emotional capital and education: Theoretical insights from Bourdieu. *British Journal of Educational Studies, 55*(4), 443–463. https://doi.org/10.1111/j.1467-8527.2007.00390.x

Authors

NOVELLA Z. KEITH (keithnov@temple.edu) is professor emerita of Urban Education at Temple University. Her work emerges from an abiding interest in participatory democracy and social justice and considers educational partnerships, community service learning, and civic engagement as spaces where these aims can be pursued. This article extends ideas presented in her recent book, *Engaging in Social Partnerships: Democratic Practices for University-Community Partnerships* (Routledge, 2015). She is currently working on the practical applications of this work with regard to cultivating capacities for democratic engagement in professionals, community partners, and students.

The Counter-Normative Effects of Service-Learning: Fostering Attitudes toward Social Equality through Contact and Autonomy

Margaret A. Brown   Jared D. Wymer   Cierra S. Cooper
Seattle Pacific University

Power dynamics are implicated in intergroup prosocial behavior (Nadler & Halabi, 2015). This research investigated two factors that influence the effect of intergroup prosocial behavior on views of social equality: amount of direct intergroup contact and type of helping. Students in a social psychology course (N = 93) were randomly assigned to a service-learning group or to a control group. The service-learning group was further subdivided into an autonomy-oriented helping group or a dependency-oriented helping group. After participating in approximately 19 hours of community service over nine weeks, service-learners had more positive views of social equality compared to the control group. This effect was strongest in autonomy-oriented helpers who had high levels of direct intergroup contact. The implications and mechanisms of service-learning as a form of counter-normative intergroup prosocial behavior are discussed.

Prosocial behavior is an integral, adaptive component of human functioning. Prosocial behavior can take many forms, including spontaneous assistance offered in emergencies, sustained community service, and the billions of dollars given each year in philanthropy. Communities richly benefit from the time, resources, and talents of prosocial people. Prosocial behavior also benefits helpers. Prosocial people become happier, healthier, and experience a greater sense of purpose in life through their service to others (Piliavin, 2003; Smith & Davidson, 2014).

Prosocial behavior that is "intergroup" (i.e., that occurs across different social groups) has the added potential benefit of increasing people's exposure to diverse group members and may result in an increased preference for social equality. Brown (2011a, 2011b) found that participating in service-learning, a form of intergroup prosocial behavior (IPB), reduced social dominance orientation (Pratto, Sidanius, Stallworth, & Malle, 1994). Social dominance orientation is an anti-egalitarian attitude that includes one's preference for group-based social hierarchy and support for discrimination against lower status groups (Sidanius & Pratto, 1999). The conditions under which these benefits of intergroup prosocial behavior are most likely to accrue have not yet been explored. The present study examines two variables hypothesized to influence the relationship between IPB and attitudes toward social equality: the amount of direct, personal contact that groups have with one another and the type of assistance offered. We begin with a brief review of the literature to provide the theoretical context for this study's design and hypotheses, focusing on the intimate relationship between IPB and power.

Power dynamics are frequently implicated in IPB. The group offering assistance (i.e., the "helpers") may possess some resource that the other group (i.e., the "recipients") lacks, and thus the transaction is founded on a status differential. The Intergroup Helping as Status Relations Model (IHSR; Nadler, 2002; Nadler & Halabi, 2006) is the most well-developed theory in social psychology to describe the connection between IPB and power dynamics. The model is based on the assumption that pervasive legitimation of social inequality (Costa-Lopes, Dovidio, Pereira, & Jost, 2013) operates within IPB, such that rather than promote equality, prosocial behavior frequently serves the ironic function of keeping high status and low status groups in their respective places (Cunningham & Platow, 2007; Halabi, Dovidio, & Nadler, 2008; Jackson & Esses, 2000; Nadler & Chernyak-Hai, 2014).

The IHSR differentiates between two types of prosocial behavior: autonomy-oriented and dependency-oriented. Autonomy-oriented helping is aimed at assisting the recipient to help him or herself by providing a partial solution such as tools that can be used to resolve the issue or need. In contrast, dependency-oriented helping provides a full solution to the recipient's need. Autonomy-oriented helping reflects the perspective that the recipient is autonomous and efficacious, whereas dependency-oriented helping reflects a more negative view of the recipient as dependent and incapable. The IHSR predicts that higher status groups will be most apt to provide dependency-oriented help to lower status groups. Dependency-oriented help keeps lower status group dependent and further entrenches existing social hierarchy. By extension, it legitimates and cements the prejudicial attitudes of high status group members toward low status group members as incompetent and weak (Nadler, 2002; Nadler & Chernyak-Hai, 2014; Nadler & Halabi, 2015).

While the IHSR model is useful for understanding typical instances of IPB, it does not apply to all forms of IPB. In a series of studies, Brown (2011a, 2011b) found that college students randomly assigned to participate in service-learning had a greater preference for social equality after the experience than a control group, as indexed by reduced social dominance orientation scores.

Service-learning is defined as:

> a course-based, credit-bearing educational experience in which students (a) participate in mutually identified and organized service activities that benefit the community, and (b) reflect on the service activity in such a way as to gain further understanding of course content and an enhanced sense of personal values and civic responsibility (adapted from Bringle & Hatcher, 1996, p. 222).

Service-learning is an atypical, "counter-normative" form of IPB for a variety of reasons (Clayton & Ash, 2004). Most salient to this research, it is collaborative and democratic (Bringle, Reeb, Brown, & Ruiz, 2016). Both groups participate in defining the need as well as the nature and parameters of the interaction. Further, service-learning is predicated on the assumption that prosocial interactions are reciprocal rather than unidirectional. Both groups learn from one another, and both groups benefit (i.e., are served) from the interaction.

Although Brown's (2011a, 2011b) research shows that IPB in the form of service-learning *can* promote more favorable attitudes toward social equality amongst high status group members, the conditions under which this effect is most likely to occur have not yet been explored. The contact hypothesis (Allport, 1954; Pettigrew & Tropp, 2006) suggests that direct, personal contact facilitates more positive intergroup attitudes. Therefore, we predict that IPB with high levels of direct contact between groups is likely to produce the best effects (Koschate, Oethinger, Kuchenbrandt, & Van Dick, 2012). Further, research on the contact hypothesis finds that the benefits of contact are enhanced when the groups have common goals and are of equal status. Helping that is autonomy-oriented is much more likely to fit with these conditions than dependency-oriented helping. In autonomy-oriented helping, both groups share the goal of genuinely and more permanently improving the condition of the recipient group; in addition, autonomy-oriented helping relies on an agentic, positive view of the recipient, which deemphasizes status differentials between groups.

In the present study, college student participants were randomly assigned to a service-learning group or control group that did not take part in community service. Within the service-learning condition, participants were subdivided into either autonomy- or dependency-oriented helping groups, and the direct contact hours that service-learners spent with the clients at the community sites was measured. While it would have been ideal to randomly assign service-learners to high and low levels of direct contact, it was not possible to achieve this without compromising the specific needs of the various service sites, which often varied from week-to-week. The dependent measure was scores on the Equality and Social Responsibility Orientation scale (ESRO; Bowman & Brandenberger, 2012), selected because it assesses attitudes toward social equality and the importance of social responsibility, and has been validated in previous research examining the outcomes of college diversity experiences including service-learning (Bowman & Brandenberger; Bowman, Brandenberger, Mick, & Smedley, 2010).

Our first hypothesis was that the service-learning condition would affect participants' attitudes. We predicted that those engaged in autonomy-oriented helping would develop more positive attitudes toward social equality than those engaged in dependency-oriented helping, and that both service-learning groups would have more positive attitudes toward social equality than the control group. Our second hypothesis was that helping type would interact with direct intergroup contact to predict attitudes toward social equality. Specifically, we expected that those in autonomy-oriented placements would be the most benefited by increased direct contact with clients at their service sites.

Method

Participants

Ninety-three students enrolled in a social psychology course at a small private university in an urban center of the Northwestern United States participated in exchange for extra course credit. Using random assignment to conditions, 47 of the participants (8 men, 39 women) were assigned to the service-learning condition, while 46 of the participants (6 men, 39 women, 1 not identified) were assigned to the control condition. The gender imbalance in the sample (83.9% women) was likely attributable to the high concentration of psychology majors in the course. At this university (and consistent with nationwide trends; Willyard, 2011), women comprise the preponderance of psychology majors. Seven other students enrolled in the course chose not to participate in the study. Three of the non-participating students were in the service-learning condition, and four were in the control condition. The mean age of participants was 20.68 ($SD = 1.66$), with the following racial/ethnic self-identification: White or European American, $n = 66$, Asian or Asian American, $n = 8$, Hispanic or Latino, $n = 6$, American Indian or Alaskan Native $n = 4$, Black or African American, $n = 2$, and Other, $n = 5$. The sample had similar numbers of non-Hispanic white/European Americans (71%) to the university population at the time of the study (68%), and to the surrounding metropolitan area during the most recent available census (year 2010; 72.7%).

Service-Learning and Control Group Procedures

On the first day of the academic quarter, students were informed of the service project component of the course. They were told that understanding the issues in one's local community was critical to informed citizenship and that it would help them to more deeply understand several of the concepts presented in the course. They were also told that the instructor was investigating the effectiveness of different pedagogical techniques for having students learn about community issues and course concepts, and they were randomly assigned to one of two groups: "service-learning" or "service research" (control). Students were informed that both groups were designed to take an equivalent amount of time, approximately 18 hours across nine weeks. Both required equal amounts of coursework (i.e., weekly journal entries and a final paper discussing their service or research project).

Participants in the service-learning group were subsequently randomly assigned to receive one of two lists of community organizations with service placements. One of the lists had autonomy-oriented placements to choose from, and one of the lists had dependency-oriented placements. The lists contained several community organizations, including food banks, nursing homes, homeless shelters, and urban youth tutoring programs. The average total time that students reported being at their service sites was 19.17 hours ($SD = 4.97$), and the average amount of direct contact they reported with the organizations' clients was 15.40 hours ($SD = 4.83$).

The research team classified the service-learning sites as autonomy- or dependency-oriented based on descriptions of the placements provided by the community organizations. An example of an autonomy-oriented placement was the Empowering Youth and Family Outreach organization, which provides tutoring and mentoring to at-risk youth. A dependency-oriented placement involved providing basic care to residents at a nursing facility (e.g., helping serve food to residents). There were 30 service-learners in autonomy-oriented placements and 17 service-learners in dependency-oriented placements. The unequal distribution of placements was due to the greater number of university partnerships with autonomy-oriented organizations, and therefore more placements were available at those sites. Nevertheless, assignment to helping type was randomized to reduce selection bias. At the end of the quarter, service-learners were asked to indicate whether they felt their service was more autonomy- or dependency-oriented (definitions were provided), and their judgments aligned with those of the research team. The number of service hours was not strictly controlled and direct contact was not randomly assigned, but a post-hoc analysis revealed no significant differences between service groups regarding the amount of total service time ($p = .20$) or hours in direct contact with clients ($p = .51$).

Even though service-learning activities may involve one-on-one interactions, service-learning experiences are considered to be an intergroup experience because the service-learning context makes group affiliations salient, and thus intergroup dynamics apply (Turner, Hogg, Oakes, Reicher, & Wetherell, 1987; van Dijk & van Engen, 2013). The clients at the service sites were different than the service-learners in a variety of salient demographic characteristics. Student service-learners were of traditional college age, in relatively good health, and most were white and of middle or upper middle socio-economic status. The clients of the service organizations included persons who were children, elderly, in poverty or working class, homeless, and ethnic minorities. Students chronicled their service experiences each week in a journal, using the structure of the DEAL model (Ash & Clayton, 2009).

The service research (control) group was given a list of weekly research topics from their instructor to investigate. For example:

> This week your journal entry will be about food insecurity, poverty, and racism. Research this topic using the Internet, library, or other sources. Below are some examples of the types of things that you could report on, but ultimately it is up to you what you choose to include: What is the poverty rate in your city?

In the United States? What income level qualifies a person to be considered living in poverty? What are the characteristics of those in poverty in this region (e.g., gender, race/ethnicity, age, etc.)? What is food insecurity? In your city, what forms of assistance are available to people who are facing food insecurity? Consider investigating specific organizations such as Solid Ground. What is their mission, what services do they provide, and how are they funded? How do racism and other forms of prejudice and oppression relate to poverty? Did you encounter anything particularly interesting or surprising in your research? What new perspectives or ideas did you encounter as a part of your research? What connections are you able to draw between classroom learning (e.g., theories on the sources of prejudice, stereotyping, and reducing prejudice) and your research?

Both the service-learning and the service research (control) groups wrote and submitted weekly journal entries, engaged in class discussion on service and its connection to course content, and wrote a final paper relating what they had learned about service to the course material. The two groups were as similar as possible except for the experiential aspect of serving in the community.

Study Procedure and Materials

The study measures were given to students during the final week of the quarter, after their service projects were completed. Students were asked some standard demographic questions, and a few questions about their service placement (for the service-learning group). Service-learners were asked to indicate the name of their service-learning site, how much total time they spent during the quarter at the service site, and how much time they spent in direct contact with clients at the site. Additionally, they were asked to classify their service as dependency-oriented (i.e., whether their service was geared to provide a full solution to the clients' needs, without much input from the client), autonomy-oriented (i.e., providing clients with tools to help address their own needs), neither, or both.

All participants received the primary assessment of Equality and Social Responsibility Orientation scale (ESRO; Bowman & Brandenberger, 2012). Bowman and Brandenberger define ESRO as "a set of attitudes and values pertaining to the recognition and denunciation of societal inequality and the importance placed on helping others" (p. 185). Their research finds that positive diversity experiences predict ESRO scores. The ESRO is comprised of seven subscales, which were presented in counterbalanced order: Responsibility for Improving Society (Nelson Laird, Engberg, & Hurtado, 2005), Openness to Diversity (Pascarella, Edison, Nora, Hagedorn, & Terenzini, 1996), Empowerment View of Helping (Michlitsch & Frankel, 1989), Situational Attributions for Poverty (Feagin, 1971), Self-Generating View of Helping (Michlitsch & Frankel, 1989), Belief in a Just World (Dalbert, Montada, & Schmitt, 1987), and Social Dominance Orientation (Pratto et al., 1994). The latter three subscales were reverse-coded, such that higher scores indicated greater equality and social responsibility orientation. All subscales were z-scored and averaged into a single, overall index of ESRO. The measure demonstrated acceptable internal reliability ($\alpha = .73$).

Participants were told that this study was investigating how experiences in social psychology courses relate to students' attitudes toward other people and social groups. Participation was voluntary and extra credit was awarded for participation. An alternative extra credit assignment was provided to avoid coercion. The survey was administered during the tenth week of the quarter. Students received a full debriefing on the last day of the course.

Results

The first hypothesis that service condition [Autonomy-Oriented Service-learning (AOSL), Dependency-Oriented Service-learning (DOSL), and Control] would influence ESRO was tested with a 3-group, one way ANOVA. There was a significant main effect, $F(2, 90) = 20.33, p < .001, \eta_p^2 = .31$, and follow-up analyses confirmed that the control condition had significantly lower ESRO scores ($M = -.32, SD = .58$) than the DOSL condition ($M = .06, SD = .36; p = .01$) and the AOSL condition ($M = .45, SD = .50; p < .001$). Additionally, ESRO scores were lower in the DOSL condition than in the AOSL condition ($p = .02$). Thus, as predicted, service-learners developed more positive attitudes toward social equality than the control group, with the autonomy-oriented helpers displaying the most positive attitudes of the three groups.

Post-hoc analyses examining the seven subscales of the ESRO individually as dependent variables revealed that all seven 3-group, one-way ANOVAs had significant overall F values (all p's < .05), consistent with the composite ESRO results described above. The specific pattern of differences between the AOSL, DOSL, and Control groups was the same as described above (i.e., the three groups significantly differed from one another, with AOSL the most positive, DOSL in the middle, and Control the least positive) for all of the individual subscales with the exception of the Responsibility for Improving Society subscale. In this case, both DOSL and AOSL groups were superior to the Control condition (p's < .01) but not different from one another ($p = .89$). In sum, use of the overall ESRO composite was a good representation of its constituent components.

To examine the second hypothesis that helping type would interact with direct contact to predict ESRO, we used a moderated regression analysis, with helping type (AOSL and DOSL) and direct contact hours as predictors. Direct contact hours was treated as a continuous predictor, and was mean-centered prior to the analysis. Helping type was coded as: AOSL = -1, DOSL = 1. An interaction term was modeled by creating a cross-product. There was a main effect of helping type, $F(1, 43) = 6.12$, $p = .02$, $\eta_p^2 = .13$, accompanied by a main effect of direct contact, $F(1, 43) = 6.06$, $p = .02$, $\eta_p^2 = .12$, and a helping type by direct contact interaction, $F(1, 43) = 3.91$, $p = .048$, $\eta_p^2 = .08$.

Simple effects tests to examine the nature of the interaction revealed that direct contact had no effect on ESRO scores among those in the DOSL condition ($t < 1$), but there was a significant effect of direct contact among those in the AOSL condition, $t(43) = 3.74$, $p = .001$. Additionally, helping type had no effect when direct contact hours were low (one standard deviation below the mean; $t < 1$), but a significant effect when direct contact hours were high (one standard deviation above the mean; $t(43) = 3.05$, $p = .005$). The nature of the effects can be seen in Figure 1.

A post-hoc moderated regression analysis that examined the effect of *non-contact* service hours (i.e., hours spent doing administrative/clerical work that did not involve direct contact with clients) found that the only significant predictor of ESRO scores was helping type, $F(1, 43) = 5.47$, $p = .02$, $\eta_p^2 = .11$. Independent of how many non-contact service hours service-learners spent at their organizations, those in AO service sites ($M = .42$) had higher ESRO scores than those in DO service sites ($M = .09$). In short, non-contact service hours did not predict attitudes toward social equality.

Discussion

Our findings supported both hypotheses. Participants who engaged in service-learning had more positive attitudes toward social equality than did a control condition (replicating previous research by Brown, 2011a, 2011b), and this effect was strongest amongst service-learners in autonomy-

Figure 1

Equality and Social Responsibility Orientation (ESRO) as a Function of Helping Type and Direct Contact

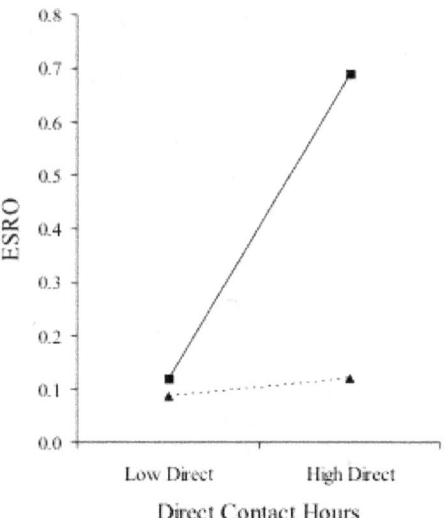

Note. Direct contact hours depicted are predicted values, one standard deviation above and below the mean.

oriented placements. Further, direct contact hours interacted with helping type, such that higher levels of direct contact with the clients of community organizations increased positive attitudes toward social equality, but only amongst service-learners engaged in autonomy-oriented helping.

These findings extend our knowledge of how IPB and views on power are related in counter-normative IPB situations such as service-learning. Nadler and colleagues' IHSR model (Nadler, 2002; Nadler & Halabi, 2006, 2015) delineates what higher status groups do in typical IPB situations, when they are free to choose what type of help to offer lower status groups. In these instances, they are most likely to provide dependency-oriented helping, which has the consequence of maintaining status hierarchies and reinforcing the prejudicial attitudes that endorse such hierarchies. However, what happens when a higher-status group is *assigned* to participate in autonomy-oriented helping? We found that participation in autonomy-oriented helping created greater endorsement of social equality, and that this effect was most pronounced when service-learners had higher levels of direct intergroup contact.

While the mechanisms and benefits of contact in improving prejudicial attitudes are well-documented, less is known about the benefits of participation in autonomy-oriented helping. Research by Nadler and Chernyak-Hai (2014; Study 4) found that low status persons who requested autonomy-oriented help were viewed as more efficacious and motivated than those who sought dependency-oriented help, and their needs were perceived as transient rather than chronic. Perhaps in our study, assigning service-learners to provide autonomy-oriented help created a more favorable impression of the clients at the community organizations, thus reducing some of the initial status differential. Also, it is possible that engaging in autonomy-oriented helping triggers a self-perception process (Bem, 1967) wherein participants come to believe that what they are doing (i.e., IPB that reduces status hierarchies) is appropriate and desirable, thus leading to the development of more positive attitudes toward social equality.

There were some limitations in our study that warrant consideration. The participants in this study were primarily young white women from a private college. The homogenous demographic of the sample limits its external validity. However, this sample represents a relatively privileged demographic, and privileged populations might be especially benefited by having their views on social equality challenged. Second, experimental control and uniformity were reduced because the experimental manipulation of service-learning took place in a naturalistic, field setting rather than in a lab. Participants in the service-learning condition served at a variety of placements with a variety of groups doing a variety of tasks. Despite this variability, serving still had significant effects on views of social equality, and autonomy-oriented placements still proved superior to dependency-oriented placements. Presumably, the variability or "noise" would weaken the power of this investigation to detect effects. A third limitation is that the amount of direct contact was not experimentally manipulated, but rather was measured, making it difficult to draw causal conclusions about its effect on attitudes toward social equality. However, participants were generally not in control of this variable. They did not choose how much time they spent with clients; rather, the service site supervisors were responsible for assigning tasks. This mitigates the possibility that participants who already had favorable views toward social equality would choose to spend more time in direct contact with clients of the organization.

While research on the IHSR has provided valuable insights into key variables (e.g., legitimacy and stability of status relations, threats to social dominance and social identity, type of helping) involved in the power dynamics of typical IPB, much is left to learn about the process and outcomes of IPB that is counter-normative. Extant research is encouraging. Help is more welcome by recipients when it is autonomy-oriented, and autonomy-oriented helping is more likely to foster reconciliation between groups (Fisher, Nadler, Little, & Saguy, 2008; Stürmer & Snyder, 2010). Service-learning is one type of counter-normative helping experience that appears to have beneficial effects on intergroup attitudes and relations (O'Grady, 2000; Rosner-Salazar, 2003). Although service-learning has received a fair amount of study, most of this research has used qualitative or non-experimental quantitative methods, rendering causal conclusions elusive (Bringle, Phillips, & Hudson, 2004; but see Brown 2011a, 2011b for exceptions).

In addition to service-learning, other forms of counter-normative IPB should be examined, particularly instances where higher status groups spontaneously choose to offer autonomy-oriented help to lower status groups. Research on motives for intergroup helping (van Leeuwen & Täuber, 2012) is a fruitful starting point. Although IPB by high status groups is at times guided by a sense of shared community and civic engagement (Omoto, Snyder, & Hackett, 2010) or core personal values such as generosity or social justice, more egoistic concerns such as impression-management can also be motivating (van Leeuwen, & Täuber, 2010). Different motivations for IPB may well have different implications for intergroup power dynamics.

Another related model that future research on the outcomes of IPB might consider is Morton's (1995) work on community service paradigms and subsequent researchers' analyses of his approach (Bringle, Hatcher, & McIntosh, 2006; Moely, Furco, & Reed, 2008). The description of charity, project, and social change types of service has some overlap with the IHSR's types of helping (i.e., roughly, the charity paradigm has some overlap with a dependency orientation and the social change paradigm has some overlap with an autonomy orientation); however, Morton's model emphasizes a more macro-level view of the service rather than perceptions of the population or person being served.

The present study found that being assigned to engage in autonomy-oriented helping, combined with higher levels of direct intergroup contact, was the best recipe for improving service-learners' endorsement of social equality and social responsibility. Given that higher status groups are inclined to give dependency-oriented help to lower status groups, and given that people are inclined to affiliate with similar others rather than with outgroups, compiling the full list of ingredients for this recipe will require effort, intentionality, and a clearer understanding of the antecedents and mechanisms of counter-normative IPB.

References

Allport, G. W. (1954). *The nature of prejudice*. Cambridge, MA: Addison-Wesley.

Clayton, P. H., & Ash, S. L. (2009). Generating, deepening, and documenting learning: The power of critical reflection in applied learning. *Journal of Applied Learning in Higher Education, 1*(1), 25–48. Retrieved from http://hdl.handle.net/1805/4579

Bem, D. J. (1967). Self-perception: An alternative interpretation of cognitive dissonance phenomena. *Psychological review*, 74(3), 183–200. Doi: 10.1037/h0024835

Bowman N. A. & Brandenberger, J. W. (2012). Experiencing the unexpected: Toward a model of college diversity experiences and attitude change. *The Review of Higher Education*, 35, 179–205. Doi: 10.1353/rhe.2012.0016

Bowman N. A., Brandenberger, J. W., Mick, C. S., & Smedley, C. T. (2010). Sustained immersion courses and student orientations to equality, justice, and social responsibility: The role of short-term service-learning. *Michigan Journal of Community Service Learning, 17*(1), 20–31.

Bringle, R. G., & Hatcher, J. A. (1996). Implementing service learning in higher education. *Journal of Higher Education*, 67, 221–239. Retrieved from http://www.jstor.org/stable/2943981.

Bringle, R. G., Hatcher, J.A., & McIntosh, R. E. (2006). Analyzing Morton's typology of service paradigms and integrity. *Michigan Journal of Community Service Learning*, 13(1), 5–15.

Bringle, R. G., Phillips, M. A., & Hudson, M. (2004). *The measure of service learning*. Washington, DC: American Psychological Association.

Bringle, R. G., Reeb, R. Brown, M. A., & Ruiz, A. (2016). *Service learning in psychology: Enhancing undergraduate education for the public good*. Washington, DC: American Psychological Association.

Brown, M. A. (2011a). The power of generosity to change views on social power. *Journal of Experimental Social Psychology, 47*, 1285–1290. Doi:10.1016/j.jesp.2011.05.021

Brown, M. A. (2011b). Learning from service: The effect of helping on helpers' social dominance orientation. *Journal of Applied Social Psychology, 41*, 850–871. Doi: 10.1111/j.1559–1816.2011.00738.x

Clayton, P. H., & Ash, S. L. (2004). Shifts in perspective: Capitalizing on the counter-normative nature of service-learning. *Michigan Journal of Community Service Learning*, 11(1), 59–70. Retrieved from http://hdl.handle.net/2027/spo.3239521.0011.106

Costa-Lopes, R., Dovidio, J. F., Pereira, C. R., & Jost, J. T. (2013). Social psychological perspectives on the legitimation of social inequality: Past, present and future. *European Journal of Social Psychology*, 43(4), 229–237. Doi: 10.1002/ejsp.1966

Cunningham, E., & Platow, M. J. (2007). On helping lower status out-groups: The nature of the help and the stability of the intergroup status hierarchy. *Asian Journal of Social Psychology*, 10(4), 258–264. Doi: 10.1111/j.1467–839X.2007.00234.x

Dalbert, C., Montada, L., & Schmitt, M. (1987). Glaube an die gerechte Welt als Motiv: Validnering Zweier Skalen. *Psychologische Beitrage*, 29, 596–615.

Feagin, J. R. (1971). Poverty: We still believe that God helps those who help themselves. *Psychology Today, 6*(6), 101–110, 129.

Fisher, J. D., Nadler, A., Little, J. S., & Saguy, T. (2008). Help as a vehicle to reconciliation, with particular reference to help for extreme health needs. In A. Nadler, T. E. Malloy, & J. D. Fisher (Eds.), *The social psychology of intergroup reconciliation* (pp. 447–468). Oxford, UK: Oxford University Press.

Halabi, S., Dovidio, J. F., & Nadler, A. (2008). When and how do high status group members offer help: Effects of social dominance orientation and status threat. *Political Psychology*, 29(6), 841–858. Doi: 10.1111/j.1467–9221.2008.00669.x

Jackson, L. M., & Esses, V. M. (2000). Effects of perceived economic competition on people's willingness to help empower immigrants. *Group Processes and Intergroup Relations*, 3, 419–435. Doi: 10.1177/1368430200003004006

Koschate, M., Oethinger, S., Kuchenbrandt, D., & Dick, R. (2012). Is an outgroup member in need a friend indeed? Personal and task-oriented contact as predictors of intergroup prosocial behavior. *European Journal of Social Psychology*, 42(6), 717–728. Doi: 10.1002/ejsp.1879

Michlitsch, J. F., & Frankel, S. (1989). Helping orientations: Four dimensions. *Perceptual and Motor Skills*, 69, 1371–1378.

Moely, B. E., Furco, A., & Reed, J. (2008). Charity and social change: The impact of individual preferences on service-learning outcomes. *Michigan Journal of Community Service Learning*, 15(1), 37–48.

Morton, K. (1995). The irony of service: Charity, project and social change in service-learning. *Michigan Journal of Community Service Learning*, 2(1), 19–32.

Nadler, A. (2002). Inter-group helping relations as power relations: Maintaining or challenging social dominance between groups through helping. *Journal of Social Issues*, 58, 487–502.

Nadler, A., & Chernyak-Hai, L. (2014). Helping them stay where they are: Status effects on dependency/autonomy-oriented helping. *Journal of Personality and Social Psychology*, 106, 58. Doi: 10.1037/a0034152

Nadler, A., & Halabi, S. (2006). Intergroup helping as status relations: Effects of status stability, identification, and type of help on receptivity to high-status group's help. *Journal of Personality and Social Psychology*, 91, 97–110. Doi: 10.1037/0022-3514.91.1.97

Nadler, A., & Halabi, S. (2015). Helping relations and inequality between individuals and groups. In M. Mikulincer, P. R. Shaver, J. F. Dovidio, & J. A. Simpson (Eds.), *APA handbook of personality and social psy-*

chology, Volume 2: Group processes (pp. 371–393). Washington, DC: American Psychological Association.

Nelson Laird, T. F., Engberg, M. E., & Hurtado, S. (2005). Modeling accentuation effects: Enrolling in a diversity course and the importance of social action engagement. *The Journal of Higher Education, 76*(4), 448–476. Doi: 10.1353/jhe.2005.0028

O'Grady, C. R. (Ed.). (2000). *Integrating service learning and multicultural education in colleges and universities.* Mahwah, NJ: Lawrence Erlbaum Associates.

Omoto, A. M., Snyder, M., & Hackett, J. D. (2010). Personality and motivational antecedents of activism and civic engagement. *Journal of Personality, 78*(6), 1703–1734. Doi: 10.1111/j.1467–6494.2010.00667.x

Pascarella, E., Edison, M., Nora, A., Hagedorn, L., & Terenzini, P. (1996). Influences on students' openness to diversity and challenge in the first year of college. *Journal of Higher Education, 67,* 174–195.

Pettigrew, T., & Tropp, L. (2006). A meta-analytic test of intergroup contact theory. *Journal of Personality and Social Psychology, 90,* 751–783. Doi: 10.1037/0022–3514.90.5.751

Piliavin, J. A. (2003). Doing well by doing good: Benefits for the benefactor. In C. L. M. Keyes & J. Haidt (Eds.), *Flourishing: Positive psychology and the life well-lived* (pp. 227–248). Washington, DC: American Psychological Association.

Pratto, F., Sidanius, J., Stallworth, L., & Malle, B. (1994). Social dominance orientation: A personality variable predicting social and political attitudes. *Journal of Personality and Social Psychology, 67,* 741–763. Doi: 10.1037/0022–3514.67.4.741

Rosner-Salazar, T. A. (2003). Multicultural service-learning and community-based research as a model approach to promote social justice. *Social Justice, 30*(4), 64–76. Retrieved from http://www.jstor.org/stable/29768224

Sidanius, J., & Pratto, F. (1999). *Social dominance: An intergroup theory of social hierarchy and oppression.* Cambridge, UK: Cambridge University Press.

Smith, C., & Davidson, H. (2014). *The paradox of generosity: Giving we receive, grasping we lose.* Oxford, UK: Oxford University Press.

Stürmer, S., & Snyder, M. (Eds.). (2010). *The psychology of prosocial behavior: Group processes, intergroup relations, and helping.* Oxford, UK: Wiley-Blackwell.

Turner, J. C., Hogg, M. A., Oakes, P. J., Reicher, S. D., & Wetherell, M. S. (Eds.). (1987). *Rediscovering the social group: A self-categorization theory.* Oxford, UK: Blackwell.

Van Dijk, H., & van Engen, M. L. (2013). A status perspective on the consequences of work group diversity. *Journal of Occupational and Organizational Psychology, 86*(2), 223–241. Doi: 10.1111/joop.12014

van Leeuwen, E., & Täuber, S. (2010). The strategic side of outgroup helping. In S. Stürmer & M. Snyder (Eds.), *The psychology of prosocial behavior: Group processes, intergroup relations, and helping* (pp. 81–99). Oxford, UK: Wiley-Blackwell.

Van Leeuwen, E., & Täuber, S. (2012). Outgroup helping as a tool to communicate ingroup warmth. *Personality and Social Psychology Bulletin, 38*(6), 772–783. Doi:10.1177/0146167211436253

Willyard, C. (2011). Men: A growing minority? gradPSYCH Magazine, 9(1), 40. Retrieved from http://www.apa.org/gradpsych/2011/01/cover-men.aspx

Authors

MARGARET A. BROWN (mbrown@spu.edu) is a professor of Psychology, director of the Center for Scholarship and Faculty Development, and assistant provost at Seattle Pacific University. She is an experienced service-learning practitioner and has won multiple awards for excellence in teaching. Dr. Brown also conducts rigorous, theory-based, experimental research on service-learning. Her recent co-authored book, entitled *Service Learning in Psychology: Enhancing Undergraduate Education for the Public Good,* examines the importance of civic education within the undergraduate psychology curriculum, and provides a wealth of practical advice to faculty members and department chairs for successful implementation.

JARED D. WYMER (wymer@spu.edu) is a doctoral student in the Department of Industrial and Organizational Psychology at Seattle Pacific University. His research interests include prosocial behavior in organizations, the extent to which various factors influence future self-continuity, short- and long-term time horizons, and associated individual and organizational outcomes. He looks forward to candidacy and a career in industry.

CIERRA S. COOPER (cooperc1@spu.edu) double-majored in psychology and political science at Seattle Pacific University. She was an Ames Scholar, recipient of the Barnabas Service Award, and president of the Black Student Union. Her research interests are in psychological aspects of institutionalized racism, and she intends to pursue doctoral studies in human development and public policy.

The *Social Justice Turn*: Cultivating "Critical Hope" in an Age of Despair

Kari M. Grain
University of British Columbia

Darren E. Lund
University of Calgary

Recent global headlines about suicide attacks, xenophobic rhetoric, systemic gun violence, and the continued displacement of those fleeing civil war and environmental catastrophe have foregrounded social justice issues pertaining to race, nationality, socioeconomic status, religion, and a host of other factors. We suggest in this paper that the pervasive despair of our current historical moment has necessitated the urgent development of the conceptual "Social Justice Turn" in service-learning. This move uses as a foundational starting point three trends that have been consistently marginalized but are gaining momentum in our field: a) critique of the field's roots in charity; b) a problematization of White normativity, paired with the bolstering of diverse voices and perspectives, and c) the embrace of emotional elements including tension, ambiguity, and discomfort. Finally, we offer "critical hope" (Bozalek, Carolissen, Liebowitz, & Boler, 2014; Freire, 2007) as a conceptual space in which service-learning as a field may simultaneously acknowledge the historical and contextual roots of current despair, while using this affective element as a pedagogical and curricular means to engage service-learning more intentionally as a vehicle for social justice goals.

It was grounds for despair. On September 2nd, 2015, a three-year-old Syrian boy named Alan Kurdi washed ashore on a Mediterranean beach. The drowning was not an unusual occurrence in the region, as news articles and witness reports had many times made second-page international headlines, warning of the exodus out of Syria, and calling alarm to the deplorable conditions of human trafficking boats. What made Alan's story front-page news, however, was the graphic imagery that quickly invoked in citizens around the world an emotional connection to this victim of civil war and structural inequality. Alan, one child of thousands lost to a circumstance positioned firmly in a larger web of structural restrictions and political conflict, became every person's child in the global imaginary. Countless public figures saw in Alan a child they knew and loved; former Canadian Prime Minister Stephen Harper recalled the moment he and his wife saw the photo, and it evoked memories of their own son at that age (The Canadian Press, 2015). Social media forums erupted with the hashtag #Alankurdi, mourning his death and the circumstances leading up to it, forming support groups for Syrian refugees, and organizing protests. The notorious photograph rendered the Syrian conflict and its consequences more than a distant political story; for many, Alan became an intimate personification of a civil war, and the face that ignited ethical debates about – among other things – who is granted the privilege of mobility, who has the power to patrol borders, what it means to work for social justice, and to what degree each individual, organization, and government is responsible for taking action when humans suffer.

These questions, catalyzed by the death of a child, became the *raison d'etre* of this article. In tandem with the hateful rhetoric of far right parties in Europe and elsewhere, and popularized xenophobic responses to the global refugee crisis, the death of Alan Kurdi implored us to ask what the field of service-learning and community engagement can and ought to do in light of this emotionally charged, highly divisive historical moment. Service-learning is ideally positioned to put a human face to issues of inequality and human suffering; notions of mobility, power, privilege, and responsibility are especially vital to this field in a time when the global events of 2015 and 2016 have caused a heightened sense of urgency and a widening political divisiveness between constructed binaries of black and white, migrant and refugee, police officer and citizen, right and left politics, Republican and Democrat, and more broadly, "us and them." High profile suicide attacks in Lahore, Brussels, Ougadougou, and Nice (to name only a few), escalating racialized police brutality, mass gun violence, the polarizing rhetoric of political campaigns here and abroad, and the rising rate of political and environmental refugees, have all profoundly shifted the landscape in which service-learning in higher education operates, and therefore must influence how we respond as educators, scholars, practitioners, and citizens within a field that continually navigates border crossings of all sorts.

It bears accentuating that the challenging nature of our current historical moment is not presented here as a devaluation of the struggles that marginalized communities have faced for many generations. In fact, although the current political climate seems new partly because it has only recently gained momentum within popular media, issues of racism, Islamophobia, xenophobia, misogyny, colonialism, exploitation, and oppression have been unrelenting for many years. Current injustices underlined by stories such as Alan Kurdi's, in other words, are far from new, but rather have been in continuous development, each issue of injustice gaining quiet momentum until a photo, a video, or a story finally grips the attention of mainstream media and a broader public. This recent shift – one of increased attention and intensity – demands that educators, practitioners, and institutions take stock; we argue that this has necessitated an organized, conceptual turn in higher education service-learning – one that is acutely aware of and responsive to inequality and dangerous rhetoric, and one that actively problematizes its own roots and blind spots.

With this increased attention to injustice in mind, we suggest in this paper that a *social justice turn* has (only just) begun in the field of service-learning, led by critical scholars and pedagogues; if developed intentionally and robustly, this turn will keep the field relevant amid the divisive politics of our current times. Without the social justice turn and its continued bolstering, service-learning, steeped in a history of White[1] normativity and charity, risks becoming an outdated pedagogy; it could simply lapse into an approach that inadvertently exacerbates intolerance, leaves the heavy lifting to marginalized activists, and omits criticality in favor of naïve hope. This naïve hope, as Freire (2007) forecasts, leads only to despair because it lacks a foundation of political struggle:

> Without a minimum of hope, we cannot so much as start the struggle. But without the struggle, hope, as an ontological need, dissipates, loses its bearings, and turns into hopelessness. And hopelessness can become tragic despair. Hence the need for a kind of education in hope. (p. 3)

Service-learning is thus poised, via the social justice turn, as a pedagogy that encounters injustice and divisiveness as it occurs in local and global communities, and using as a catalyst these disheartening and enraging events that could comprise grounds for despair, instead fuels itself to engage in political action toward social and economic justice.

In this paper we provide a working definition of our understanding of social justice situated within a critical conceptual framework, and outline research in which critical pedagogues and scholars have taken up related concerns within community engagement and service-learning literature. By enacting a social justice approach, service-learning has the potential to empower communities, resist and disrupt oppressive power structures, and work for solidarity with host and partner communities. Although themes related to power and privilege are far from new in service-learning, we suggest an immediate need for a shift from their marginalized position to a more central focus, thereby laying a foundation for an emergent social justice turn. In particular, we highlight three areas that signify a conceptual transformation in the field of service-learning that has already begun to take place in its earliest form: (a) the problematization of charity and salvationism; (b) a critique of White normativity paired with the burgeoning diversification of authors and perspectives; and (c) a pedagogical and curricular embrace of emotions – especially those related to tension, ambiguity, and discomfort. Finally, we offer "critical hope" (Bozalek, Carolissen, Liebowitz, & Boler, 2014; Freire, 2007) as a concept that can assist the service-learning field in moving through/working with the despair and cynicism that seems to have intensified in light of recent events.

Theoretical Framework

Using a theoretical framework inspired by critical social justice pedagogy (Freire, 1970; Kumashiro, 2009; Sensoy & DiAngelo, 2012) and critical race feminism (Bannerji, 2000; hooks, 2003; Razack, 1998), we outline social justice service-learning scholarship that has pushed the field toward this conceptual turn, describe the key tenets of the proposed transition that have already begun to take place, and suggest further developments that our field must consciously enhance if it is to remain relevant in a politically divided global atmosphere. We acknowledge that higher education institutions perpetuate inequality through hegemony, patriarchy, classism, and White normativity (Bannerji, 2000; hooks, 2003; Razack, 1998), all of which must be countered by higher education service-learning practices and scholarship (Verjee, 2012). Central to the extension of the social justice turn, we advocate for a continued diversification of voices in the field, and adopt a firm anti-oppressive stance toward the hate speech highlighted by outspoken politicians and social media groups. We offer the notion of "critical hope" (Bozalek et al.,

2014; Freire, 2007) as a helpful tool for thinking about and moving through some of the "difficult knowledge" (Britzman, 1998) that service-learning participants (community partners, students, faculty, and staff) often encounter. When inequality is foregrounded in service-learning programs and in the broader society in which they are situated, it is these "pedagogies of crisis," as Kumashiro (2009) describes them, with which service-learning participants and affected communities must grapple.

Literature Review: Evidence of a Social Justice Turn in Service-Learning

The discussion of social justice is not new in the field of service-learning, as practitioners and scholars in the past decade or so have called for "justice-learning" (Butin, 2007), "a pedagogy of interruption" (Bruce, 2013), "critical service-learning" (Mitchell, 2008), "social justice sense-making" (Mitchell, 2013), and "antifoundational service-learning" (Butin), among others. Some volumes have focused on the intersection of social justice and service-learning (e.g., Calderon, 2007; Cipolle, 2010; Tinkler, Tinkler, Jagla, & Strait, 2016) and various publications have pointed to the goal of using this approach as a project in the development of a citizens oriented in, expressing commitment to, and highly valuing social justice (Battistoni, 2002; Mitchell).

Unfortunately, the term "social justice" is sometimes used loosely to describe programs and approaches that – behind the label – are not foundationally premised on social justice at all. Therefore, our discussion of a social justice turn will be preceded by a working definition of social justice as we understand it. Beyond a general idea, what exactly does this term mean in the context of engaging collaboratively with community, and how can it encapsulate more than just an emblem for those issues of fairness that we claim to be important to service-learning? Too often, the notion is used vaguely, and with little analysis of its meaning, roots, and the myriad ways it is taken up. While social justice carries a rich academic and grassroots history, and has prompted innumerable debates, we define it following the tenets set forth by Sensoy and DiAngelo (2012), who refer to "specific theoretical perspectives that recognize that society is stratified (i.e., divided and unequal) in significant and far-reaching ways along social group lines that include race, class, gender, sexuality, and ability" (p. xviii). Working against social injustice means adhering to the following commitments:

> recognizing that relations of unequal social power are constantly being enacted at both the micro (individual) and macro (structural) level, understand our own positions within these relations of unequal power, think critically about knowledge, and act on all of the above in service of a more socially just society. (p. xix)

Drawing on the emancipatory work of Freire (2007/1994), we see social justice goals as encompassing a struggle to equalize unequal power relations and call into question hegemonic assumptions and processes. By our conception, social justice requires a strong sense of humility in facing the unknown and the uncertain as well as a willingness to listen to those with whom we collaborate toward common goals. Service-learning as social justice often draws on the work of anti-racist, participatory action research, critical pedagogy, and feminist scholars to examine and resist political, economic, and social inequities that permeate educational institutions and broader society (e.g., Freire, 1970, 1973; Gorski, Zenkov, Osei-Kofi, & Sapp, 2012; hooks, 2003; Kumashiro, 2009; Rosenberger, 2000). In our conceptualization of social justice, we also recognize that the very act of generating a definition can exclude multiple perspectives and render some voices unheard. Therefore, borrowing from Bruce (2013), we position the "relational" element of service-learning also as a characteristic of our form of social justice. In other words, while we see the importance of explicitly discussing the theoretical foundations and assumptions of the term in question, we also consider "social justice" open to transformation based on varying contexts and different lived experiences of (in)justice(s). This will be discussed in greater detail when we delve into the role of ambiguity and discomfort in the social justice turn. While the above topics imbricated in social justice are not new to the literature, there has been a recent proliferation of research that deals with them. With the staggering variability of programs organized under the banner of service-learning, it is unsurprising that the field may be critiqued for its capacity to reify harmful stereotypes, reproduce racism, and reinscribe the exhausted First- versus Third-World dichotomy, while promoting in mainly privileged university students a self-congratulatory sense of having altruistically helped those in need (Cipolle, 2010; Diprose, 2012; Grusky, 2000; Purpel, 1999; Vaccaro, 2009). Other critiques outline concerns over the community impact and exploitation (Butin, 2003, 2010; Cipolle, 2010), emotional voyeurism (Bowdon & Scott, 2002; Butin, 2006; Langstraat & Bowdon, 2011; Purpel, 1999), and the inaccessibility of the pedagogy for marginalized students (Butin, 2006; Verjee & Butterwick, 2014), among others. As Einfeld and Collins (2008) illustrate through their research with an AmeriCorps service-learning program, the exposure to inequality and the development of relationships with marginalized or underprivileged communities does not necessarily lead students to a desire for social change. Many of the scholarly voices deeply critical of service-learning, however, are the same ones that point to its potential as a highly effective, emotional, and transformational pedagogy that serves community needs while also teaching students about diversity, power and privilege, social justice, responsibility, civic mindedness, global citizenship, and more (e.g., Catlett & Proweller, 2016; Cipolle, 2010; Grusky, 2000; Hartman & Kiely, 2014; Kiely, 2004; Kraft & Dwyer, 2000; Lund, Bragg, Kaipainen, & Lee, 2014; Lund & Lee, 2015; Schensul & Berg, 2004; Sharpe & Dear, 2013). Herein lies the greatest dilemma within the field of service-learning: It has the capacity to exacerbate inequality when done poorly, and to be a promising equalizing force when done well. Its effectiveness in advancing the goals of social justice, rather than causing harm, we argue, is contingent upon a conscious shift in the conceptualization of service-learning – the social justice turn–one that has already begun in three particular areas.

Critiquing Charity and Salvationism

The first and most notable sign of a social justice turn can be observed in the popularization of a critique of charity and salvationism. According to Bruce (2013), a charity approach to service-learning involves the troubling notion that we, as a group – typically learners, volunteers, students, and faculty – have something that that they, as a distant, other group – of marginalized, impoverished, or "at-risk" people – do not have, and so we aim to help them. This deficit-model thinking reinscribes students and institutions as privileged and powerful, and recipient communities as lacking, thereby perpetuating a server-served dichotomy (Bruce, 2013; Cipolle, 2010). Several publications contain warnings, preambles, and problematizations of a charity-based approach to service-learning – and in fact, it has become unusual to *omit* this vital issue in any major volume or publication in the field (e.g., Bringle & Hatcher, 2011; Calderon, 2007; Cipolle, 2010; Gorski et al., 2012; Johnson, 2014; Morton, 1995; Nieto, 2000; Oden & Casey, 2007). While various scholars differ in their suggestion for *where exactly* the field should move, the resounding consensus seems to be oriented in a direction away from charity and salvationism, and toward, to some extent, an examination of power and privilege (e.g., Hartman & Kiely, 2014). Recent advances in service-learning on a global level, for example, cite the fact that international service-learning (ISL) is too narrow in its conception of crossing borders (Hartman & Kiely, 2014). Instead, Hartman and Kiely propose that "global service-learning" (GSL) is a "community-driven service experience" that examines power relations, inequality, and a broad set of global issues through critically reflective practice (p. 60).

In yet another example, the foreword to O'Grady's (2000) edited volume on service-learning and multiculturalism contains the following statement: "This book challenges the perception of community service as charity, replacing it with the notion of civic responsibility in a pluralistic but unequal society" (Nieto, 2000, p. ix). While Morton (1995) offers three models of service, including charity, project, and social change, each with its own strengths, he suggests that the social change model particularly offers great potential for societal transformation. Others call assertively for a transition from charity approaches to a "social change" model that was taken up by the Black Panther Party in the 1960s and 1970s (Oden & Casey, 2007). Kajner, Chovanec, Underwood, and Mian (2013) share research that highlights the use of critical pedagogy frameworks to support students in activist community placements, while Lewis (2004) outlines the complexities of her own college's attempted transition from a charity-based approach – described as a consensus perspective of society – toward a social justice approach. This apparent bifurcation of aims is also reflected in Mitchell's (2008) influential article, which distinguishes between traditional and critical approaches, the former of which underscores service and student learning without due emphasis on structural inequality, and the latter of which focuses on – and takes action against – structural and institutionalized injustice.

While charity and salvationism are frequently problematized in the literature, global citizenship, as an oft-cited central goal of service-learning, is critiqued for its implicit goal of helping the needy Other (Jefferess, 2008). In his sharp critique of modern theorizations of global citizenship, Jefferess frames global citizenship rhetoric as a form of modern day imperialism, contending that,

> the form of imperialism has changed: race discourse and the language of inferiority and dependence have been replaced by that of culture talk, nation-building, and global citizenship. The notion of aid, responsibility, and poverty-alleviation retain the Other as an object of benevolence. The global citizen is somehow naturally endowed with the ability and inclination to 'help' the Other. (p. 28)

This inclination, he claims, is rooted in a sense of pity, and so it follows that service-learning as a pedagogy that invokes global citizenship may be critiqued as such. This helping narrative is further problematized by claims that it invokes a new form of imperialism and colonialism, wherein good intentions only function to reiterate a striking power differential: "Many acts of helping within service learning projects . . . may in fact be acts of complicity in the reproduction of structural and cultural inequalities" (Bruce, 2013, p. 36). The term "service" in fact has been contested for its negative connotations to the extent that Maas-Weigert (1998) suggested dropping it altogether and instead using the term "community based learning" to underline reciprocity and community relationships. This popularized critique of service-learning – that, despite its best intentions, it has the capacity to do harm through its focus on "helping" or "serving" the broken Other – is a promising indication that the social justice turn is ripe to take place in the field.

The commitment to an ongoing problematization of structural inequality and charity-based notions of service-learning, while a key tenet of the social justice turn, does not come without its complexities and pitfalls; an underlying desire for innocence can subtly manifest as a key driving factor in social justice work. Drawing on the work of Stein (2016) and Tuck and Yang (2012), we can develop an awareness of our "moves to innocence," which can be described as "those strategies or positionings that attempt to relieve the settler of feelings of guilt or responsibility without giving up land or power or privilege, without having to change much at all" (p. 10). Thus, while a subversion of charity approaches to service-learning are key to the development of the social justice turn, the critique itself is not enough; in fact, Stein (2016) cautions against the use of "critique as self-immunization," whereby "we may position ourselves as outside of critique or complicity" (p. 18). She suggests instead, an awareness of our habitual moves to innocence, an approach infused with humility, and "a commitment to sit with, listen to, learn from, and even be undone by the discomfort of knowing that even as we seek to dismantle structures of capture and containment, we remain answerable for our differential complicity within them" (p. 20). In other words, even in our quest to "do the right thing," we cannot distance ourselves from the complexity of our identity and positioning within constellations of structural inequality.

Critiquing White Normativity and Bolstering Diversity

Keeping complexity in mind, we shift our attention to a second indication of a nascent conceptual and practical shift in our field: the problematization of both entrenched White normativity and the underrepresentation of diverse voices. This awareness has resulted in not only the development of an important critique, but also a budding profusion of diverse topics and voices that present insights into issues of race, gender, ability, nationality, religion, culture, and many others. This section offers examples of literature that critique White normativity and proffer counter-narratives from diverse voices, people, and communities.

McIntosh (1989) wrote that White normativity is developed through a privileging of "White" knowledge and behavior as somehow neutral and ideal. ISL in particular has been problematized for its tendency to cater to White, middle- to upper-class students (Green, 2003; Mitchell, Donahue, & Young-Law, 2012; York, 2016). As Butin (2006) reminds us in his summary of the limits of service-learning in higher education, "service-learning may ultimately come to be viewed as the 'Whitest of the White' enclave of postsecondary education" (p. 482). Building on this, Mitchell, Donahue, and Young-Law (2012) caution us that done poorly, this approach may become merely a "pedagogy of Whiteness," wherein programs embody "strategies of instruction that consciously or unconsciously reinforce norms and privileges developed by, and for the benefit of, white people" (p. 613). Consequently, as Butin (2006) points out, institutions and pedagogues sometimes make overarching assumptions that their service-learning students do indeed fit the normative identity described as "White, sheltered, middle-class, single," thereby running the risk of further catering to a privileged group while also failing to acknowledge the shifting demographics toward more diverse higher education student bodies (p. 481).

Extending this line of inquiry, Bocci (2015) examines service-learning texts and the construction of historical narratives in the field to expose ways in which White normativity is expressed through both an overrepresentation of White voices (e.g., leaders, scholars, practitioners, and students) and a dominance of White narratives, histories, and ways of knowing. Her analysis illustrates how the field's scholarship emphasizes the White conceptual roots of service-learning by highlighting White, Anglo founding theorists such as John Dewey and William James, while downplaying non-Anglo thinkers such as Paulo Freire, W. E. B. DuBois, and Alain Locke. A continuing history of White normativity and dominance is a key issue that critical pedagogues and scholars have begun to problematize in service-learning. Further, the urgency of this dialogue is made more salient with the silencing and marginalization of non-White voices, non-hegemonic perspectives, and bolstered by divisive global events of recent years that exacerbate the marginalization of vulnerable groups of people.

It bears stressing here that we write this article as White scholars in a field and academic culture that continues to be dominated at the institutional and societal level by White voices (see Lund & Carr, 2015). No social justice turn in service-learning can develop without highlighting this problematic reality, examining our own complicity in such inequality, and working to change it at a structural level. One way to do this is to draw on Butin's (2005) assertion that the unit of analysis should not be service-learning programs themselves but rather the institutions in which they operate and by which they are constrained. Furthermore, our field can benefit from observing and asking questions of other fields and disciplines that have found success in their diversity and inclusion of many voices and multiple ways of knowing. Significantly, we can learn much from listening to the voices of those who choose *not* to engage in the field of service-learning for some of the reasons noted above.

Fortunately, the profusion of voices and perspectives in service-learning scholarship – while it still has a long way to go – is beginning to offer counter-narratives and important considerations for the progressive development of the field. Through her service-learning counter-storytelling research with women of color at the University of British Columbia, Verjee (2012) proposes "a transformative vision of service-learning engagement" which calls for institutional accountability and critical examination of hegemony as a prerequisite for genuine, mutually beneficial relationships with the community. Donahue and Luber (2015) highlight the heteronormative nature of traditional service-learning, calling for the "queering of service-learning." They suggest that approaching community engagement work through the lens of queer theory and with attention paid to LGBT issues may trouble normative assumptions and lead students to unlearn binary thinking, often leading to moments of "crisis" as described by Kumashiro's (2002) pedagogy of crisis. Furthermore, drawing on her extensive experience in community engagement and social justice work, Mitchell (2015) continues to push the field toward more critically reflective engagement with diverse students, staff, and communities; her work resonates with many, and she recently received a standing ovation for her keynote panel presentation at the 2015 IARSLCE conference in Boston. The examples above highlight a small portion of the myriad efforts being put forth by practitioners and scholars to present alternative narratives that enrich a rapidly diversifying field. This paper positions the profusion of these voices – and the many unheard people who work to engage marginalized and disempowered communities daily – as foundational to the social justice turn.

Embracing Emotion: Tension, Ambiguity, and Discomfort

A third change that evidences the birth of the social justice turn can be observed in the recent pedagogical and curricular embrace of critical emotion studies (e.g., Langstraat & Bowden, 2011) and the focus on tension, ambiguity, and discomfort. There is little doubt that service-learning has the capacity to be an emotional journey in which participants, including students, community partners, host communities, faculty, staff, and others, may encounter varying types of difference and are necessarily put in a position to question their own ontologies, ethics, and ways of knowing. This is reflected in service-learning's effectiveness as a transformative pedagogy rooted in Kolb's (1984) notions of experience, action, and reflection. Transformation and questions of identity and being, however, can entail great discomfort, ambiguity, and tension – all of which are becoming increasingly embraced by practitioners and pedagogues in the early days of the social justice turn (e.g., Mills, 2012; Sharpe & Dear, 2013). Donahue and Luber (2015) point out that service-learning – and particularly those examples that invoke queer theory or work with queer communities – can enact what Kumashiro (2009) describes as a "pedagogy of crisis" wherein students' critical examination and unlearning of outdated assumptions can cause great emotional distress. Emotional crises can arise when students come to realize that they have behaved in oppressive ways or have unfairly benefitted from – or been disadvantaged by – an inequitable system. Adding to the complexity, other students may encounter intense emotions when they feel they have been marginalized, or are expected to speak for/on behalf of a group they are perceived to represent. How are educators to respond to and teach through varying types of affective engagement? These possibly harrowing experiences, while seeming to be destabilizing in their discomfort, have great transformative potential, and service-learning scholarship confirms the expectation that students *should* encounter and grapple with discomfort.

Building on the field's engagement with ambiguity, Butin (2007) proposes that service-learning is a "paradigmatic example of postmodern pedagogy" which effectively resists the quest for finality and closure, and "works to disturb students' notions of static truth" (p. xiii). Extending this notion, Bruce (2013) offers Biesta's (2006, 2010) "pedagogy of interruption" as a way to frame service-learning that is "relational" in that it can neither be scripted nor provide any sense of closure or sureness, particularly pertaining to the meaning of justice. This notion of ambiguity, on the one hand, can stand in direct contradiction to some social justice approaches, which may at times over-emphasize the (often undefined) goals of empowerment, solidarity, and equity. On the other hand, our specific conception of social justice is rooted in a sense of humility, which recognizes that "justice" is differently defined, and that those who script the definitions and have the voice to publicly make claims, are not necessarily representative of those who experience injustice. Furthermore, in line with Bruce's relational service-learning, justice may be conceived differently across varying contexts, and cannot be pre-defined previous to the encounter with the Other. The social justice turn recognizes the limitations of pre-defined notions of justice, and emphasizes in its conceptualization the important role of ambiguity, and an ongoing openness to new characterizations of social justice from a range of perspectives and throughout ongoing historical transformations.

Critical Hope: "An Action-Oriented Response to Contemporary Despair"

Is there a way that those who struggle with despair in our present moment can find common ground – and work together – with those who remain hopeful? In writing this paper, we called up vivid memories of conference rooms, social situations, and service-learning field experiences, wherein – grossly simplified – individuals labeled as "idealists" came nose-to-nose with those labeled "cynics." The former sometimes perceive the cynics as "killjoys" – outspoken radicals who struggle with the current neoliberal university environment and who do not recognize that service-learning is a win-win-win pedagogy that fulfills our university's public service mandate, teaches students effectively through hands-on experience, and collaborates with communities on projects that are important to them. The latter sometimes perceive the idealists as focusing too intently on the needs of the powerful institution and privileged students while devaluing historicity, identity, structural violence, and the voices and desires of partner communities.

Similarly, in the case of Alan Kurdi, for example, those labeled idealists might recognize the horror of this tragedy but position it simultaneously as a moment that can catalyze change, build bridges of compassion, and bring people together for a cause.

The cynics, in response, might gesture to a long history of global exploitation and conflict leading to his death, the abhorrence of a system that stipulates who has rights to mobility and who does not, and the fact that there have been numerous victims before and after Alan who also deserve justice. "Critical hope" (Boler, 2004; Bozalek et al., 2014; Freire, 2007) offers a conceptual, *relational* space in which *both* perspectives – and the many nuanced, complex variations similar to them – can coexist simultaneously. In fact, it is very likely that versions of two such bifurcations will exist in simultaneity and in constant tension within the same individual.

Critical hope is, on the one hand, a conceptual and theoretical direction and, on the other, "an action-oriented response to contemporary despair" (Bozalek et al., 2014, p. 1). As an idea, it is inspired by the praxis and frameworks of critical theory, particularly those emerging from the Frankfurt School, neo-Marxist critiques, and the work of Freire (Bozalek et al., 2014; Freire, 1970, 2007). It can be summarized as "an act of ethical and political responsibility that has the potential to recover a lost sense of connectedness, relationality, and solidarity with others" (Zembylas, 2014, p. 14). We propose that the social justice turn in service-learning is premised on, and can be aided by, the necessary tension between criticality – of privilege, charity, hegemony, representation, history, and inequality – along with a hope that is neither naïve nor idealistic, but that remains committed to ideals of justice, reflexivity, and solidarity. The criticality and hope that underlie the social justice turn in service-learning cannot be disaggregated but rather must work in tandem with one another at all times. Kezar and Rhoads (2001) identify a number of tensions that persist in the field, highlighting the question of service-learning's central learning outcomes: Is it meant to bolster social responsibility, enhance understanding of multiculturalism and empathy, or foster thinking and writing skills? In short, these authors ask, is the pedagogy of service-learning approached with a cognitive or affective understanding of learning? Critical hope not only creates space for *both,* but insists upon their interplay as a foundational requirement.

Bozalek, Carolissen, Liebowitz, and Boler (2014) outline two ways that critical hope can be used: First, it may serve as a "unitary and unified concept which cannot be disaggregated from either hopefulness or criticality" (p. 1), and second, it may function as an analytical concept that honors and theorizes the affective, the political, the spiritual, and the intellectual. Zembylas (2014), drawing on Boler (2004), Freire, (1994), and Duncan-Andrade (2009), distinguishes critical hope from other less progressive notions: "naïve hope" (Boler, 2004; Freire, 1994) that can be summarized as "blind faith that things will get better" (Zembylas, 2014, p. 13); "hokey hope" that is rooted in individualistic, tired narrative that folks who just "pull themselves up by their bootstraps" can overcome any barriers and live out their dreams (Duncan-Andrade, 2009); "mythical hope" that is premised on "the false narrative of equal opportunity, emptied of its historical and political contingencies" (Duncan-Andrade, p. 182); and "hope deferred," which, while founded on progressive ideals, can get caught up in the process of critiquing inequitable systems and structures while stopping short of active engagement due to the belief that no pedagogical approach can have actual transformative potential because of the broader barriers extant throughout and beyond the education system (Duncan-Andrade). In contrast with these notions, critical hope engages with both the critical and the emotional (Zembylas):

> To say that someone is critically hopeful means that the person is involved in a critical analysis of power relations and how they constitute one's emotional ways of being in the world, while attempting to construct, imaginatively and materially, a different lifeworld. (p. 13)

Overlaying some of the key tenets of critical hope onto our understanding of service-learning can assist those who feel torn between a strong sense of both optimism and pessimism. Service-learning, as a pedagogy that crosses cultural, racial, national, and disciplinary borders (to name only a few), is rich with opportunities to analyze power relations; such border crossing frequently generates intensely emotional experiences, which offers all partners occasions for reflection on the ways in which emotions are determined and affected by hegemony, privilege, and social conditioning. Finally, the aspect that distinguishes service-learning from other forms of experiential learning is oriented in the construction of what Zembylas (2014) calls "a different lifeworld" (p. 13) – service activities led by the communities most affected. In short, critical hope provides a conceptual space in which those invested in the social justice turn in service-learning may concurrently take into account both the despairing events of our current historical moment along with the varied, often unjust histories of those involved, while also moving forward with the development of programs and partnerships that may well generate changes that decrease suffering and dismantle unjust structures. After all, as Apple (2015) reminds us, "despair and cynicism only help those in dominance" (p. xvi).

Social Justice Service Learning: Three case studies

In our work, we see critical hope enacted through programs designed to do more toward fostering social justice through critical learning and systemic change rather than more temporary transformational experiences for individuals. One example of a promising community-engaged program is offered by Catlett and Proweller (2016) whose work reveals how "feminist-informed community based service-learning experiences can be a vehicle for advancing social justice" (p. 65). They use critical feminist theoretical perspectives to engage university students in reflection and dialogue about youth relationship violence, activism, and community work. In particular, they work with students in a year-long engagement that involves both a 10-week service-learning placement and a deeper involvement with an established dating violence prevention program called "Take back the halls: Ending violence in relationships and schools." The authors emphasize the importance of service-learning being "existentially disturbing" (Butin, 2010, p. 20) and unsettling in order to uncover the systemic nature of inequality, injustice, and complicity.

The program design and pedagogical approaches outlined by Catlett and Proweller (2016) include a number of components that both promoted and assessed learning through the university course and its service-learning component while facilitating the anti-violence program with high school students. They enacted activities and assessments that appear to work toward a kind of critical hope with their course. Students engaged in in-depth qualitative interviews at the beginning and again at the end of the program, focusing on their lessons learned, their interest in the program on interpersonal violence, and the lives of urban youth. They also wrote reflective "Who Am I" papers at the beginning of the academic quarter, which they revisited and revised at the end of the term, exploring particularly their own multiple identities and life experiences as well as similar reflections on the lives of the students with whom they worked. All components of the program were created and viewed through a feminist lens, fostering greater depth of critical engagement toward social justice along with significant insights aimed at both individual and collective transformation. As the authors describe it,

> feminist-informed community based service-learning directs attention to the root causes of social problems, compelling student learners to go beyond superficial examination of social inequity to deeper exploration of the systemic bases of intersecting forms of power

and oppression. . . . And to locate themselves within intersecting axes of privilege and oppression . . . [with a focus on] accountability – identifying the ways in which we are implicated in intersecting systems of inequality and developing criteria against which we measure our accountability to the communities with whom we are engaged. (pp. 68–69)

Results of their research on this program show that "the learning environment should be an authentic community in which students feel safe and supported to engage in non-judgmental, open-ended inquiry, exploring critical connections between material learning in the classroom and their personal experiences" (p. 85). Not surprisingly, students' learning experiences were uneven and disquieting, often fraught with discomfort, and data showed "evidence of confusion, ambivalence, and even resistance" (p. 86) as students grappled with their own implication in systems of inequity as well as empowered as part of a broader effort toward social change.

Another service-learning approach with postsecondary students that shows promise in enacting the ideals of critical hope is through the development of critical social justice programs involving co-curricular "alternative breaks" that afford students the opportunity to develop crucial understandings of the root causes and complexities of social issues in host communities. Sumka, Porter, and Piacitelli (2015) outline promising models and examples of this approach as well as key components of the program. When designed to foster in students a nuanced understanding of systems and the identities of those working within them, alternative break program participants "are better able to address those issues with humility, a broader perspective, and sensitivity to complexity. . . . to work with an eye toward structural change and capacity building" (p. 13).

Creating a detailed plan for alternative breaks that includes components required by the Break Away organization, for example, allows students to gain the quality and depth of understanding that will foster greater success in attaining social justice goals. Their eight components include the following: (a) strong, direct, "hands-on" service in activities that address unmet social needs; (b) an alcohol and drug free environment; (c) attention to diversity and social justice focusing on power, privilege, and oppression; (d) a strong orientation to the values and mission of the community partner prior to departure; (e) effective education with multiple perspectives on social issues; (f) adequate training in the skills and tasks necessary for the particular project; (g) opportunities for reflection both individually and as a group; and (h) reorientation to internalize and transfer lessons learned, sharing their experience to continue to raise awareness on social issues as well as taking action through direct service and advocacy (Sumka, Porter, & Piacitelli, 2015, p. 21). These programs share with community-based service-learning a commitment to reciprocal partnership development, attention to a critical understanding of power and privilege, a strong educational foundation, and a commitment to social action (p. 17). Aligning their work with the critical service-learning model articulated by Mitchell (2008), the authors demonstrate how thoughtfully designed alternative break programs can be part of the necessary social change that addresses "structural systems of inequality, injustice, oppression, and marginalization" (Sumka et al., p. 18). They assert that

> by engaging in community driven direct service that addresses root causes of social issues and preparing participants to continue the work of social change throughout their lives, alternative breaks can be part of the greater community working toward a more just society. (p. 18)

An underlying principle that guides these programs is the promotion of a critically informed active citizenship that attends to social justice through gaining a personal connection to social issues, an understanding of the root causes, and a commitment to collective action against oppression and inequity.

As a final example, and with some self-consciousness, we offer a community-driven university program that reflects how service-learning can work toward these goals, one in which we have both played central roles. Author Lund is co-founder of the Service-Learning Program (SLP) for pre-service teachers and continues to teach in the program at the University of Calgary, in Alberta, Canada, and Grain worked at a nonprofit agency that is a Community Partner in the program as well as serving on the community-based Working Group that acts as a steering committee for the program. Founded in 2011 by Lund and Lianne Lee, along with a team of community and campus collaborators, the SLP (Lund, 2016) provides pre-service teachers with weekly opportunities to examine theory and engage in critical reflection and hands-on experiences with young people through community agency programs. The integration of teacher education for social justice, critical service-learning models, and anti-oppressive pedagogical approaches through a social justice framework support students in translating their learning when they enter classrooms as teachers.

One of the most significant strengths of the SLP and the collaborative model from which it was built is its long-term focus on implementing system-level strategies that contribute to the quality of life for diverse children, youth, and their families. The SLP has taken a permanent place in the Faculty of Education and has grown to include agencies working with immigrant and refugee children, youth with disabilities, youth with LGBTTQ identities, and Indigenous children and youth. Each agency is offered the opportunity to send key leaders to participate in the Working Group to offer continual feedback into the program, now planning for its sixth iteration. Further, it includes a 5-year ongoing research component that includes pre- and post-semester interviews as well as classroom and field observations. This has resulted in a robust data set that offers rich insights into reciprocal community engagement, fostering cultural humility, and critical teacher education for social justice (e.g., Lee & Lund, 2016; Lund & Lee, 2015).

A Tool for Social Justice Service-Learning

If critical hope calls for reflection and action on topics such as solidarity and equity, one of our key roles as service-learning educators and practitioners is to offer students experiences that interrogate their own assumptions *in tandem with* tools that assist them in accessing those assumptions and working to change them, move beyond them, and act upon them at a systemic level. A useful tool for the identification of relevant issues in social justice service-learning can be found in Andreotti's (2012) "HEADS UP" framework, which is predicated on critical literacy in global engagement and uses an acronym to highlight the complexities of "Hegemony, Ethnocentrism, Ahistoricism, Depoliticization, Salvationism, Uncomplicated solutions and Paternalism" (p. 1). Andreotti suggests that HEADS UP can move learners away from naïve hope and toward a stance of "skeptical optimism and ethical solidarities" (p. 2) by prompting important conversations about the "problematic historical patterns of thinking and relationships" summarized by the terms in the above list. If service-learning students are able to identify and problematize their own complicity in a notion such as Salvationism (one of the seven highlighted), they can extend their critical reflection by asking specific questions about that term, which Andreotti provides in her tool. For example, she offers this question in relation to Salvationism: "does this initiative acknowledge the self-centered desire to be better than/superior to others, and the imposition of aspirations for singular ideas of progress and development that have historically been part of what creates injustice?" (p. 2). Given the great diversity of student project placements under the banner of service-learning, this tool can be a catalyst for important modes of reflection and dialogue, particularly to consider not only how a given project can serve the goals of community members but also how a given project might inadvertently reify stereotypes or harmful ideas. In addition to these social justice considerations, and echoing what many social justice service-learning scholars have ideated, we suggest that service-learning steeped in critical hope attends specifically to a variety of identity markers that render some people marginalized or oppressed based on ability, race, gender, gender identity, sex, socioeconomic status, nationality, religion, mental health, and many more.

Conclusion

In conceiving and writing this article, we debated how to best integrate some global and localized events that have captured the hearts and minds of so many people around the world. What does the dangerous rhetoric in the wake of Brexit, for example, have to do with our relatively small and specialized academic field? How does the Black Lives Matter movement play out in service-learning research and practice? How does racialized police brutality factor in to our commitment to community engagement? How does the systemic problem of missing and murdered Indigenous women affect Canadian universities' curricular, pedagogical, and community engagement practices? Why did an image of Alan Kurdi washed up on a Greek beach invoke us to reflect on our global responsibility in response to a distant civil war and widespread Islamophobia? Weeks after Alan's image first appeared in the news, and not long after, we observed too much social media Islamophobia to wrap our heads around, we settled into a kind of despair, and finally turned our attention to these questions. Our social circles seemed awash with fear, and people we had thought to be reasonably astute had become voices of intolerance. We wondered how service-learning could respond to issues that had come to paint an increasingly troubling social and political landscape in which we conduct our work. How can we, as educators, practitioners, and activists in service-learning, engage with diverse students and communities, some of whom are facing their greatest challenges of oppression and marginalization in recent history? And what of those practices in our field that inadvertently contribute to inequality and injustice? How are we ourselves complicit?

We ask these questions not because we know the answers, but because now more than ever we seek the wisdom and solidarity of our service-learning partners and colleagues, and we deeply believe that our field needs to engage in the conversation about our proverbial tipping point that will individually and collectively move us along in the social justice turn. Each individual and community will respond differently to gripping news stories and personal injustice(s), so how might we begin a dialogue (and then move beyond dialogue) about those highly emotional learning moments that render us too devastated to be silent, too angry to be idle, or too frustrated to keep doing the same thing over and over?

The result of our reflection became this manuscript, an intellectually premised argument not only that a social justice turn has begun in service-learning, led by visionary critical scholars like Mitchell, Butin, Bruce, and others, but also an impassioned argument that a social justice turn must continue, not only as a reaction to "a world gone mad," but as a continuous commitment to taking action and critically reflecting upon issues that affect us, our communities, students, faculty, and local and global partners. The promising exemplars identified above provide merely a glimpse into the kinds of bold engagements that might continue to point us in the right direction. We believe that the future of the social justice turn – while it is fueled by initiatives that *do* work – could be equally strengthened by examining those initiatives that "backfired," "failed," or did not serve the goals of social justice within the field. In fact, we suggest that learning from our mistakes in the enactment of critical hope is as vital as learning from our successes, and such a task requires vulnerability and risk-taking. We do not attempt in this paper to create or reveal a new or universalizing solution to the highly contextual problems that plague our societies and our field; instead, this article is a reminder of an idea that is quite old: that as times change so too must our educational approaches. And times, changing (or rather, being exposed) as violently and swiftly as they have been recently, require equally responsive transformations – not simply individually, but also in our families, our faculties, our classrooms, our institutions, and our quiet, back-room conversations. Service-learning can remain highly relevant *if* it continues to shift away from charitable volunteer approaches and White normativity, toward an embrace of ambiguity and discomfort, and with an acceptance that hope and struggle toward social justice are contradictory yet *complementary* allies in our work.

Just as service-learning from a social justice perspective is not undertaken to absolve privileged individuals and communities of guilt or complicity in issues of inequality, the response to global injustices such as the death of Alan Kurdi must not be used as a strategy to absolve individuals and institutions of structural, self-implicating critiques. Alan represents a victim who invoked in many a highly empathetic and compassionate response because he is understood to be an innocent child. But what of victims who are not perceived as innocent, and with whom the masses have more trouble identifying and empathizing? The selective nature of compassion and empathy is as vital a conversation as any in the future of the social justice turn in service-learning, and by extension, so is how to avoid using the narratives of innocent victims as a means to affirm the "goodness" of those who respond. Thus, key to the conceptual turn is the notion that service-learning must neither be centered on students' and institutions' desire to "do good" nor their own definitions of justice but, rather, it must be driven by community collaborations, common goals, and definitions that emerge differently over time and geography. In this way, as Bruce (2013) suggests, the pedagogy's *relational* characteristic becomes of paramount importance; there are many (sometimes incommensurable) approaches to social justice that can neither be scripted nor predetermined, and yet it is vital to outline what is desired by all collaborators when service-learning is oriented from this perspective.

The social justice turn is simultaneously a conflict-ridden struggle against inequality, xenophobia, and oppression, and an insistence on education's responsibility as a conduit of hope – not the naïve kind disaggregated from conflict, but the kind that understands struggle as a necessary component of change. This turn understands itself to be (as with education more broadly) continuously obsolete, and therefore, continuously "turning" conceptual curves in response to – and in anticipation of – broader global issues that determine our field's priorities. As Butin (2007) reminds us, "if service-learning is to avoid becoming overly normalized, we must continuously question and disturb our assumptions, our terms, and our practices" (p. xi). The social justice turn is premised upon an ongoing cycle of critiquing, reimagining, re-acting, and responding to the issues highlighted by our current moment, and undergirded by varied histories of resisting oppression. Just because social justice dialogues and voices are becoming louder in our field and in mainstream media does not mean that institutions and broader structures themselves are changing – and this transformation we take as one of our key goals moving forward. Building this struggle on a foundation of critical hope offers a conceptual space in which those who are justifiably immobilized, nonplussed, or enraged by continued examples of injustice may find solidarity with those who are stubbornly hopeful and oriented in the possibilities and potentialities of service-learning – and indeed education – to move through, with, and beyond despair.

Notes

We would like to acknowledge the efforts of Tima Kurdi (Alan's aunt) and other family members of Alan Kurdi for their efforts to educate others about the plight of Syrian refugees. We also thank them for their message of hope in the face of their personal tragedy. Tima Kurdi's sentiments have been instrumental in the development of this paper, and she has provided us with valuable written feedback throughout ongoing conversations. We hope that this article reflects her efforts and generates some social and structural changes in the areas of education and service-learning. Tima Kurdi's TedxTalk can be viewed at http://tedxeastvan.com/tima-kurdi/

[1] We use the upper case here to signify that this word represents a racialized category that is a social construction, and not simply the color.

References

Andreotti, V. (2012). Editor's Preface: HEADS UP. *Critical Literacy: Theories and Practices, 6*(1), 1–3.

Apple, M. (2014). Foreword. In V. Bozalek, B. Leibowitz, R. Carolissen, & M. Boler (Eds.), *Discerning critical hope in educational practices* (pp. xii-xxii). New York: Routledge.

Bannerji, H. (2000). *The dark side of the nation: Essays on multiculturalism, nationalism and gender.* Toronto, ON: Canadian Scholars' Press.

Battistoni, R.M. (2013). Civic learning through service learning. In J. A. Clayton, R. G. Bringle, & J. A. Hatcher (Eds.), *Research on service learning: Conceptual frameworks and assessment* (pp. 111–132). Sterling, VA: Stylus.

Bowdon, M., & Scott, B. (2002). *Service learning in technical and professional communication.* New York: Longman.

Bozalek, V., Carolissen, R., Leibowitz, B., & Boler, M. (2014). Introduction. In V. Bozalek, B. Leibowitz, R. Carolissen, & M. Boler (Eds.), *Discerning critical hope in educational practices* (pp. 1–8). New York: Routledge.

Bozalek, V., Carolissen, R., Leibowitz, B., & Boler, M. (Eds.). (2014). *Discerning critical hope in educational practices.* New York: Routledge.

Bringle, R. G., & Hatcher, J. A. (2011). International Service Learning. In R. G. Bringle, J. A. Hatcher, & S. G. Jones, (Eds.), *International service learning: Conceptual frameworks and research* (pp. 3–28). Sterling, VA: Stylus.

Britzman, D. (1998). *Lost subjects, contested objects: Toward a psychoanalytic inquiry of learning.* New York: Suny Press.

Bruce, J. (2013). Service learning as a pedagogy of interruption. *International Journal of Development Education and Global Learning, 5*(1), 33–47. https://doi.org/10.18546/IJDEGL.05.1.03

Butin, D. (2003). Of what use is it? Multiple conceptualizations of service learning within education. *Teachers College Record, 105*(9), 1674–1692. https://doi.org/10.1046/j.1467–9620.2003.00305.x

Butin, D. (2005). *Service-learning in higher education.* New York: Palgrave Macmillan. https://doi.org/10.1057/9781403981042

Butin, D. (2006). The limits of service-learning in higher education. *The Review of Higher Education, 29*(4), 473–498. https://doi.org/10.1353/rhe.2006.0025

Butin, D. (2007). Justice-learning: Service-learning as justice-oriented education. *Equity & Excellence in Education, 40*(2), 177–183. https://doi.org/10.1080/10665680701246492

Calderon, J. (Ed.). (2007). *Race, poverty, and social justice: Multidisciplinary perspectives through service-learning.* Sterling, VA: Stylus.

The Canadian Press. (2015, September 3). Harper: Alan Kurdi image heartbreaking, but doesn't change need to fight ISIL. *The Huffington Post.* Retrieved from http://www.huffingtonpost.ca/2015/09/03/Alan-kurdi_n_8084778.html

Catlett, B. S., & Proweller, A. (2016). Disruptive practices: Advancing social justice through feminist community based service-learning in higher education. In A. Tinkler, B. Tinkler, V. Jagla, & J. Strait (Eds.), *Service-learning to advance social justice in a time of radical inequality* (pp. 65–94). Charlotte, NC: Information Age Publishing.

Cipolle, S. B. (2010). *Service-learning and social justice: Engaging students in social change.* Plymouth, UK: Rowman & Littlefield.

Dewey, J. (1916). *Democracy and education.* New York: Macmillan.

Diprose, K. (2012). Critical distance: Doing development education through international volunteering. *Area, 44*(2), 186–192. https://doi.org/10.1111/j.1475-4762.2011.01076.x

Donahue, D., & Luber, M. (2015). Queering service learning: Promoting anti-oppressive action and reflection by undoing dichotomous thinking. In J. C. Hawley (Ed.), *Expanding the circle: Creating an inclusive environment in higher education for LGBTQ students and studies* (pp. 209–224). Albany, NY: State University of New York Press.

Einfeld, A., & Collins, D. (2008). The relationships between service learning, social justice, multicultural competence, and civic engagement. *Journal of College Student Development, 49*(2), 95–109. https://doi.org/10.1353/csd.2008.0017

Freire, P. (1970). *Pedagogy of the oppressed.* New York: Seabury.

Freire, P. (1973). *Education for critical consciousness.* New York: Seabury.

Friere, P. (2007/1994). Pedagogy of hope. New York: Continuum.

Gorski, P. C., Zenkov, K., Osei-Kofi, N., & Sapp, J. (Eds.). (2012). *Cultivating social justice teachers: How teacher educators have helped students overcome cognitive bottlenecks and learn critical social justice concepts.* Sterling, VA: Stylus.

Green, A. E. (2003). Difficult stories: Service-learning, race, class, and whiteness. *College Composition and Communication, 55*(2), 276–301. https://doi.org/10.2307/3594218

Grusky, S. (2000). International service learning: A critical guide from an impassioned advocate. *American Behavioral Scientist, 43*(5), 858–867. https://doi.org/10.1177/00027640021955513

Hartman, E., & Kiely, R. (2014). Pushing boundaries: Introduction to the global service-learning special section. *Michigan Journal of Community Service Learning, 21*(1), 55–63.

hooks, b. (2003). *Teaching community: A pedagogy of hope.* New York: Routledge.

Jefferess, D. (2008). Global citizenship and the cultural politics of benevolence. *Critical Literacy: Theories and Practices, 2*(1), 27–36.

Johnson, M. (2014). Introduction. In P. Green & M. Johnson (Eds.), *Crossing boundaries: Tension and transformation in international service-learning* (pp. 1–11). Sterling, VA: Stylus.

Kajner, T., Chovanec, D., Underwood, M., & Mian, A. (2013). Critical community service- learning: Combining critical classroom pedagogy with activist community placements. *Michigan Journal of Community Service Learning, 19*(2), 36–48.

Kelly, D. M., & Brandes, G. M. (2001). Shifting out of 'neutral': Beginning teachers' struggles with teaching for social justice. *Canadian Journal of Education, 26*(4), 437–454. https://doi.org/10.2307/1602176

Kezar, A., & Rhoads, R. (2001). The dynamic tensions of service learning in higher education. *The Journal of Higher Education, 72*(2), 148–171. https://doi.org/10.2307/2649320

Kiely, R. (2004). A chameleon with a complex: Searching for transformation in international service-learning. *Michigan Journal of Community Service Learning, 10*(2), 5–20.

Kolb, D. (1984). *Experiential learning: Experience as the source of learning and development.* Upper Saddle River, NJ: Prentice Hall.

Kraft, R. J., & Dwyer, J. (2000). Service and outreach: A multicultural and international dimension. *Journal of Higher Education Outreach and Exchange, 6*(1), 41–47.

Kumashiro, K. (2009). *Against common sense: Teaching and learning toward social justice* (2nd ed.). New York: Routledge.

Langstraat, L., & Bowdon, M. (2011). Service learning and critical emotion studies: On the perils of empathy and the politics of compassion. *Michigan Journal of Community Service Learning, 17*(2), 5–14.

Lee, L., & Lund, D. E. (2016). Infusing service-learning with social justice through cultural humility. In A. S. Tinkler, B. E. Tinkler, J. R. Strait, & V. M. Jagla (Eds.), *Service-learning to advance social justice in a time of radical inequality* (pp. 359–381). Charlotte, NC: Information Age Publishing.

Lewis, T. L. (2004). Service-learning for social change? Lessons from a liberal arts college. *Teaching Sociology, 32*(1), 94–108. https://doi.org/10.1177/0092055X0403200109

Lund, D. E. (2016). *Service-Learning Program.* Werklund School of Education. Calgary, AB: University of Calgary. Retrieved from http://werklund.ucalgary.ca/upe/service-learning-programht

Lund, D. E., Bragg, B., Kaipainen, E., & Lee, L. (2014). Preparing preservice teachers through service-learning: Collaborating with community for children and youth of immigrant backgrounds. *International Journal of Research on Service-Learning in Teacher Education, 2*, 1–32.

Lund, D. E., & Carr, P. R. (Eds.). (2015). *Revisiting the great White north? Rethinking Whiteness, privilege, and identity in education* (2nd Ed.). Rotterdam, The Netherlands: Sense.

Lund, D. E., & Lee, L. (2015). Fostering cultural humility among pre-service teachers: Connecting with children and youth of immigrant families through service-learning. *Canadian Journal of Education, 38*(2), 1–30. Retrieved from http://www.cje-rce.ca/index.php/cje-rce/article/view/1744/1756. https://doi.org/10.2307/canajeducrevucan.38.2.10

Maas-Weigert, K. (1998). Academic service learning: Its meaning and relevance. *New Directions for Teaching and Learning, 73*, 3–10. https://doi.org/10.1002/tl.7301

McIntosh, P. (1989/2013). White privilege: Unpacking the invisible knapsack. In H. S. Shapiro, M. C. Davis, & P. Fitzpatrick (Eds.), *The institution of education* (pp. 215–218). Boston: Pearson.

Mills, S. D. (2012). The four furies: Primary tensions between service-learners and host agencies. *Michigan Journal of Community Service Learning, 19*(1), 33–43.

Mitchell, T. D. (2007). Critical service-learning as social justice education: A case study of the citizen scholars program. *Equity & Excellence in Education, 40*(2), 101–112. https://doi.org/10.1080/10665680701228797

Mitchell, T. D. (2008). Traditional vs. critical service-learning: Engaging the literature to differentiate two models. *Michigan Journal of Community Service Learning, 14*(2), 50–65.

Mitchell, T. D., Donahue, D. M., & Young-Law, C. (2012). Service learning as a pedagogy of whiteness. *Equity & Excellence in Education, 45*(4), 612–629. https://doi.org/10.1080/10665684.2012.715534

Mitchell, T. D. (2013). How service-learning enacts social justice sensemaking. *Journal of Critical Thought and Praxis, 2*(2), 6.

Nieto, S. (2000). Foreword. In C. O'Grady (Ed.), *Integrating service learning and multicultural education in colleges and universities* (pp. ix-xi). Mahwah, NJ: Lawrence Erlbaum Associates.

Morton, K. (1995). The irony of service: Charity, project and social change in service-learning. *Michigan Journal of Community Service Learning, 2*(1), 19–32.

Oden, R. S., & Casey, T. A. (2007). Advancing service learning as a transformative method for social justice work. In J. Calderon (Ed.), *Race, poverty, and social justice: Multidisciplinary perspectives through service learning* (pp. 3–22). Sterling, VA: Stylus.

Pickron-Davis, M. C. (1999). *Black students in community service learning: Critical reflections about self and identity.* Unpublished doctoral dissertation, University of Pennsylvania, Philadelphia.

Purpel, D. (1999). *Moral outrage in education.* New York: Peter Lang.

Razack, S. (1998). *Looking white people in the eye.* Toronto, ON: University of Toronto Press.

Schensul, J., & Berg, M. (2004). Youth participatory action research: A participatory approach to service-learning. *Michigan Journal of Community Service Learning, 10*(3), 76–88.

Sensoy, O., & DiAngelo, R. (2012). *Is everyone really equal? An introduction to key concepts in social justice education.* New York: Teachers College Press.

Sharpe, E., & Dear, S. (2013). Points of discomfort: Reflections on power and partnerships in international service-learning. *Michigan Journal of Community Service Learning, 19*(2), 49–57.

Stein, S. (2016). (Dis)assembling the modern subject of higher education. Manuscript submitted for publication.

Sumka, S., Porter, M. C., & Piacitelli, J. (2015). *Working side by side: Creating alternative breaks as catalysts for global learning, student leadership, and social change.* Sterling, VA: Stylus.

Tinkler, A., Tinkler, B., Jagla, V., & Strait, J. (Eds.). (2016). *Service-learning to advance social justice in a time of radical inequality.* Charlotte, NC: Information Age.

Tuck, E., & Yang, K.W. (2012). Decolonization is not a metaphor. *Decolonization: Indigeneity, Education & Society, 1*(1).

Vaccaro, A. (2009). Racial identity and the ethics of service-learning as pedagogy. In S. Evans, C. Taylor, M. Dunlap, & D. Miller (Eds.), *African Americans and community engagement in higher education: Community service, service-learning, and community-based research* (pp. 119–133). Albany, NY: State University of New York Press.

Verjee, B. (2012). Critical race feminism: A transformative vision for service-learning engagement. *Journal of Community Engagement and Scholarship, 5*(1), 57–69. https://doi.org/10.1057/9781137441102_3

Verjee, B., & Butterwick, S. (2014). Conversations from within: Critical race feminism and the roots/routes of change. In S. Iverson & J. James (Eds.), *Feminist community engagement* (pp. 42–73). New York: Palgrave MacMillan.

Williams, R. L., & Ferber, A. L. (2008). Facilitating smart-girl: Feminist pedagogy in service learning in action. *Feminist Teacher, 19*(1), 47–67. https://doi.org/10.1353/ftr.0.0027

York, T. (2016). More than a desire to serve: A mixed methods exploration of low-income, first-generation college students' motivations to participate in service-learning. In A. Tinkler, B. Tinkler, V. Jagla, & J. Strait (Eds.), *Service-learning to advance social justice in a time of radical inequality* (pp. 7–39). Charlotte, NC: Information Age.

Zembylas, M. (2014). Affective, political and ethical sensibilities in pedagogies of critical hope: Exploring the notion of 'critical emotional praxis.' In V. Bozalek, B. Leibowitz, R. Carolissen, & M. Boler (Eds.), *Discerning critical hope in educational practices* (pp. 11–25). New York: Routledge.

Authors

KARI GRAIN (kari.grain@gmail.com) is a doctoral candidate and Vanier Scholar in the Department of Educational Studies at the University of British Columbia, where she currently works in the Centre for Teaching, Learning and Technology. Grain also develops curriculum and pedagogy for service-learning and experiential education courses across UBC. Previously held positions include service-learning manager at the University of Calgary and division manager of education programs for an immigrant and refugee settlement organization. Grain's master's thesis on volunteer teacher programs in Rwanda garnered the Michele Laferriere Award for top Canadian thesis in comparative education. Her research interests include social justice and global service-learning, international development, critical emotion and affect studies, and the politics of hope in global engagement efforts. Her current fieldwork uses photovoice and community-based research to examine community impacts of an international service-learning program in rural Uganda. Grain serves as assistant editor for the upcoming *Wiley International Handbook of Service-Learning for Social Justice.*

DARREN E. LUND (dlund@ucalgary.ca) is a professor in the Werklund School of Education at the University of Calgary, where his research examines social justice activism. Before earning his

PhD from the University of British Columbia, Darren was a high school teacher for 16 years. Darren has published over 300 articles, chapters, and books, and has been recognized with many honors, including the *2015 Alberta Teachers' Association Educational Research Award* and the *2012 Scholar-Activist Award* from the American Educational Research Association. Lund was also named a *Reader's Digest National Leader in Education* and one of Red Deer's *Top Educators of the Century*. Darren is co-founder of the award-winning *Service-Learning Program for Pre-Service Teachers*, and the editor of the upcoming *Wiley International Handbook of Service-Learning for Social Justice.*

Pathways to Adult Civic Engagement: Benefits of Reflection and Dialogue across Difference in Higher Education Service-Learning Programs

Dan Richard
University of North Florida

Cheryl Keen
Walden University

Julie A. Hatcher
Indiana University-Purdue University Indianapolis

Heather A. Pease
Loyola University Chicago

The current study explores the relationship between participation in college service-learning (SL) experiences, in both academic courses and co-curricular programs, and post-college civic engagement. Using data from a purposeful sample of 1,066 alumni from 30 campuses who participated in the 20th Anniversary Bonner Scholars Study, we explored the extent to which SL experiences during the college years were related to civic outcomes post-graduation, particularly in terms of civic-minded orientations, volunteering, and civic action. When evaluating various attributes of SL programs (e.g., curricular, co-curricular programming, types of reflection, dialogue across difference, interactions with others), two components were particularly salient. Dialogue with others across difference was the strongest predictor of cultivating civic outcomes after college. In addition, both structured and informal reflection independently contributed to civic outcomes (i.e., civic-mindedness, voluntary action, civic action). The results suggested the Pathways to Adult Civic Engagement (PACE) model, which can be used to examine SL programming in higher education and to guide future research to understand how variations in SL program attributes influence civic outcomes years after graduation.

The well-being of American democracy is dependent upon the active participation of its citizens and professionals in both political and community life. This voluntary impulse for engagement is shaped, in part, by traditions learned in families, clubs, religious organizations, and schools (Daloz, Keen, Keen, & Parks, 1996; Wilson, 2000). Each of these social organizations is vital to cultivating civic commitments (Kim, Flanagan, & Pykett, 2015). Higher education has a unique responsibility to prepare graduates with the necessary disciplinary knowledge for their careers as well as with the skills and dispositions to be active citizens through both their personal and professional lives (Sullivan & Rosen, 2008). The National Task Force on Civic Learning and Democratic Engagement (2012) and the Association of American Colleges & Universities (Reich, 2014) recently reiterated to institutions of higher education that their mission should focus on civic engagement.

Research suggests that the college years are indeed a crucial period in the development of civic identity and engagement (Colby, Ehrlich, Beaumont, & Stephens, 2003; Kneflekamp, 2008; Mitchell, Richard, Battistoni, Rost-Banik, Netz, & Zakoske, 2015). Civic outcomes for college students include a wide and complex range of dimensions, including civic knowledge, skills, dispositions, and behaviors related to civic identity, sense of social responsibility, and intentions to participate in politics as well as community engagement and voluntary action (Beaumont, 2012; Hatcher, 2011; Hatcher, Bringle, & Hahn, 2016). Understanding the conditions under which higher education institutions are best able to support civic outcomes among graduates would enrich student learning, help college administrators enact coordinated and impactful academic and co-curricular service-learning (SL) programs, and support the engagement of alumni in the public sphere.

SL, defined broadly as a course-based activity or as a co-curricular program (Jacoby, 2015), is on the rise in American higher education. Concomitantly, research on SL is increasingly prevalent. There have been a number of critiques regarding the quality of SL research in higher education (Butin, 2013; Finley, 2011; Giles & Eyler, 2013). The research on SL often is focused on one course or one program and rarely uses multi-campus sampling strategies. Oftentimes, the research fails to identify clearly the various dimensions of the SL course design (Finley, 2011), thus attributing the outcomes to SL rather than to the specific characteristics of, or variations within, the SL experience itself (Giles & Eyler, 2013). The quality of the SL experience is rarely associated with the variations in student outcomes (Hatcher, Bringle, & Muthiah, 2004). Additionally, the majority of research on SL in higher education is focused on the short-term impact of the academic or co-curricular SL experiences on student outcomes (Conway, Amel, & Gerwien, 2009; Yorio & Ye, 2012), using end-of-course assessments or program evaluation strategies. Research is also limited on alumni who have completed participation in college-level SL programs and who may now be involved in their communities post-graduation (Mitchell, Battistoni, Keene, & Reiff, 2013). Another limitation is that empirical studies on SL programs, regardless of methodological approach, often lack a theoretical or conceptual model, thus limiting the ability to evaluate the theory or conceptual model under various contexts and conditions (Hatcher et al., 2016, Steinberg, Bringle, & McGuire, 2013).

In the current study, we used data from a large, multi-campus, formative program-wide evaluation to address some of these critiques in research on SL. Based on our analysis and interpretation of the data derived from a large, multi-institutional survey and informed by the literature, a general model emerged that can be evaluated and used to improve the design of SL programs. We explored how experiences within SL programs (i.e., reflection activities, informal interactions with mentors and peers, curricular components, co-curricular experiences, community interactions) relate to post-graduate civic outcomes (i.e., civic-mindedness, voluntary action, civic action). The conceptual model is a framework for researchers and practitioners to evaluate the relationships among key elements of SL programs and civic outcomes after graduation. First, we will describe some of the theoretical literature and previous research that informed the development of the model. Second, we will describe the model, the methods, and the results used to generate and test the model. Third, we will explore the implications and limitations of this work.

Service Learning Program Features

Curricular SL Courses

High quality SL experiences, both course-based and co-curricular, have several attributes based on principles of good practice (Council for the Advancement of Standards in Higher Education, 2015; Hahn & Hatcher, 2015; Jacoby, 2015; National Youth Leadership Council, 2008). These attributes have important implications for generating civic outcomes (Stokamer & Clayton, 2016). Research on credit-bearing SL has demonstrated its value for supporting academic learning (Conway et al., 2009; Warren, 2012), critical thinking (Conway et al.), and deep learning (Hahn & Hatcher, 2015). Academic SL in the senior year is related to political and social involvement (Kilgo, Pasquesi, Sheets, & Pascarella, 2014). Curricular SL provides opportunities for structured reflection, oftentimes in the form of assignments, and structured reflection has been found to deepen the meaning of the service experience and increase the reported quality of the learning experience (Ash & Clayton, 2004; Hatcher et al., 2004; Mabry, 1998; Sturgill & Motley, 2014).

Co-curricular Programs and Experiences

Less evidence exists on the impact of co-curricular SL programs. In a large-scale study across 38 campuses, Finley and McNair (2013) found that increased involvement in SL programs correlated with self-reported deep learning, practical competence, personal and social development, and general education outcomes. Finley and McNair's data, however, did not specify whether the SL experiences occurred in the curricular or co-curricular settings. Instead, researchers asked whether SL was happening on campus and whether students were engaged. SL experiences and engagement with racial/cultural diversity during college were associated with adult volunteerism 13 years later (Bowman, Brandenberger, Lapsley, Hill, & Quaranto, 2010). Bowman, Park, and Denson (2014) found that participation in ethnic group organizations on campus, which often involves service, was positively associated with civic engagement 6 years later. Vogelgesang and Astin (2000), using data from more than 22,000 students, found that students participating in service only (not connected to a course but assuming some informal reflection was involved) showed learning gains in civic outcomes similar to those who had course-based SL when compared with students who did not participate in service at all. However, while those who volunteer during college have been more likely to continue to do so after they graduate compared to those who did not, Vogelsang and Astin (2005) found the rate of volunteering diminished 6 years after graduation.

Reflection

Reflection is an essential part of SL (Hatcher et al., 2004, Jacoby, 2015). Reflection is characterized as the hyphen between "service" and "learning" and noted as what distinguishes SL from volunteerism or community service (Giles & Eyler, 2004). Reflection fosters students' ability to make meaning from experience (Bringle & Hatcher, 1999; Eyler & Giles, 1999), increases critical thinking (Ash & Clayton, 2004), and supports the development of civic outcomes, including a social justice orientation (Mitchell, 2014). Fenzel and Peyrot (2005) and Vogelgesang and Astin (2000) found that reflection in SL programs, as opposed to community service without reflection, led to more community responsibility and personal political involvement among alumni. Reflection within SL has been found to contribute to moral reasoning (Boss, 1994) and changes in beliefs about one's own impact on society (Astin & Sax, 1998), including self-efficacy and commitment to activism (Astin, Vogelgesang, Ikeda, & Lee, 2000). Reflection is instrumental in adult identity development (Jones & Abes, 2004; Mezirow, 2000; Mitchell et al., 2015) and in being attentive to the needs of others (Jones & Hill, 2003; Daloz et al., 1996). Additionally, reflection is an essential component to professional practice for it can deepen insight and generate new and improved action (Brookfield, 1995; Schön 1987).

Dialogue across Difference

Another important attribute of SL courses is dialogue across perceived difference (Keen & Hall, 2009). Dialogue across difference might happen informally at service sites, in conversations with peers while traveling to and from a service site, or in structured reflection in a class or co-curricular program activity (Keen & Hall, 2009). When faced with racial, class, ability, or gender diversity, interactions with people who have different backgrounds and experiences can provide the cognitive dissonance necessary for intellectual and personal development (Bowman, 2011; Bowman & Brandenberger, 2012; Diaz & Perrault, 2010; Gurin, Dey, Hurtado, & Gurin, 2002; Hudson & Hunter, 2014). Dialogue across difference provides opportunities for students to experience diversity and develop a pattern of empathy for others, and this can lead to action on behalf of others. Niehaus and Rivera's (2015) analysis of a multi-campus survey of students who participated in alternative spring break trips, which are typically SL oriented programs, found that the trips provided a setting that facilitated informal interactions with diverse others. Holsapple (2012) identified interactions across difference as one of five main outcomes related to openness to diversity outcomes and reported across 55 studies of credit-bearing SL courses. Morton and Bergbauer (2015), in a description of SL programs that target long-term impact, highlighted the importance that dialogue across difference has on student learning and civic engagement. They noted, students learn ". . . that the personal growth they experience by participating in difficult conversations and working in complex, diverse environments can increase their desire and willingness to participate in communal and public life" (p. 28).

Dialogue across difference, when well-planned, produces important civic outcomes. Jones, Robbins, and LePeau (2011) found that students participating in short-term immersion programs including co-curricular SL deepened their understanding of social issues through sustained interaction with community members facing poverty and homelessness. However, the benefits of dialogue across difference may not always be fully realized. Research has pointed to the need for facilitators of SL programs to be careful in assuming whether or not participating students have experienced the poverty, illiteracy, or racism that the students are doing service to ameliorate. Assuming a dimension of difference may prompt students who identify with targeted social categories to experience feelings of the other, particularly students of color or those who are aware of class differences between themselves and their college peers (Mitchell et al., 2012; Seider, 2013; Seider & Hillman, 2011).

Civic Outcomes

The goal of SL programs is to affect student outcomes. In a comprehensive review of research on civic outcomes, Hemer and Reason (2016) concluded that civic outcomes for college students are multifaceted, being classified into categories such as civic knowledge, civic skills, civic attitudes and values, and civic behaviors and participation. Together, these four dimensions of civic outcomes contribute to the formation of civic identity. This complexity in defining civic outcomes is evident in the other literature reviews (Finley, 2011) as well as rubrics designed to evaluate civic engagement (American Association of Colleges & Universities, 2009) and civic knowledge (Civic Rubrics for Knowledge and Values, 2016). For the purposes of the current study, civic outcomes included both civic-mindedness and civic action.

Civic-mindedness, for the purposes of this study, is "a way of thinking about, and paying attention to, the public good and the well-being of society" (Checkoway, 2014, p. 77) and is defined as "a person's inclination or disposition to be knowledgeable of and involved in the community, and to have a commitment to act upon a sense of responsibility as a member of that community" (Steinberg, Hatcher, & Bringle, 2011, p. 429). Civic-mindedness includes knowledge (e.g., technical knowledge within the discipline, knowledge of contemporary social issues), skills (e.g., listening, consensus building, working with diverse others), dispositions (e.g., valuing community engagement, being a social trustee of knowledge), and behavioral intentions to be involved in political and voluntary action (Steinberg et al.). In terms of life after college, civic-mindedness also includes the added domains of how one thinks about their work as a vocation and the public purposes of their profession (Hatcher, 2008). Civic-minded professionals have the public interest at the forefront of their professional work and a sense of civic responsibility to conduct their work to advance the social good (Dzur, 2004; Sullivan, 2005).

Civic action among adults focuses on a range of behaviors (as opposed to behavioral intentions and dispositions) from volunteering to voting to leading boycott campaigns. Finlay, Flanagan, and Wray-Lake (2011), for example, using indicators of civic action such as volunteering, civic organizational involvement, and voting, found that individuals with a college education, compared to those without a college education, sustained levels of civic involvement gained during the AmeriCorps program. Rockenbach, Hudson, and Tuchmayer (2014) found that entering college students who volunteered or did community service the year before entering college still found service to be important 6 years later. In addition, cohort-based service-scholarship programs are an effective means to support the development of civic action (Mitchell et al., 2014).

Research Question

In the current study, we explored three central aspects of college SL programs: (a) curricular and co-curricular experiences; (b) formal and informal reflection with others; and (c) dialogue across difference. We expected that variations in these elements would support the development of civic outcomes, specifically, civic-minded orientations, volunteering, and civic action. We suggest a model to address the interactions among these elements. The data provided by the Bonner Alumni Study provided a unique opportunity to ask the research question: What is the relationship among SL program experiences and the relative impact of these elements, in the context of the others, on civic outcomes post-graduation?

Method

Context and Setting

In 2010, as part of the 20th anniversary celebration of the Bonner Scholar Program (BSP), the Corella and Bertram F. Bonner Foundation (Bonner Foundation) funded a comprehensive, formative, program-wide evaluation to understand a variety of outcomes of the BSP as self-reported by alumni participants. Two members of the research team developed an online questionnaire and BSP alumni from 34 institutions of higher learning were invited to participate in the study. By design, BSP goals across colleges and universities are remarkably similar. Campus program leaders attend training sessions and receive resource materials designed to reach a set of common learning outcomes. However, campus programs have unique elements, due in part to implementation of the BSP in a variety of institutional contexts and across a number of years, which results in variation across individual student experiences. All BSPs intentionally recruit traditionally-aged college students with financial need, most of whom are Pell Grant eligible, who show an interest in and commitment to community service and engagement.

One BSP goal is to enable students to develop a sense of meaning and purpose that extends into the students' personal, professional, and civic lives. Each campus program typically involves 40–80 students in a weekly minimum of 10 hours of community service, training, retreats, and reflection over 4 years. Participants in the first decade of the program did not have many opportunities for curricular SL, but BSP participants in the second decade of the program may have taken a variety of SL courses based on availability at their respective campuses. The majority of BSP students serve at three or more service sites over the course of their college career, and many return to the same service site over multiple semesters to develop a greater understanding of community issues within the context of that local service site. By the third and fourth years in the program, BSP students typically take on expanded leadership roles and responsibilities both on campus and in their communities. By the fourth year, BSP students develop a capstone-level project that integrates their academic pursuits and career interests with the 1640 hours of service and program activities (Bonner Network, 2015). The service-based scholarship program uses best practices in co-curricular student development programs (Butin, 2013; Hoy & Johnson, 2013) and aligns with other models of college student development and best practices of higher education (Astin et al., 2000; Baxter-Magolda, 2000; Blaich, Pascarella, Wolniak, & Cruce, 2004; Keeling, 2004; Kuh, Kinzie, Schuh, & Whitt, 2005).

Sample

The Bonner Foundation retrieved addresses for 75% of the total alumni pool from 30 campuses (N = 3,304) and sent 2,141 emails for whom email addresses were available and 1,163 postcards to those for whom only mailing addresses were available. The campuses were largely small liberal arts colleges in the U.S., many in Appalachia, including some elite institutions and two historically Black universities. Liberal arts colleges, such as the ones attended by participants in this sample, tend to provide more opportunities for interaction with diverse others than other types of colleges and universities (Hu & Kuh, 2003).

Respondents totaled 1,066 (70% female; 75% White), representing a 32% response rate. A design flaw in a small number of survey items resulted in some participants not completing questions that offered nine options instead of five, with 680 participants (63%) completing all measures (a 21% response rate). Response rates obtained in this study are in line with response rates achieved in other online surveys (see Nulty, 2008, for a review). In each analysis, the sample size was the maximum number of respondents available given the available data for the variables included in the analysis. The age range of alumni who responded to the survey was between 22 and 50, with a mean age of 29 and a modal age of 32, with 10% of the sample older than 35. The average alumni respondent was 9 years post-graduation.

Measures Representing Modeled Variables

The questionnaire designed for use in the 20th Anniversary Bonner Scholars Survey included items about past college activities and experiences as well as current activities and opinions related to personal and professional life. Past college activities and experiences included participation in Bonner leadership activities; types of co-curricular service experiences; enrollment in curricular SL; types and perceived value of reflection activities; and perceived value of conversations and interactions with Bonner Scholars, faculty, and peers in formal and informal settings who supported learning. One survey question asked about the importance for their learning of "people who were very different from me." Current activities and opinions included benefits of the BSP, attitudes about work, employment sector, level of college debt, life satisfaction, participation in national service programs, and volunteer and voting patterns (Bonner Foundation, 2016). For the purposes of the Pathways to Adult Civic Engagement (PACE) model, and this current article, we focused on understanding the key variables during college that led to civic-minded orientations, volunteering, and civic activities in post-college life.

Curricular and co-curricular SL. Bonner alumni reported on the number of SL courses they took during college, ranging from 0 to 11 or more. Sixty-six percent of respondents had taken at least one SL course. Only 16% of respondents completed five or more SL courses, therefore this variable was recoded from 0 to 5, with 5 representing five or more courses. Alumni indicated the frequency of their participation in co-curricular service and leadership experiences sponsored by the Bonner Program. These frequencies were recoded and converted into Z-scores, then summed to create two indexes (Distefano, Zhu, & Mîndrilă, 2009): immersive service experiences (i.e., service trips, summers of service, international service experiences; Cronbach's α = .38) and leadership experiences (i.e., Bonner conferences, COOL conferences, regional conferences, training programs; Cronbach's α = .51). The reliability for these co-curricular experiences was less than optimal. The lower reliabilities might reflect differences in SL program experiences across the 30 campuses or might reflect a need for further development and clarity of these concepts.

Reflection and dialogue. The Bonner program, by design, places a high level of emphasis on reflection and interaction with others. To understand the contributions of these activities to student outcomes, alumni responded to a set of questions about reflection and meaningful conversations with others. These questions included:

- Reflection is intentionally thinking about experience. Reflection includes making meaning from an experience, gaining understanding or insight, and results in taking new action. The next set of questions ask you to think about the types of reflection activities you used during college and which activities you found to be helpful to your learning.
- In college, learning occurs in a variety of ways. When you think back upon your college experience, how valuable were conversations and interactions with others in challenging and supporting your learning?

Bonner alumni responded on a 7-point rating Likert-type scale with higher scores representing more value for each type of reflection and each type of conversation and interactions with others, using a range from *1 = Not at all important to my learning* to *7 = Extremely important to my learning*.

From this data, two indexes were created. The variable named formal dialogue and reflection was defined along two dimensions, including classroom experiences (3 items; the importance of conversation with faculty in classroom settings, with students in classroom settings, conversations with faculty/staff in formal settings; Cronbach's α = .71) and structured assignments (3 items; the helpfulness of course writing projects to document learning from an experience, structured reflection activities in a class or organization or Bonner program, writing in a journal; Cronbach's α = .62). Although journal writing can be done in informal settings, many course-based SL experiences require journal writing and therefore it was considered to be a part of formal reflection in this study.

The variable named informal dialogue and reflection was defined along the dimensions of informal dialogue with peers and informal dialogue with faculty/staff. The concept of informal dialogue with peers represented responses across seven items on how important and helpful, for example, were conversations with Bonners in informal settings, conversations with other students in service experiences, and informal dialogue with others (Cronbach's α = .84). The concept of informal dialogue with faculty/staff represented responses across four items on how important and helpful, for example, were conversations with faculty/staff in informal settings and conversations with a mentor or advisor (Cronbach's α = .73). The variable of dialogue across difference was defined by responses to a single item about the importance of conversations with others who are very different from me. The survey did not specify the types of difference across which alumni would have had these conversations, simply conversations with people the alumni perceived were different from them on any dimension.

Civic outcomes. Questions regarding the civic outcomes of the BSP included the Civic-Minded Professional Scale (CMP; Hatcher, 2008), three items from Vogelgesang and Astin's (2000) Life After College survey, and 12 items from AmeriCorps's alumni survey (Corporation for National and Community Service, 2004). The CMP scale is comprised of 23 items (Cronbach's α = .91) and assesses professionals' identity, dispositions, and commitments related to civic action for the public good. Items include statements such as my personal values and beliefs are well integrated and aligned with my work and career and I feel very comfortable recruiting others to become more involved in the community. Alumni rated their agreement with these statements on a 7-point Likert-type scale from 1 = Strongly Disagree to 7 = Strongly Agree, with higher average scores representing high levels of civic orientation as a professional ($M = 5.65$, $SD = .75$).

Alumni also indicated their current levels of voluntary and civic action in their community. Alumni indicated (h)ow many different organizations have you volunteered through in the last 12 months? Seventy-seven percent of alumni reported volunteering in one or more organizations within the past year, and 2% reported volunteering in eight or more organizations. The number of organizations within which alumni volunteered served as a measure of current levels of voluntary action ($M = 2.01$, $SD = 1.69$). Each alumnus also indicated the frequency with which she/he had completed a number of civic actions such as contacted public official to express opinion, signed a written or email petition, and didn't buy product because of values of company, on a 7-point rating scale with 1 = Never and 7 = Always. The average response across 12 civic actions ($M = 3.21$, $SD = 1.21$) served as an index of current civic engagement (Cronbach's α = .87).

Results

The data from the 20th Anniversary Bonner Scholars Study gave us the opportunity to analyze a large data set, explore patterns among variables, and develop the Pathways to Adult Civic Engagement (PACE) model. After mining the extensive survey data in a graduate research class, for developing the PACE model and this current article we focused on understanding the key variables during college that led to civic-minded orientations, volunteering, and civic activities in adult life. We investigated not simply whether the components of the model independently contributed to civic outcomes but also to what extent the interactions among components were influential in producing civic outcomes. A general model emerged from analysis of the data (Figure 1).

Civic Outcomes

Having a civic-minded orientation, as measured by the CMP scale, was associated with more frequent civic action and with volunteering after graduation. BSP alumni who reported higher levels of civic-minded orientation also reported participating more frequently in a variety of civic actions [$r(681) = .51$, $p < .001$] and reported volunteering for a greater number of different organizations within the past 12 months [$r(679) = .40$, $p < .001$]. Thus, the development of professional orientations that integrate civic identity and work (CMP) was associated with current civic action.

Figure 1
Pathways to Adult Civic Engagement (PACE) Model

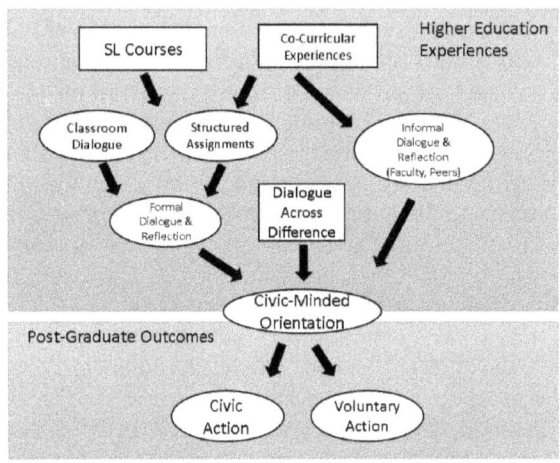

Table 1
Correlations among Civic Outcomes

	Civic-minded Orientation	Civic Action Index	M	SD
Civic-minded Orientation			5.65	.75
Civic Action Index	.51**		3.21	1.31
Voluntary Action	.40**	.36**	2.01	1.69

Note: **p < .001 (2-tailed).

Dialogue across Difference

The PACE model suggests the central importance of asking college students to reflect upon their conceptions about the community and about their place in it. An important mechanism in this process, as proposed by the PACE model, is engaging during college in challenging dialogue across perceived difference. To test this influence on future alumni civic action, we conducted a mediation analysis (Baron & Kenny, 1986). The more BSP alumni rated dialogue with people who were very different from me as important to their learning during their college experiences the more frequently these alumni reported currently engaging in different types of civic action [$r(653) = .30$, $p < .001$] and the more they reported volunteering at a number of different community organizations [$r(657) = .15$, $p = .001$]. Thus, the more BSP alumni found dialogue across difference important during their college experiences (across curricular and co-curricular SL programs), the more they were committed to volunteering and civic action after graduation. Dialogue with people "who were very different" also was strongly associated with responses on the CMP scale [$r(654) = .45$, $p = .001$], suggesting that dialogue across difference was supportive of the development of a civic-minded orientation to one's work life.

Figures 2A and 2B show the mediation model with coefficients for the relationship between dialogue across difference and civic action when the relationship with CMP is statistically controlled. Sobel tests and resulting coefficients indicate that the relationship between dialogue across difference and civic actions was not mediated, but the magnitude of the relationship was modified or moderated by CMP ($Z = 9.04$, $p < .001$). The relationship between dialogue across difference and volunteering, on the other hand, was completely mediated by CMP, $Z = 7.94$, $p < .001$ (see Figures 2A and 2B for coefficients). Thus, the relationship between meaningful dialogues across difference during college was related to civic and voluntary action after graduation when those dialogues contributed to a deep sense of professional commitment to civic action and service.

Figures 2A and 2B
Civic-Minded Orientations Moderate the Relationship between Dialogue across Perceived Difference and Civic Action (Figure 2A) and Mediates the Relationship between Dialogue across Difference and Voluntary Action (Figure 2B)

Figure 2A

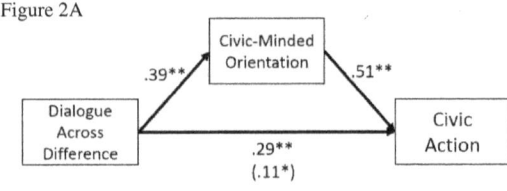

Figure 2B

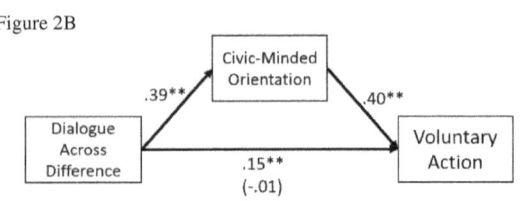

Note. Coefficients represent standardized estimates with partial coefficients in parentheses.
*$p < .05$; **$p < .001$.

Reflection and Dialogue

The development of commitments to civic action through personal and professional identity depends on a number of factors, only some of which relate

Table 2
Bivariate Correlations indicating Associations among Various types of Reflection and Dialogue during College Civic-Minded Orientation after Graduation

	Civic-minded Orientation	Dialogue Across Difference	Classroom Experiences	Structured Assignments	Peer Informal Dialogue
Dialogue Across Difference	.44**				
Classroom Experiences	.32**	.57**			
Structured Assignments	.27**	.36**	.34**		
Peer Informal Dialogue	.40**	.66**	.56**	.47**	
Faculty/Staff Informal Dialogue	.37**	.54**	.70**	.31**	.53**

Note. **$p < .001$

Table 3
Simultaneous Regression Predicting Civic-Minded Orientation after Graduation from Various types of Reflection and Dialogue during College.

	B	SE	β	t-value	Tolerance
(Constant)	3.69	.15			
Dialogue Across Diff	.16	.03	.27	5.34**	.49
Classroom Experiences	−.03	.03	−.04	−.85	.45
Structured Assignments	.04	.02	.08	2.08*	.77
Peer Informal Dialogue	.09	.04	.13	2.49*	.46
Faculty/Staff Informal Dialogue	.10	.03	.16	3.18**	.47

Notes. Dependent Variable = Civic-minded Orientation;
B = Unstandardized Coefficients, SE = Standard Error, β = Standardized Coefficients
*$p < .05$; **$p < .01$, ***$p < .01$

to dialogue across difference. Students find opportunities to engage in dialogue and reflection in SL courses, co-curricular programming, and many other college experiences. We tested the interrelationships among reported dialogue and conversations alumni reported across a number of academic and co-curricular experiences in college with civic-minded orientation using multiple regression analyses. Table 2 provides a summary of the bivariate correlations among the included variables, and Table 3 provides the multiple regression analysis results. Overall, reports of valuable dialogue during college experiences predicted civic-minded orientations after graduation, Adjusted $R^2 = .23$, $F(5,624) = 39.18$, $p < .001$. Among the various opportunities for reflection and dialogue (see Table 3), the best predictor of a civic-minded orientation after graduation was the opportunity to dialogue with people who were very different ($β = .27$). The only type of dialogue that was not related to a civic-minded orientation (while controlling for other forms of reflection and dialogue) was structured reflection and dialogue as part of a course ($β = -.04$). The lack of relationship with course reflection and dialogue, however, might be a function of the interrelationship among course-related dialogue and informal dialogue with faculty and staff as well as with dialogue across perceived difference (see Table 2). In addition, the alumni from the first decade of the 20-year BSP likely had fewer opportunities to take SL courses, as the number of such courses likely increased over time.

Curricular and Co-curricular SL Support Civic-Minded Orientations

Reflection and dialogue are supported by curricular and co-curricular SL experiences during college. To investigate the relationship among these experiences and their connection with the development of a civic-minded orientation, we employed hierarchical regression. Table 4 provides bivariate correlations among curricular and co-curricular SL experiences and a civic-minded orientation (CMP). Table 5 provides coefficients for both a simultaneous regression and a hierarchical regression controlling for reflection and dialogue variables listed in Table 3. This analysis determines the unique contribution of taking SL courses and participating in co-curricular programming when dialogue and reflection during these experiences are statistically allowed to influence the results (simultaneous regression) and when reflection and dialogue during these experiences are specifically controlled in the analysis, showing the unique contribution of coursework and co-curricular experiences without

Table 4
Various types of Reflection and Dialogue during College Correlated with Civic-Minded Orientation after Graduation

	CMP	SL Courses	Immersive Service Experiences
SL Courses	.15**		
Immersive Service Exp.	.15**	.12**	
Leadership Experiences	.28**	.26**	.16**

Notes. CMP = Civic-Minded Professional score; SL = Service Learning
**$p < .001$

Table 5
Simultaneous Regression Predicting Civic-Minded Orientation after Graduation from the Frequency of Service Learning (SL) Courses and the Frequency of Co-Curricular Experiences (Model 1) and Hierarchical Regression while Controlling for Reflection and Dialogue (Model 2)

Model 1	B	SE	β	t-value	Tolerance
(Constant)	4.48	.16			
SL Courses	.03	.02	.08	1.93	.93
Immersive Service Exp.	.15	.04	.11	2.75**	.97
Leadership Experiences	.22	.04	.24	6.16***	.92
Model 2					
(Constant)	3.87	.15			
SL Courses	.01	.02	.03	.78	.93
Immersive Service Exp.	.08	.04	.10	2.33*	.97
Leadership Experiences	.10	.03	.12	2.90**	.92

Notes. Dependent Variable = Civic-Minded Professional score;
B = Unstandardized Coefficients, SE = Standard Error, $β$ = Standardized Coefficients
*$p < .05$; **$p < .01$, ***$p < .01$

the influence of reflection and dialogue.

The frequency of taking SL courses in college was associated with a civic-minded orientation after graduation, $r(646) = .15, p < .001$ (see Table 4). For Bonner alumni, however, a civic-minded orientation was more strongly associated with Bonner leadership experiences ($r(646) = .28, p < .001$. Students enrolled in the BSP likely engage in leadership experiences and SL courses simultaneously. The simultaneous regression analysis indicates that curricular SL and co-curricular SL experiences overall were associated with a civic-minded orientation after graduation, $R^2 = .09, F(3,644) = 22.32, p < .001$. When reflection activities were specifically controlled to determine the unique influence of curricular SL and co-curricular SL experiences, the hierarchical regression indicates that these college-level experiences continue to predict a civic-minded orientation after graduation [$R^2 = .03, F(3,595) = 6.36, p < .001$], albeit a smaller amount. An examination of the pattern of coefficients indicates that the relationship between leadership experiences and immersive service experiences during college with a civic-minded orientation exists beyond what could be accounted for by the reflection and dialogue experiences involved in these experiences. One interpretation of the pattern of coefficients is that the influence of SL courses on a civic-minded orientation after graduation seems to occur through the reflection, dialogue activities, and assignments associated with those course-based experiences.

Discussion

Research on SL, particularly course-based SL, has engendered much attention, and this study suggests that SL, particularly co-curricular SL, provides a rich learning environment for civic outcomes after college. SL provides opportunities for both formal and informal reflections and conversations with others. These conversations occur with peers, faculty, community members, or community site supervisors, and may involve dialogue across difference. These conversations, both formal and informal, may promote moral and cognitive reflection at service sites, in the classroom, and in informal discussion settings on campus or in the van going to or returning from service sites. The PACE model emphasizes the importance of reflection and dialogue as it provides opportunities for the development of a civic orientation toward and commitment to service in one's community.

Barnhardt, Sheets, and Pasquesi (2015) found that liberal arts colleges with a mission reflecting commitment to service, typical of BSP host institutions, might be more successful at developing civic action in their alumni than comprehensive undergraduate institutions and research-focused institutions. The Wabash alumni study (Kilgo et al., 2014), however, found that doing course-based SL might contribute more to sustaining civic outcomes than pre-college service experiences. SL experiences with adequate opportunities for dialogue and reflection may prevent the modest decline in civic engagement after college. Further research could establish whether the relationship among program elements and civic outcomes might be maintained outside of the unique mission of liberal arts schools.

Limitations

In the current project, dialogue across difference served as a key experience in predicting civic orientations and civic action after graduation, yet this was based on a single-item measure. The development of a pluralistic orientation (see Engberg & Hurtado, 2011), for example, might mediate some of the effects that dialogue across difference has in predicting civic engagement after college. We have limited data about the developmental experiences in young adulthood (Arnett, 2004) that might influence civic engagement after college. Bonner Scholars may have pursued uniquely developmental experiences. Future research could establish additional variables that are important for these program elements to have their full effect. The Difficult Dialogues project (O'Neil, 2006; Placier, Kroner, Burgoyne, & Worthington, 2012) sponsored by the Ford Foundation has worked to develop successful practices to sustain dialogues on campus among students who perceive important differences going into the dialogues in both curricular and co-curricular settings.

The 20th Anniversary Bonner Scholars Survey formatively evaluated the BSP program, and this might limit the applicability of findings to other colleges' co-curricular and service-based scholarship program. The constructs of 'leadership' and 'immersive service experiences' were based on specific questions related to BSP programs. This may have led to an undue emphasis on these types of experiences. The alumni answered many questions about their current practices, and the relationships among a variety of program experiences and current behavior suggest the importance of these program variables. Future research could explore additional program attributes of theoretical interest along with attributes identified in the current study to explore possible overlap or extension of concepts related to civic action after graduation.

Common to prior research on SL in classes or programs into which students self-select, this study was based on data from college graduates who either self-selected to apply for the BSP or were selected by admissions offices to be a part of this service-based scholarship program. Participants also self-selected to participate in the study. This self-selection bias may have influenced the results in that respondents may have been among those BSP alumni who were most satisfied with their Bonner experience. The best way to control for self-selection bias in quasi-experimental designs is to control for pre-existing variables; however, this approach was not possible in that we did not have any information about the participants before college. One way to address the concern about response bias due to self-selection is to ensure a reasonable response rate, which we were able to establish. Additionally, the pattern of the correlations suggest, however, that higher amounts of reflection, dialogue, and SL experiences were associated with higher amounts of civic outcomes in one's adult and professional lives, even for those who self-selected into the program.

Implications

These findings are particularly relevant to advancing the use of service-based scholarships as curricular or co-curricular strategy for engaging students in developmentally conducive learning opportunities and institutional strategy for developing civic-minded alumni, particularly among college students who are Pell Grant eligible, which is the case for most Bonner Scholars. Findings from this current study are consistent with those from the Sam H. Jones Community Service Scholarship (Hatcher, Bringle, Brown, & Fleischhacker, 2006), a campus-funded program at Indiana University-Purdue University Indianapolis (Hahn, Hatcher, & Graunke, 2016). Evidence from both studies indicates that service-based scholarship programs provide opportunities for high-ability low-income students to be successful in college and in professional life. Many foundations (e.g., Lumina) are interested in finding ways to improve degree completion among low-income students. Similarly, as states move toward outcome metrics in higher education, one of the metrics to determine performance funding for public institutions may be based on the number of students with a Pell Grant who complete a bachelor's degree.

The PACE model suggests that faculty and staff need to provide opportunities for informal dialogue with faculty and peers, particularly if they want educational experiences to result in civic-minded alumni. Our findings bear out decades-long research by Astin (1993) showing the importance of informal discussion with peers as well as by Schoem and Hurtado (2001) who documented the outcomes of dialogue across boundaries of perceived difference. Whereas informal reflection appears prominently in the PACE model, we learned that structured and unstructured reflection work together to support civic outcomes.

The Civic-Minded Professional (CMP; Hatcher, 2008) scale, previously validated with a sample of higher education faculty, shows promise as an instrument for studying civic-mindedness among alumni and across a range of professional fields. In the current study, scores on the CMP scale were strongly associated with measures of volunteerism and civic action among BSP alumni years after graduation. Researchers interested in evaluating the long-term community impact of SL courses and co-curricular programs might consider assessing the extent to which a civic-minded orientation leads to community benefit through the civic actions of their alumni.

Research on higher education, as with research on K-12 education, also suggests that teaching approaches that stress collaborative and experiential work and projects, including group inquiry, political internships, simulations, and open and critical discussion, are often important for promoting civic learning and civic action in college students (Astin, 1993; Battistoni & Hudson, 1997; Beaumont, 2012; Kuh et al., 2005). Although extensive research is available on SL, dialogue across difference is not often included in quantitative collection tools nor in observations or interview protocols. Even more challenging might be arranging college classes, enrollment, and major selection so that such perceived diversity, as well as reflection and dialogue regarding those differences, is part of students' experiences.

When changing the mission and sustaining a commitment to fostering civic engagement amongst graduates seems too far a reach, the PACE model suggests that smaller program designs can bring desired results to a cohort within a larger institution. Coordinated programs at the institutional level and across institutions can be difficult to implement and manage. Smaller programs that include a coordinated set of key elements referenced by the PACE model may find success with a smaller number of students. This general PACE model likely has its greatest impact as programs across multiple institutions and settings find ways to emphasize these key elements as a way of fostering and encouraging a civic-minded orientation among their program participants, graduates, and future professionals.

Notes

BSP campuses participating in the study include Allegheny College, Berea College, Berry College, Carson-Newman College, Centre College, Concord College, Davidson College, Earlham College, Ferrum College, Guilford College, Lees-McRae College, Lynchburg College, Mars Hill College, Maryville College, Middlesex County College, Morehouse College, Oberlin College, Rhodes College, Spelman College, Stetson University, The College of New Jersey, University of Richmond, Warren Wilson College, Waynesburg University, West Virginia Wesleyan College, and Wofford College.

References

American Association of College and Universities (AAC&U). (2009). *Civic engagement VALUE rubrics*. Retrieved from https://www.aacu.org/civic-engagement-value-rubric.

Arnett, J. J. (2004). *Emerging adulthood: The winding road from the late teens through the twenties*. New York: Oxford University Press.

Ash, S. L., & Clayton, P. H. (2004). The articulated learning: An approach to guided reflection and assessment. *Innovative Higher Education*, 29(2), 137–154. https://doi.org/10.1023/B:IHIE.0000048795.84634.4a

Astin, A. W. (1993). *What matters in college*. San Francisco: Jossey-Bass.

Astin, A. W., & Sax, L. J. (1998). How undergraduates are affected by service participation. *Journal of College Student Development*, 39(3), 251–263.

Astin, A.W., Vogelgesang, L. J., Ikeda, E. K.; & Yee, J. A. (2000). How service learning affects students. Retrieved from http://heri.ucla.edu/pdfs/hslas/hslas.pdf.

Barnhardt, C. L., Sheets, J. E., & Pasquesi, K. (2015). You expect what? Students' perceptions as resources in acquiring commitments and capacities for civic engagement. *Research in Higher Education*, 56, 622–644. https://doi.org/10.1007/s11162-014-9361-8

Baron, R. M., & Kenny, D. A. (1986). The moderator-mediator variable distinction in social psychological research: Conceptual, strategic, and statistical considerations. *Journal of personality and social psychology*, 51(6), 1173–1182. https://doi.org/10.1037/0022-3514.51.6.1173

Battistoni, R. M., & Hudson, W. E. (1997). *Experiencing citizenship: Concepts and models for service-learning in political science*. Stylus Publishing, LLC.

Baxter Magolda, M. B. (2000). Interpersonal maturity: Integrating agency and communion. *Journal of College Student Development*, 41(2), 141–156.

Beaumont, E. (2012). What does recent research suggest about civic learning and civic action in young adults 18–30? Some insights and foundations for further work. Spencer Foundation. Retrieved from http://www.spencer.org/resources/content/3/9/2/documents/elizabethbeaumont.pdf

Blaich, C. F., Pascarella, E. T., Wolniak, G. C., & Cruce, T. M. (2004). Do liberal arts colleges really foster good practices in undergraduate education? *Journal of College Student Development, 45*(1), 57–74. https://doi.org/10.1353/csd.2004.0013

Bonner Network (2015). Student development and leadership. Retrieved from http://bonnernetwork.pbworks.com/w/page/13113175/Student%20Development%20and%20Leadership.

Bonner Foundation (2016). Student Impact Survey. Retrieved from http://bonnerwikiv2.pbworks.com/w/page/104743603/Bonner%20Student%20Impact%20Survey%20-%20Overview .

Boss, J. A. (1994). The effect of community service work on the moral development of college ethics students. *Journal of Moral Education, 23*(2), 183–198. https://doi.org/10.1080/0305724940230206

Bowman, N. A. (2011). Promoting participation in a diverse democracy A meta-analysis of college diversity experiences and civic engagement. *Review of Educational Research, 81*(1), 29–68. https://doi.org/10.3102/0034654310383047

Bowman, N. A., & Brandenberger, J. W. (2012). Experiencing the unexpected: Toward a model of college diversity experiences and attitude change. *The Review of Higher Education, 35*(2), 179–205. https://doi.org/10.1353/rhe.2012.0016

Bowman, N., Brandenberger, J., Lapsley, D., Hill, P., & Quaranto, J. (2010). Serving in college, flourishing in adulthood: Does community engagement during the college years predict adult well-being? *Applied Psychology: Health and Well-Being, 2*(1), 14–34. https://doi.org/10.1111/j.1758-0854.2009.01020.x

Bowman, N. A., Park, J. J., & Denson, N. (2015). Student involvement in ethnic student organizations: Examining civic outcomes 6 years after graduation. *Research in Higher Education, 56*, 127–145. https://doi.org/10.1007/s11162-014-9353-8

Bringle, R. G., & Hatcher, J. A. (1999). Reflection in service-learning: Making meaning of experience. *Educational Horizons, 77*, 179–185.

Brookfield, S. (1995). *Becoming a critically reflective teacher*. San Francisco: Jossey-Bass.

Butin, D. W. (2013). Transformation is just another word: Thinking through the future of community engagement in the disrupted university. In A. Hoy & M. Johnson (Eds.), *Deepening community engagement in higher education* (pp. 245–252). New York: Palgrave Macmillan.

Checkoway, B. (2014). Civic minded professors. In J. Reich (Ed.), *Civic engagement, civic development, and higher education* (pp. 77–79). Washington, DC: Bringing Theory to Practice.

Civic Rubrics for Knowledge and Values: A National Collaboration. (2016). Civic Knowledge Rubric. Retrieved from https://civiclearningrubric.wordpress.com/civic-knowledge-rubric/

Colby, A., Ehrlich, T., Beaumont, E., & Stephens, J. (2003). *Educating citizens: Preparing America's undergraduates for lives of moral and civic responsibility*. San Francisco: Jossey-Bass.

Conway, J. M., Amel, E. L., & Gerwien, D. P. (2009). Teaching and learning in the social context: A meta-analysis of service-learning's effects on academic, personal, social, and citizenship outcomes. *Teaching of Psychology, 36*, 233–245. https://doi.org/10.1080/00986280903172969

Corporation for National and Community Service (2004). Serving country and community: A longitudinal study of service in AmeriCorps (Report). Cambridge, MA, Abt Associates.

Council for the Advancement of Standards in Higher Education (2015). Civic engagement and service-learning programs. Retrieved from http://standards.cas.edu/getpdf.cfm?PDF=E86EC8E7-9B94-5F5C-9AD22B4FEF375B64

Daloz, L. A., Keen, C. H., Keen, J. P., & Parks, S. D. (1996). *Common fire: Lives of commitment in a complex world*. Boston: Beacon Press.

Diaz, A., & Perrault, R. (2010). Sustained dialogue and civic life: Post-college impacts. *Michigan Journal of Community Service Learning, 17*(1), 32–43.

Distefano, C., Zhu, M., & Mîndrilă, D. (2009). Understanding and using factor scores: Considerations for the applied researcher. *Practical Assessment, Research & Evaluation, 14*(20), 1–11.

Dzur, A. W. (2004). Democratic professionalism: Sharing authority in civic life. *The Good Society, 13*(1), 6–14. https://doi.org/10.1353/gso.2004.0026

Engberg, M. E., & Hurtado, S. (2011). Developing pluralistic skills and dispositions in college: Examining racial/ethnic group differences. *The Journal of Higher Education, 82*, 416–443. https://doi.org/10.1353/jhe.2011.0025

Eyler, J., & Giles Jr, D. E. (1999). *Where's the learning in service-learning?* San Francisco: Jossey-Bass.

Fenzel, L. M., & Peyrot, M. (2005). Comparing college community participation and future service behaviors and attitudes. *Michigan Journal of Community Service-learning, 12*(1), 23–31.

Finlay, A. K., Flanagan, C., & Wray-Lake, L.(2011). Civic engagement patterns and transitions over 8 years: The AmeriCorps national study. *Developmental Psychology, 47*(6), 1728–1743. https://doi.org/10.1037/a0025360

Finley, A. (2011). *Civic learning and democratic engagements: A review of the literature on civic engagement in post-secondary education*. Paper prepared for the U. S. Department of Education as part of Contract: ED-OPE-10_C-0078. Retrieved from http://www.aacu.org/sites/default/files/files/CLDE/LiteratureReview.pdf

Finley, A., & McNair, T. (2013). Assessing underserved students' engagement in high impact practices. (Report) Washington D.C.: American Association of College and Universities.

Giles, Jr., D. E., & Eyler, J. (2013). Review essay: The endless quest for scholarly respectability in service-learning research. *Michigan Journal of Community Service Learning, 20*(1), 53–64.

Gurin, P., Dey, E. L., Hurtado, S., & Gurin, G. (2002). Diversity in higher education: Theory and impact on educational outcomes. *Harvard Educational Review, 72*(3), 330–366. https://doi.org/10.17763/haer.72.3.01151786u134n051

Hahn, T. W. & Hatcher, J. A. (2015). The relationship between enrollment in service learning courses and deep approaches to learning: A campus study. *PRISM: A Journal of Regional Engagement, 4* (2), 55–70. Retrieved from http://encompass.eku.edu/prism/vol4/iss2/1.

Hahn, T. W., & Hatcher, J. A. (2015, September 30). *What about service-learning matters? Using a taxonomy to identify variables to improve research and practice* [Webinar]. In IARSLCE *Webinar Series*. Retrieved from https://www.youtube.com/watch?v=O3W27s3-XTw.

Hahn, T. W., Hatcher, J. A., & Graunke, S. S. (2016). *Service scholarships, persistence and retention*. Research Brief, Center for Service and Learning, Indianapolis, IN.

Hatcher, J. A. (2008). The public role of professionals: Developing and evaluating the Civic-Minded Professional scale. (Doctoral dissertation). Retrieved from Pro Quest Dissertation and Theses, AAT 3331248, 2008.

Hatcher, J. A. (2011). Civic knowledge and engagement. In J. Penn (Ed.), *Measuring complex general education learning outcomes. Jossey-Bass Quarterly Sourcebooks* (pp. 81–92). San Francisco: Jossey-Bass.

Hatcher, J. A., Bringle, R. G., Brown, L. A., & Fleischhacker, D. A. (2006). Indiana University-Purdue University Indianapolis: Supporting student involvement through service-based scholarships. In E. Zlotkowski, N. V. Longo, & J. R. Williams (Eds.), *Students as colleagues: Expanding the circle of service-learning leadership* (pp. 35–48). Providence, RI: Campus Compact.

Hatcher, J. A., Bringle, R. G., & Hahn, T. W. (2016). *Research on student civic outcomes in service learning: Conceptual frameworks and methods. Volume 3: IUPUI Series on Service Learning Research*. Sterling, VA: Stylus Publishing.

Hatcher, J. A., Bringle, R.G., & Muthiah, R. (2004). Designing effective reflection: What matters to service-learning? *Michigan Journal of Community Service learning, 11*(1), 38–46.

Hemer, K. M., & Reason, R. D. (2016, in press). Civic outcomes in higher education. In J. A. Hatcher, R.G. Bringle, & T. W. Hahn (Eds), *Research on student civic outcomes in service learning: Conceptual frameworks and methods* (pp. 25–43). Sterling, VA: Stylus.

Holsapple, M. A. (2012). Service-learning and student diversity outcomes: Existing evidence and directions for future research. *Michigan Journal of Community Service Learning, 18*(2), 5–18.

Hudson, M., & Hunter, K. O. (2014). Positive effects of peer-led reflection on undergraduates' concept integration and synthesis during service-learning. *International Journal of Teaching and Learning in Higher Education, 26*(1), 12–25.

Hu, S., & Kuh, G. D. (2003). Diversity experiences and college student learning and personal development. *Journal of College Student Development, 44*(3), 320–334. https://doi.org/10.1353/csd.2003.0026

Jacoby, B. (2015). *Service-learning essentials: Questions, answers, and lessons learned*. San Francisco: Jossey-Bass.

Jones, S. R., Robbins, C. K., & LePeau, L. A. (2011). Negotiating border crossing: Influences of social identity on service-learning outcomes. *Michigan Journal of Community Service Learning, 17*(2), 27–42.

Jones, S. R., & Abes, E. S. (2004). Enduring influences of service-learning on college students' identity development. *Journal of College Student Development, 45*(2), 149–166. https://doi.org/10.1353/csd.2004.0023

Jones, S. R., & Hill, K. E. (2003). Understanding patterns of commitment: Student motivation for community service involvement. *The Journal of Higher Education, 74*(5), 516–539. https://doi.org/10.1353/jhe.2003.0036

Keeling, R. (Ed.). (2004). *Learning reconsidered: A campus-wide focus on the student experience*. Washington, DC: American College Personnel Association and National Association of School Personnel Administrators.

Keen, C., & Hall, K. (2009). Engaging with difference matters: Longitudinal student outcomes of co-curricular service-learning programs. *The Journal of Higher Education, 80*(1), 59–79. https://doi.org/10.1353/jhe.0.0037

Kilgo, C. A., Pasquesi, K., Sheets, J. K. E., & Pascarella, E. T. (2014). The estimated effects of participation in service-learning on liberal arts outcomes. *The International Journal of Research on Service-Learning and Community Engagement, 2*(1), 18–31.

Kim, T, Flanagan, C. A. & Pykett, A. A. (2015). Adolescents' civic commitments in stable and fledgling democracies: The role of family, school, and community. *Research in Human Development, 12*(1), 28–43. https://doi.org/10.1080/15427609.2015.1010344

Knefelkamp, L. (2008). Civic identity: Locating self in community. *Diversity and Democracy: Civic Learning for Shared Futures, 11*(2), 1–3.

Kuh, G. D., Kinzie, J., Schuh, J. H., & Whitt, E. J. (2005). Never let it rest: Lessons about student success from high-performing colleges and universities. *Change: The Magazine of Higher Learning, 37*(4), 44–51. https://doi.org/10.3200/CHNG.37.4.44–51

Mabry, J. B. (1998). Pedagogical variations in service-learning and student outcomes: How time, contact and reflection matters. *Michigan Journal of Community Service Learning, 5*, 32–47.

Mezirow, J. (2000). *Learning as transformation: Critical perspectives on a theory in progress*. San Francisco: Jossey-Bass.

Mitchell, T. D. (2014). How service-learning enacts social justice sensemaking. *Journal of Critical Thought and Praxis, 2*(2), 1–26.

Mitchell, T. D., Battistoni, R. M., Keene, A. S. & Reiff, J. (2013). Programs that build civic identity: A study of alumni. *Diversity and Democracy*, Summer, *16*(3), 22–23.

Mitchell, T. D., Richard, F. D., Battistoni, R. M., Rost-Banik, C., Netz, R., & Zakoske, C. (2015). Reflective practice that persists: Connections between reflection in service-learning programs and in current life. *Michigan Journal of Community Service Learning, 21*(2), 49–64.

Morton, K., & Bergbauer, S. (2015). A case for community: Starting with relationships and prioritizing community as method in service-learning. *Michigan Journal of Community Service Learning, 22*(1), 18–32.

National Task Force on Civic Learning and Democratic Engagement. (2012). *A crucible moment: College learning and democracy's future.* Washington, DC: Association of American Colleges and Universities.

National Youth Leadership Council (2008). K-12 service-learning standards for quality practice. Retrieved from https://nylc.org/standards/ .

Niehaus, E., & Rivera, M. (2015). Serving a stranger or serving myself: Alternative breaks and the influence of race and ethnicity on student understanding of themselves and others. *Journal of College and Character, 16*, 209–224. https://doi.org/10.1080/2194587X.2015.1091360

Nulty, D. (2008). The adequacy of response rates to online and paper surveys: What can be done? *Assessment & Evaluation in Higher Education, 33*(3), 301–314. https://doi.org/10.1080/02602930701293231

O'Neil, R. M. (2006). The difficult dialogues initiative. *Academe, 92*(4), 29–30. https://doi.org/10.2307/40253462

Placier, P., Kroner, C., Burgoyne, S., & Worthington, R. (2012). Developing difficult dialogues: An evaluation of classroom implementation. *The Journal of Faculty Development, 26*(2), 29–36.

Reich, I. N. (Ed.). (2014). *Civic engagement, civic development, and higher education: New perspectives on transformational learning.* Washington, D.C.: Bringing Theory to Practice.

Rockenbach, A. B., Hudson, T. D., & Tuchmayer, J. B. (2014). Fostering meaning, purpose, and enduring commitments to community service in college: A multidimensional conceptual model. *The Journal of Higher Education, 85*, 312–338. https://doi.org/10.1353/jhe.2014.0014

Schoem, D. L., & Hurtado, S. (2001). *Intergroup dialogue: Deliberative democracy in school, college, community, and workplace.* Ann Arbor, MI: University of Michigan Press. https://doi.org/10.3998/mpub.11280

Schön, D. A. (1987). *Educating the reflective practitioner: Toward a new design for teaching and learning in the professions.* San Francisco: Jossey-Bass.

Seider, S. (2013). Two key strategies for enhancing community service learning. *Journal of College and Character, 14*(1), 79–84. https://doi.org/10.1515/jcc-2013-0011

Seider, S., & Hillman, A. (2011). Challenging privileged college students' othering language in community service learning. *Journal of College and Character, 12*(3), 1–7. https://doi.org/10.2202/1940-1639.1810

Stokamer, S. T., & Clayton, P. H. (2016). Civic learning through service learning: Instructional design and research. In J. A. Hatcher, R. G. Bringle, & T. W. Hahn (Eds.), *Research on student civic outcomes in service learning: Conceptual frameworks and methods* (pp. 45–65). Sterling, VA: Stylus.

Sullivan, W. M. (2005). *Work and integrity: The crisis and promise of professionalism in America* (2nd Edition). San Francisco: Jossey-Bass.

Sullivan, W. M. & Rosin, M. S. (2008). *A new agenda for higher education: Shaping a life of the mind for practice.* San Francisco: Jossey-Bass.

Steinberg, K. S., Bringle, R. G., & McGuire, L.E. (2013). Attributes of high-quality research on service learning. In P. H. Clayton, R. G. Bringle, & J. A. Hatcher (Eds.), *Research on service learning: Conceptual frameworks and assessment, Vol 2A: Students and Faculty* (pp. 27–53). Sterling, VA: Stylus.

Steinberg, K., Hatcher, J. A., & Bringle, R. G. (2011). A north star: Civic-minded graduate. *Michigan Journal of Community Service Learning, 18*(1), 19–33.

Sturgill, A., & Motley, P. (2014). Methods of reflection about service-learning: Guided vs. free, dialogic vs. expressive, and public vs. private. *Teaching and Learning Inquiry: The ISSOTL Journal, 2*(1), 81–93. https://doi.org/10.20343/teachlearninqu.2.1.81

Vogelgesang, L. & Astin, A. (2000). Comparing the effects of community service and service-learning. *Michigan Journal of Community Service Learning, 7*, 25–34.

Vogelgesang, L. J., & Astin, E. W. (2005). Research Report# 2: Post-college civic engagement among graduates. Higher Education Research Institute: University of California, Los Angeles.

Warren, J. L. (2012). Does service-learning increase student learning?: A meta-analysis. *Michigan Journal of Community Service Learning, 18*(2), 56–61.

Wilson, J., 2000. Volunteering. *Annual Review of Sociology, 26*, 215–240. https://doi.org/10.1146/annurev.soc.26.1.215

Yorio, P. L., & Ye, F. (2012). A meta-analysis on the effects of service-learning on the social, personal, and cognitive outcomes of learning. *Academy of Management Learning and Education, 11*(1), 9–27. https://doi.org/10.5465/amle.2010.0072

Authors

DAN RICHARD (drichard@unf.edu) is the director of the Office of Faculty Enhancement and associate professor in the Department of Psychology at the University of North Florida. He also serves as the section co-editor of the Advances in Theory and

Methodology Section of the *International Journal of Research on Service Learning and Community Engagement*. He is the lead researcher assessing student-learning outcomes related to UNF's Quality Enhancement Plan on community-based transformational learning. He teaches service-learning courses in research design and statistics as well as a course on revenge and the lasting impact of community resentment on individuals making a transition from prison back to the community.

CHERYL KEEN (cheryl.keen@waldenu.edu) serves as core faculty in the Ph.D. in Education program at Walden University. Previously she served as dean of faculty, co-dean of students, and director of the Center for Community Learning at Antioch College, 15 years as senior researcher for the Bonner Foundation, and several years as evaluator of the Volunteers Exploring Vocation program. Before that she directed the New Jersey Governor's School on Public Issues and the Future of New Jersey, and was the Millicent Fenwick Research Professor for Public Issues and Education at Monmouth University. Cheryl Keen's co-authored book, *Common Fire: Leading Lives of Commitment in a Complex World* (Beacon Press, 1996), anchors the focus of her scholarly outreach.

JULIE HATCHER (jhatcher@iupui.edu) is executive director of the Center for Service and Learning and associate professor of Philanthropic Studies in the Lilly Family School of Philanthropy at Indiana University Purdue University Indianapolis. Her scholarship and research relates to community engagement in higher education and she has responsibilities for leading the research and scholarship of CSL. Julie is a member of the campus Community Engagement Leadership Team within the Office of Community Engagement. She also serves on the National Advisory Board for the Carnegie Classification for Community Engagement and was part of the rubric development team for AAC&U Civic Engagement Rubric and the Civic Knowledge Rubric.

HEATHER PEASE (heather.pease@outlook.com) is currently a doctoral candidate in Research Methodology at Loyola University Chicago. Her dissertation topic is social scientists' conceptualization and implementation of research ethics and integrity. Heather is also a former student of Dan Richard. Their mentor-mentee relationship began as a result of a service-learning graduate course in quasi-experimental design in 2010.

SLCE Future Directions Project: Sustaining a Dialogue, Challenging the Movement

Sarah Stanlick
Lehigh University

Edward Zlotkowski
Bentley University & Puppet Showplace Theater

In 2015 – twenty years after the article "Does Service-Learning Have a Future?" in which Zlotkowski (1995) called attention to the importance of institutionalizing service-learning as an academic endeavor, complete with strong disciplinary connections, professional development and resources for faculty, and high pedagogical standards – the SLCE Future Directions Project (SLCE-FDP) opened a broad conversation on the future of service-learning and community engagement (SLCE). Believing that earlier question to be largely settled at this point, the project poses new questions: "What are our visions now for the future of SLCE, why, and what will it take to get there?" and "How can we leverage the movement to advance those ends – intentionally, inclusively, and with integrity?" (Stanlick & Clayton, 2015, p. 78).

From the beginning of the project, we have sought to honor and incorporate voices, experiences, and perspectives often marginalized in traditional academic writing. We have tried to bring together diverse perspectives and experiences, including in our project design an attempt to avoid academic jargon and an over-reliance on traditionally accepted (academic) knowledge centers. But we also readily acknowledge that we have a long way to go on this front: There are many voices yet to be heard. We seek to envision the future together as an inclusive, ever-expanding learning community that adopts a frame of bold vision, tangible action, and appreciative inquiry.

Functioning as an international learning community, the SLCE-FDP operates in three primary venues: an interactive website (www.slce-fdp.org); an ever expanding set of in-person conversations on campuses, in communities, and at conferences; and special sections of the *Michigan Journal of Community Service Learning (MJCSL)*. Across all of these venues we invite colleagues to envision a bold future for the SLCE movement, and we are happy to report that the responses we have received over the past year have given us much food for thought on a broad range of ideas and viewpoints.

Our earliest contributors themselves brought a wide range of perspectives to the table: their own diverse personal and professional identities (undergraduate students, community leaders, social entrepreneur, and new as well as established faculty and staff members, to name just a few) and thought pieces that spanned many issues and settings. They grappled with the challenges and tensions of both local and global engagement, the identities held by all partners in SLCE (who variously self-define as practitioners, scholars, and practitioner-scholars), the dynamics of working within and outside of the academy, and issues of privilege and power. Priorities for the future of the SLCE movement articulated in that first set of thought pieces include, by way of example, the importance of asset-based course design in the first year (Bauer, Kniffin, & Priest, 2015); students, community partners, and faculty seeing themselves as colleagues in SLCE who relate with one another and contribute to the work in non-hierarchical ways (Hicks, Seymour, & Puppo, 2015); looking at institutional transformation through the lens of deep, pervasive, and integrated second order change (Saltmarsh, Janke, & Clayton, 2015); and designing global service-learning with strong critical reflection and a focus on the challenges of re-entry into home communities (Pisco, 2015). The 2015 contributors have also used their thought pieces to advance their work in various ways: to gather contributors to a thematically similar edited volume, in professional development activities on their campuses, as a foundation for other writing, as a starting point for other collaborations with the same co-authors, and to share their thinking with colleagues, to name a few examples.

Since the publication of the first set of thought pieces in November of 2015, we have utilized several strategies to expand participation in the project. In addition to soliciting additional thought pieces, we have facilitated discussions at several conferences, hosted multi-partner dinner conversations, promoted interaction through our online learning community space, and collected input from many individuals and a few SLCE organizations on the idea of developing a national plan to guide the future evolution of SLCE – a strategy proposed in a 2015 essay by Howard and Stanlick. We have gathered ideas from colleagues across the United States – from Hawaii and Alaska through Iowa and Chicago to New England and the Appalachian Mountains – as well as abroad (e.g., Canada, Ireland, and Hong Kong). Ideas, questions, and feedback have been varied, critical, and constructive. The thread that runs through all of this work has been a deep commitment to nudging the SLCE movement and our world toward a better future. It is in this spirit that we present the Fall 2016 contributions to the SLCE Future Directions Project.

This special section shares thought pieces from 19 contributors, including the 4 lead project facilitators and the project's doctoral Fellow. This group also includes graduate students, volunteers with local and international community organizations, leaders of nonprofit organizations, campus administrators, new and veteran faculty members, consultants, and well-established SLCE scholars. They have produced six thought pieces that, in their own way and through their own lenses, respond to the following questions: *What are our visions now for the future of SLCE? Why? What will it take to get there?* In this set of thought pieces, contributors call the movement to . . .

- Focus on empowerment of all stakeholders in community-university partnerships and break down narratives of heroic "helping" in order to move toward transformative reciprocity [Stanlick & Sell]
- Listen to and learn from the ways community organizations navigate the tensions of enacting democratic engagement in a world that makes doing so difficult – specifically tensions around being asset-based, co-creative, place-based, and process-oriented [Whitney, Muse, Harrison, Edwards, & Clayton]
- Create and value "front doors" into SLCE-related careers in the form of engaged graduate education – specifically, doctoral programs that transcend single disciplines and that incorporate SLCE practice and scholarship [Kniffin, Shaffer, & Tolar]
- Reimagine assessment so that it walks the talk of the values of democratic engagement–
- specifically, explore and implement "values engaged assessment" as a counternormative way of framing assessment authentically [Bandy, Bartel, Clayton, Gale, Mack, Metzker, Nigro, Price, & Stanlick]
- Critically reflect on such concepts as charity and justice in an age of neoliberal forces and address the difficulty and opportunity to advance justice-focused work in that environment [Blosser]
- Integrate into SLCE the lens of critical university studies (CUS) as a way to examine the motivations of universities in engaging in SLCE, to account for the social and economic privilege that spurs such engagement, and to cultivate among all partners awareness of the need for moral vigilance regarding the academy's commitments to engagement [Fine]

In addition to these thought pieces, this special section includes an essay by Kniffin and Howard that continues the discussion opened in a 2015 piece on the possibility of developing a national strategic plan for SLCE. Their essay shares responses to that proposal gathered over the past year through a survey of national SLCE organizations and through several discussions we have held at conferences and other venues as well as ideas for what such a plan might contain and how it might best be developed.

In the following paragraphs we explore three themes that emerge in our reading of the six thought pieces: the importance of holding tension, the influence of neoliberalism, and the disruption and distribution of power.

Holding Tension

Awareness of a variety of tensions emerges in this set of thought pieces; in that spirit, much of the thinking we see in them is framed more in terms of both/and rather than either/or. There seems to be a necessary and prevalent feature of SLCE that calls for navigating difficult waters and tangled expectations, motivations, and goals. Many of the contributors speak to a heightened sense of the moral, social, and political compromises practitioner-scholars may feel compelled to make in their SLCE work as a function of pressures related to institutionalization. With these challenges along every dimension of engaged work realized and illuminated, the authors get to the difficult work of trying to address and design for these tensions in productive and just ways.

In the thought piece by Whitney and colleagues, titled "Learning from and with Community Organizations to Navigate the Tensions of Democratic Engagement," stories from two community-based organizations highlight tensions between our commitments to democratic engagement and the internal and external norms and pressures that make living out those commitments difficult. The authors share some of the ways these organizations attempt to navigate these tensions. They also remind us that community engagement is happening in many instances without the involvement of higher education institutions and suggest not only that there is much to be learned from such examples but also that the presence of academic institutions in SLCE often further complicates matters and exacerbate tensions, especially when members of those institutions bring technocratic tendencies into partnerships with community organizations.

In "Critical University Studies, Globalization, and the Future of Service Learning," Fine turns a similar critical lens more directly on the academy. He prompts us to acknowledge the privilege and the sometimes problematic motivations that may underlie institutions' presumed commitments to engagement and urges us to incorporate critical reflection that explicitly examines institutions' agendas and the otherwise unquestioned assumptions about the meanings of service and partnership embedded in SLCE as a result of corporatizing and globalizing forces.

In "Beyond Superheroes and Sidekicks: Empowerment, Efficacy, and Education in Community Partnerships," Stanlick and Sell provide another look at tensions between cultural norms and the requirements of democratic partnerships. Having partnered for several years, they call our attention to the ways in which a variety of common incentives – for example, the ways institutions and society often frame student leadership in hierarchical terms and the ways grant opportunities often encourage new programs and interventions over support processes already in place – can result in a "power dynamic that prizes [the] role of hero . . . [while] relegate[ing] community partners to the role of sidekick, or worse, recipient." While narratives praising individual leadership, social entrepreneurship, and helping have gained much prominence, the authors remind us that partnership work requires humility, mutual empowerment, and co-creation.

The thought piece by Bandy and colleagues on "Values-Engaged Assessment: Reimagining Assessment through the Lens of Democratic Engagement" works with a similar tension. The authors explore the experience of being "torn between the democratic values [they] want to enact and often technocratic, neoliberal norms [they] feel pressured to accommodate in assessment." They encourage us not to shy away from this tension or be shut down by it but rather to embrace it and leverage it to critique and change underlying paradigms. Rather than thinking of assessment as a necessary evil to appease external entities and ensure financial support, they invite us to view it instead as an opportunity to more authentically live out our values. Nodding to tensions within tensions, this thought piece acknowledges that the values of democratic engagement on which what they refer to as "values-engaged assessment" rests are themselves contested and sometimes in tension with one another, not only with the dominant narratives of our society.

Neoliberalism's Influence on Higher Education and SLCE

Related to the first theme, holding tension, is the influence of neoliberal forces on higher education. As noted above, Bandy and colleagues point to "neoliberal norms" and the pressure to accommodate those expectations in the assessment of SLCE and the tension that causes when institutionally powerful forces have to be appeased within the assessment process. On the hopeful side, however, they write, "It is our conviction that the assessment work of SLCE practitioner-scholars can embody and nurture a set of relationships, practices, and modes of inquiry that is potentially transformative of technocratic and neoliberal tendencies in our institutions." In support of such a paradigm shift, they model and invite reimagining the values that underlie assessment – values such as rigor – through the lens of democratic engagement. The extent to which the authors of these thought pieces help us recognize the complexity of our work as SLCE practitioner-scholars in an age of pervasive neoliberalism is both critical and encouraging.

In "Resisting the Siren Song: Charting a Course for Justice," Blosser identifies the many ways in which we agree to practices and policies we know are insufficient, as a result of the reality of the many neoliberal forces exerted on our work from within and beyond the academy. As he says towards the end of his thought piece: "The hard part about justice work . . . . is that to do it we may have to push back against the stakeholders we have spent years cultivating . . . [who] we still need . . . if we are to exist within the higher education system." Indeed, he suggests that "the future of the movement will depend on the ability of SLCE leaders to recognize and navigate neoliberal incentives, using them to further our objectives but resisting the urge to let the work be co-opted."

Fine is equally clear about the influence of neoliberalism. He notes that "to look back on the past twenty years and forward to the next is to acknowledge higher education's rapid corporatization and internationalization" and expresses concern that "as higher education, deeply influenced by neoliberalism's pressures to marketize, adopts the structure and value systems of big business, it risks placing private interest before public concern." Powerfully arguing that SLCE "does not emerge in a vacuum" and that "resources are not innocent," Fine urges us to "engage with SLCE's ethical complications rather than assuming, in advance, that all SLCE efforts are inherently good." The reality of higher education's being implicated in neoliberalism requires that we look critically at, for example, such seemingly innocuous language as "global citizenship" and interrogate the market-driven commitments and assumptions that may otherwise remain hidden.

Disruption and Distribution of Power

Another theme we see recurring throughout the thought pieces as well as in the essay by Kniffin and Howard involves the disruption and distribution of power. Questions about who holds power to make decisions, generate scholarship, affect change, and create partnerships cut across contexts – whether within the academy or community organizations, local or national – and across roles – from nonprofit leader to faculty member to graduate student, to name a few examples.

Fine calls us to make the academy and its priorities a focus of critical analysis. The field of Critical University Studies (CUS), which he suggests SLCE learn from and use as a lens through which to examine our institutions, helps us see more clearly the ways in which higher education institutions enter into relationships with communities not as benign agents of assistance but as players with their own agendas. CUS "strategically implicates both individuals and communities in the moral muddle that is SLCE's relation to the global, corporate university," thus challenging traditional power structures and examining the motives of powerful and perhaps power-seeking institutions through the lenses of justice and ethics. "Teaching our partnerships" – reflecting critically on them in terms of whose agendas they serve, for example – can empower students to ask disruptive questions of their institutions.

Another approach to such power disruption can be found in the thought piece by Stanlick and Sell. The authors warn us of narratives that are created about and sometimes within community partnerships that can be disempowering and can reinforce hierarchical power dynamics that undermine the flourishing of communities and of the SLCE movement. Mechanisms must be put in place to ensure that all partners have a voice and that their voices are heard – a proposition that requires vulnerability and humility and can be threatening to academic institutions in which certitude and expertise have long been lionized. They offer as examples of such shared power co-creation of programming and research, reciprocal engagement on boards and relevant committees, and cultivating humility through critical reflection on the part of all stakeholders.

The thought piece by Whitney and colleagues explicitly shifts power to community voices in that it consists of stories from community organizations and calls for the SLCE movement to seek out, listen to, and learn from examples of democratic engagement that have no necessary connection to higher education. Given their candid sharing of the challenges they face in trying to be asset-oriented, co-creative, place-based, and process-focused as well as the details of how they navigate and even leverage the difficulties, we can learn much from these and other community organizations about "persistence and resilience in the face of the very norms we seek to disrupt and replace with more hopeful and empowering alternatives." Indeed, the authors suggest that such structures for decision-making, program development, communication, and power sharing can serve as models for democratic partnerships that do and do not include academic institutions.

In "Winding Pathways to Engagement: Creating a Front Door," Kniffin, Shaffer, and Tolar bring our attention to the need to empower graduate students – a traditionally underrepresented and, in some cases, marginalized population – to thrive in their identities as community-engaged practitioner-scholars rather than to settle for limited opportunities patched together within traditionally siloed academic programs. Their call for the development of "front doors" – more explicit and formalized points of entry into SLCE-related careers – disrupts the power of the disciplines as the default home of scholars. In an academy without such "front doors," "students without a high level of persistence, the resources to devote significant time and attention to the search for a program, and/or strong connections in the field may never find appropriate pathways, with the consequence that the SLCE movement may lose their participation and leadership." Power translates into influence, and graduate students who have been invited into the SLCE movement and enabled to co-create knowledge with faculty and community colleagues and mentors as an integral part of their education will have the capacities to lead change as professionals and citizens, both within and beyond the academy. Power also translates into responsibility, and the authors therefore insist that "individuals already working in SLCE have a responsibility to make the invitation into this work compelling and clear – to institutionalize, formalize, and broaden pathways toward engagement."

Conclusion

The authors of this set of thought pieces remind us that, whether we like it or not, there will always be tensions as we wear our many hats, balance our many expectations, engage many voices, and envision the future together. There is no such thing as an ideologically pure or politically neutral SLCE endeavor. Further, there is often a tendency to respond to social and conceptual challenges by polarizing phenomena and dismissing one set of alternatives, and we are pleased to see the authors of these thought pieces not only avoid doing that but in many ways model an alternative in their acknowledgements of complexities and tension points.

In addition, much of where we stand now rests on where we have been and what developments have brought us to the current moment: the transformation of higher education, the rapid pace of technology, and the geopolitical environment that produces the "wicked problems" with which we must grapple. However appealing it may seem, we cannot simply toss away our academic constraints unless we wish to return to the days of operating entirely as a form of volunteerism. We often see a related phenomenon in the tendency to bypass important contributions from years past instead of building on or adapting them. While we may have radically underestimated how difficult it would be to do engaged work with integrity from inside the academy, we should also be careful not to underestimate the value of the projects, programs, and partnerships we have helped create.

What is clear from the work of our colleagues in these thought pieces – whether within the academy or deeply entrenched in community organizations – is that the winds of change are blowing. One need look no further than our current political climate – institutionally, locally, nationally, and internationally – to see that we are a world at a pivot point. We are demanding more just, equitable, and inclusive forms of governance and representation; and regardless of political party or ideological leaning, the sociopolitical environment is one of increasing calls for agency, empowerment, and deep collaboration. This is a moment of opportunity for SLCE to be a movement and a mechanism to help nurture the development of engaged citizens who can help usher in democratic change. Through engaged scholarship and high-impact practices as well as responsible anchor-institution initiatives that challenge and shape our colleagues, our communities, and ourselves, we can model the way for our institutional and governmental structures and demand the type of fair and just treatment that our world needs now more than ever. SLCE provides a space for interactions among those voices and stakeholders to share perspectives, goals, and visions for a better world. What can we do in partnership and how do we get to that better world? Please enjoy the thought pieces sourced for this special section of the MJCSL and think about the ways in which you yourself might help nudge the movement and the world forward with your work.

References

Bauer, T., Kniffin, L. E., & Priest, K. L. (2015). The future of service-learning and community engagement: Asset-based approaches and student learning in first-year courses. *Michigan Journal of Community Service Learning*, 2(1), 89–92.

Hicks, T., Seymour, L., & Puppo, A. (2015). Democratic relationships in service-learning: Moving beyond traditional faculty, student, and community partner roles. *Michigan Journal of Community Service Learning*, 2(1), 105–108.

Howard, J., & Stanlick, S. (2015). A call for a national strategic plan. *Michigan Journal of Community Service Learning*, 22(1), 128–132.

Pisco, K. (2015). Deepening service abroad: A call for reciprocal partnerships and ongoing support. *Michigan Journal of Community Service Learning*, 2(1), 93–96.

Saltmarsh, J., Janke, E. M., & Clayton, P. H. (2015). Transforming higher education through and for democratic civic engagement: A model for change. *Michigan Journal of Community Service Learning*, 2(1), 122–127.

Stanlick, S., & Clayton, P. H. (2015). Introduction: Special section on the SLCE Future Directions Project. *Michigan Journal of Community Service Learning*, 22(1), 78–82.

Zlotkowski, E. (1995). Does service-learning have a future? *Michigan Journal of Community Service Learning*, 2(1), 123–133.

Authors

SARAH E. STANLICK (ses409@lehigh.edu) is the founding director of Lehigh University's Center for Community Engagement and a professor of practice in Sociology and Anthropology. She previously taught at Centenary University and was a researcher at Harvard's Kennedy School, assisting the U.S. Ambassador to the United Nations, Samantha Power. She has published in journals such as *The Social Studies* and the *Journal of Global Citizenship and Equity Education*. Her current interests include inquiry-based teaching and learning, global citizenship, transformative learning, and cultivating learner agency.

EDWARD ZLOTKOWSKI (ezlotkowski@bentley.edu) is professor emeritus of Literature and Media Studies at Bentley University. He is the founding director of the Bentley Service-Learning Center and has been a senior associate at the American Association for Higher Education, Campus Compact, and the New England Resource Center for Higher Education. He devotes much of his time to literacy initiatives and is a community partner with Puppet Showplace Theater in Brookline, Massachusetts.

Beyond Superheroes and Sidekicks: Empowerment, Efficacy, and Education in Community Partnerships

Sarah Stanlick
Lehigh University

Marla Sell
Bethany Christian Services Refugee Resettlement

In his 1995 article "Does Service-Learning Have a Future?" Edward Zlotkowski calls us to heed the recommendations of Kendall (1990) in *Combining Service and Learning: A Resource Book for Community and Public Service*. To support the work of service-learning and community engagement (SLCE) being done in a high-quality, sustainable way, Kendall offers three Principles of Good Practice: (a) integrating service-learning programs into the central mission and goals of the schools and agencies where they are based; (b) establishing a balance of power between educational and community partners; and (c) wedding reflection to experience.

Today, we find ourselves still grappling with Kendall's recommendations, notably establishing a balance of power in partnerships. For example, we are just scratching the surface of understanding the difference between technocratic and democratic partnerships (Saltmarsh, Hartley, & Clayton, 2009), and funding mechanisms still largely define higher education institutions as the catalysts for community-engaged research and social impact interventions. This thought piece focuses on these partnerships challenges, calling the SLCE movement to live the principles of what the two of us think of as *transformative reciprocity* – a deep, thick collaboration that holds the possibility for all stakeholders to be transformed by the partnership (Jameson, Clayton, & Jaeger, 2010) – and thereby cultivate partnership power dynamics that are just, fair, and inclusive.

How do we establish a balance of power in genuine, life-giving ways – ways that support the self-actualization and growth of all stakeholders? How do we ensure that partnerships are flexible, inclusive, and encouraging of the growth of everyone involved? And how do we avoid the pitfalls of dysfunctional helping when power is unbalanced and community partners are diminished or paralyzed by the social and economic privilege of the academy? In what ways can we build a culture of humility and reciprocity to bring about a balanced power dynamic?

Through our experience building a strong, sustained community-university partnership, we have seen first-hand the importance of and obstacles to reciprocity in relationships. Albeit well-intentioned, the messages young people receive from many directions as first-year students (if not before) – that they should become innovative entrepreneurs – over-emphasize a particular conception of leadership: one that assumes technocratic power centered on innovative individuals at the top of social hierarchies. Similar expectations of faculty, staff, and community partners – for instance, as expressed in many funding opportunities – encourage us to *found* and *create* new programs, initiatives, and research projects rather than to enhance those that already exist or to support the work of colleagues. The role of follower or nurturer is implicitly or explicitly discouraged, and a power dynamic is thus created that elevates single individuals into the role of "hero." The value placed on that role is wrapped up in the ideal image of ourselves as helpers. This superhero mentality can lead to bold action, but it can also relegate others – often, community partners – to the role of sidekick, or worse, *recipient*.

Our bold call for the SLCE movement is to name and avoid the superhero mentality and to focus instead on *connecting* and *sustaining*, with the goal of collective empowerment at the forefront. According to Freire (1970), education and engagement are political acts that can bring about empowerment. We see reflected in both society at large and within partnerships unbalanced power, personified as a distinction between oppressors and the oppressed. The remedy to that power imbalance is education, through which the oppressed regain their sense of humanity and agency. Freire also affirms the need for oppressors – those who hold privilege and power in a way that marginalizes and disempowers others – to honestly acknowledge power imbalance and re-examine their role through "conscientization" (critical consciousness). By addressing those imbalances, we move toward partnerships in which all partners are truly empowered and thus in the best position to contribute to lasting change.

Let us recast our roles as multifaceted, empowered partners and leave behind the notion of community-campus partnerships as binaries that often devalue half of the partnership. Let us take care in our rush to provide assistance and right wrongs that we not assume a role that disempowers and reduces agency. As Illich (1968) reminds us, the road to hell is paved with good intentions: Good intentions without consideration of community voice can create damaging power structures. It is only through mutual empowerment and transformative reciprocity that we can work toward a future that is co-created and just.

About our Partnership

First, we must establish the context within which we operate and which gives rise to our thinking about partnerships. Marla has worked with refugee resettlement agencies in Allentown, Pennsylvania for over a decade and is currently the director of the Refugee Resettlement program for Bethany Christian Services, the sole refugee resettlement agency in the Lehigh Valley. Sarah is a faculty member and director of the Center for Community Engagement at Lehigh University, located in neighboring Bethlehem, Pennsylvania. We have worked together over the last six years to provide meaningful, reciprocal SLCE opportunities to Lehigh students, our new neighbors, the resettlement agency, and ourselves. While our roles have shifted and agencies have come and gone over the years, the constant has been our partnership: weathering the changes through our commitment to strong communication and empowerment of all stakeholders.

Through our partnership, we have catalyzed deep learning, research, and engagement from first-year projects to senior capstones. An ongoing SLCE practicum involves third-year students in facilitating cultural orientation classes to support refugees' transition to the United States. Each semester we formally evaluate the SLCE activities and impacts, address concerns, and make changes to maintain flexibility and responsiveness to new opportunities. Our partnership process includes frequent meetings to check in and share concerns, lessons learned, new information, and opportunities. Programming is co-planned and supported through grants identified and pursued together. Further, Sarah participates in reviews by the state and the State Department to represent the partnership and connect the work that is being done under the auspices of the partnership as part of a larger effort to provide holistic services within a wide network of support systems (e.g. counseling programs, English as a second language training). These reviews are necessary for continued federal and state support of the refugee resettlement agency and demonstrate the importance and functioning of our partnership to meet the state's priority for high-quality refugee resettlement and support.

This partnership has also helped our community maintain focus on the most important issues facing refugees resettling in the Lehigh Valley. Attention to the influx of Syrian refugees in 2015 and 2016 to the area has piqued new interest – positive and negative – within the academy on a national level. Evidence of this is found in a plethora of new classes, conference presentations, research projects, and initiatives such as Every Campus a Refuge, which houses refugee families on campuses. It has illuminated a wide variety of kind-hearted, motivated individuals who seek to help as well as a lack of knowledge about the refugees who have been coming to the Lehigh Valley and the process of resettlement. Refugees who come to the Lehigh Valley, despite the pervasive thought that they are only Syrian, also come from the Karen, Chin, and Kachin minority groups of Burma, Democratic Republic of Congo, Sudan, Iraq, and Eritrea, for example. The process by which they come to the United States is rigorous, with pre-arrival checks from a variety of agencies, which can take years. Finally, the (mis)understanding of refugees as inherently "in need" and "thankful for any support they get" is a stereotype. Most had rich lives in their home countries and are highly educated professionals. They are individuals who have agency, confidence, and a determined spirit. The partnership between the resettlement agency and the university has been intentionally asset-based to nurture both empowerment and transformation for our stakeholders and new neighbors as they transition to life in our community.

With this long-standing relationship in mind, we realize there are lessons learned worth sharing both as evidence of the value of transformationally reciprocal partnerships and as an example of the partnership's operational and philosophical mechanics for those interested in creating or maintaining something similar. We have three high priority goals for the future of the SLCE movement in mind: the need to cultivate humility and reciprocity, avoiding the narrative of heroes and protectors, and the difficult task of illuminating when service can be a disservice. At the center of these goals is the balance of power to ensure that transformational reciprocity can take place when power and agency are held in different measure by multiple stakeholders.

Mechanisms for Empowerment: Valuing Humility and Reciprocity

Valuing humility in our students and ourselves needs to be a top priority as we navigate the waters of reciprocal, meaningful community engagement. Humility – an intentional acknowledgement of one's modest, humble role in the larger world – serves as the essential currency of respectful, meaningful partnerships as it inherently places the emphasis on the greater good rather than on personal ego. Cultivating humility can lead to better outcomes for community organizations and students alike, while preparing students to be humble, effective practitioners (Lund & Lee, 2015). Humility is also a necessary element of adopting a more democratic form of SLCE and thereby honoring power sharing, asset recognition, and a shared sense of responsibility to one another for successful and ethical community partnerships.

Hand-in-hand with humility is reciprocity, a moral norm first introduced in academic literature by Gouldner (1960) when he described it as a pattern of mutual benefit and gratification between parties. In the context of SLCE, the term reciprocity holds and communicates an essential value of our work. Sigmon (1979) focused the concept of reciprocity on reciprocal learning, affirming that meaningful service-learning is realized when stakeholders – community partner and educational institution alike – are transformed by the experience. Jameson, Clayton, and Jaeger (2010) make the distinction between thin (mutual and transactional) and thick (transformational and co-creative) reciprocity – noting that they can coexist but that only the latter facilitates an empowering level of "co-ness." The two of us stress the need for such *transformational reciprocity* in order to deepen relationships and ensure that all who work in partnership are supported as agents of change and collective empowerment within and beyond their role in SLCE.

So, how do we cultivate transformational reciprocity? Critical reflection, disorientation, and critical thinking are essential to the concept of praxis, which provides learners – students, educators, and community partners alike – with a continuous cycle of learning and growth. As a constant cycle of re-evaluation of our values, mistakes, and triumphs, praxis can cultivate a sense of a larger purpose in the world and responsibility to one another. This is particularly valuable when working with the knotty and multi-faceted issues of equity and inclusion for refugees. For instance, students who may be grappling with long-held political beliefs that have heretofore been unchallenged meet refugee families face-to-face and, because of this experiential connection, may reconsider their attitudes, perspectives, and beliefs. They may then receive information about differences in refugee resettlement processes between the U.S. and Europe and wrestle with national security perceptions and realities that the two different contexts provide. Such challenges to their established understandings invite ongoing making and remaking of their place in the world and their beliefs.

In addition, appreciating our differences and holding in tension different beliefs in order to move toward a shared goal strengthens attitudes and behaviors of humility and reciprocity. The refugee resettlement agency has volunteers and supporters from many different religious and political traditions. Evangelical Christians, observant Muslims, and liberal atheists may work side-by-side, called to resettlement work for very different reasons and intersecting in some ways while diverging in others. Open lines of communication and shared decision-making are key to ensuring each partner has an equitable investment in the partnership. Further, the praxis mentality the two of us cultivate within and through our partnership ensures that each stakeholder feels valued and that there are mechanisms to continuously solicit input and feedback to sustain a healthy, engaged, and peaceful community.

Avoiding the Narrative of Superheroes and Sidekicks: Valuing Empowerment and Co-Creation

Another pitfall SLCE scholar-practitioners must take care to avoid is dysfunctional rescuing: compensating for past power differentials by well-intentioned, but disempowering "helping." For instance, a student team could assume refugees coming to the United States would be in need of English as a Second Language (ESL) training. Without consulting those who are already providing language services, the students contact the resettlement agency directly with a curriculum of their own creation and a request for space to hold classes. Such planning and design that happens outside of the partnership relegates the community partner to a powerless or supporting position. It also ignores both the professional ESL teachers who offer such classes already and the work of the agency to mobilize resources, suggesting – implicitly or explicitly – that the agency is not doing enough to support the refugees. In the face of pushback from the agency on actual needs or opportunities, the students and faculty may insist that they worked hard on the curriculum and that the resources of their institution are much greater, reaffirming the presumed power differential. Assumptions regarding what refugees need and what the organization needs, even after hearing what they have voiced as their own priorities, can arise and persist when trust has not been built and when communication is not in place.

Much of this desire to swoop in and "save" is

motivated by a place in the heart that wants to be *helpful*. Bauer, Kniffin, and Priest (2015) address a similar concern in first-year service-learning, as they designed programming to be more asset-based in order to support their students in learning to appreciate community voice, assets, and expertise. While it is a noble desire to want to "help," we must examine our own motivations when entering into a partnership with the community, especially one in which the power dynamic has traditionally been skewed to one side.

Empowerment of all stakeholders – in that they are able to exercise agency, commitment, and support – should be the goal per Freire's (1970) vision of a just and flourishing society. Anything short of that allows for the creation of systems that exploit and perpetuate inequality. Palmer (2011) calls our attention to the fact that "insight and energy give rise to new life as we speak out and act out our own version of truth, while checking and correcting it against the truths of others" (p. 47). If we do not hold ourselves to check ourselves and reflect truth in our partnerships, we miss the accidental injustices we might continue to create. And, in so doing, we reinforce systems that disempower partners and discourage co-creation.

Further, there is sometimes a disconnect between the story we want to hear and the story that holds a more complete view of the situation. For example, a campus communications office could want to run an inspirational story on an exceptional faculty member making change in a community through grant-supported research, when the reality is more complex and multi-layered than that. This type of storytelling happens for a number of reasons – for instance, expectations of the institution or funding agency, frustration with the slow pace of change or resource allocation – yet it is important to address and avoid the danger of perpetuating myths that disempower. Ultimately, stories that put one stakeholder in the focus as a sort of hero or savior can create long-term damage by setting up a power dynamic that is dysfunctional.

When is Service a Disservice?

Community engagement professionals and practitioner-scholars steeped in SLCE often end up taking on the role of the buzzkill. Young, enthusiastic, and optimistic faces come to us brimming with hope for the future and with big ideas for initiatives they wish to undertake. In their chapter "Mainstream or Margins?" Stanton, Giles, and Cruz (1999) explore the dilemmas and tradeoffs of making change from inside the system using institutional mechanisms or from outside the walls throwing rocks and shaking up norms. We argue that there is a necessary tension between those two extremes where real change occurs, and it is within that tension that we as stakeholders, partners, and community members often undergo the most transformation.

Understanding the continuum of service – the variety of ways in which individuals can engage with communities, from philanthropy to community-engaged research – and the ways in which we can and should engage – or not – based on community voice is essential. The pragmatist – in our experience, the one who manages risk, holds partners to shared values, and advises contemplation – is not always an easy role to play and can often bring scorn from those who wish to jump to *doing* in a situation that might need *considering*. We often hear questions that run the gamut from deep, reflective inquiry to well-intentioned but ill-considered action: *If there is a need, why can't I just set up a GoFundMe account? I have a bunch of clothes I collected; why can't I just drop them off? How do I found a nonprofit?* It is our duty as responsible stakeholders, facilitators, teachers, and partners to trouble the motivations, assess the situation, and keep an open dialogue to ensure that our work is living the values to which we subscribe.

Conclusion

In the HBO television comedy *Silicon Valley*, Gavin Belson, a character embodying the Steve Jobs-esque visionary cliche, addresses his staff after his company suffers a particularly frustrating loss to a smaller upstart company. Defeated, he realizes that his company will not be the one responsible for propelling forward a new type of technology that could be revolutionary. In frustration he yells, "I don't know about you people, but I don't want to live in a world where someone else makes the world a better place better than we do!"

Through satire we hold up a mirror to ourselves. This may seem like a silly anecdote, but it perfectly illustrates an attitude we often see in newcomers to resettlement work. Most have an abundance of goodwill and enthusiasm in their hearts. Many want to be *originators* and *creators* when it is *connectors* and *sustainers* that are actually needed. If we are truly invested in the empowerment of all stakeholders – community, in its most inclusive sense – we must face the hard truth that we could come to a point where our helpfulness, our love, and our intense desire for change are not helpful or valid – indeed, we may already be there. Truly engaging in the community in a way that is in the mold of Freire's vision of education and partnership is at its core about the development of capacity and agency as the forces driving social and civic change. Community partners, researchers, students, and educators should, through these endeavors, feel agency as we move to a deeper level of co-ness. In that model, where value is placed on empowerment, we have to accept that our roles might morph, with the role of superhero and sidekick becoming obsolete and a new, equitable partnership full of opportunity emerging strongly.

References

Bauer, T., Kniffin, L. E., & Priest, K. L. (2015). The future of service-learning and community engagement: Asset-based approaches and student learning in first-year courses. *Michigan Journal of Community Service Learning, 22*(1), 89–93.

Freire, P. (1970). *Pedagogy of the oppressed.* New York: Continuum.

Gouldner, A. W. (1960). The norm of reciprocity: A preliminary statement. *American Sociological Review, 25,* 161–178. https://doi.org/10.2307/2092623

Illich, I. (1968/1990). To hell with good intentions. In Jane C. Kendall & Associates (Eds.), *Combining service and learning, Volume 1: A resource book for community and public service* (pp. 314–320). Raleigh, NC: National Society for Internships and Experiential Education.

Jameson, J. K., Clayton, P. H., & Jaeger, A. (2010). Community engaged scholarship as mutually transformative partnerships. In L. Harter, J. Hamel-Lambert, & J. Millesen (Eds.), *Participatory partnerships for social action and research* (pp. 259–277). Dubuque, IA: Kendall Hunt.

Lund, D. E., & Lee, L. (2015). Fostering cultural humility among pre-service teachers: Connecting with children and youth of immigrant families through service-learning. *Canadian Journal of Education, 38*(2), 1–30. https://doi.org/10.2307/canajeducrevucan.38.2.10

Palmer, P. J. (2011). *Healing the heart of democracy: The courage to create a politics worthy of the human spirit.* San Francisco: John Wiley & Sons.

Saltmarsh, J., Hartley, M., & Clayton, P. H. (2009). *Democratic engagement white paper.* Boston: New England Resource Center for Higher Education.

Sigmon, R. L. (1979). Service-learning: Three principles. *Synergist, 8,* 9–11.

Stanton, T. K., Giles, D. E., Jr., & Cruz, N. I. (1999). *Service-learning: A movement's pioneers reflect on its origins, practice, and future. Jossey-Bass Higher and Adult Education Series.* San Francisco: Jossey-Bass.

Zlotkowski, E. (1995). Does service-learning have a future? *Michigan Journal of Community Service Learning, 2*(1), 123–133.

Authors

SARAH E. STANLICK (ses409@lehigh.edu) is the founding director of Lehigh University's Center for Community Engagement and a professor of practice in Sociology and Anthropology. She previously taught at Centenary University and was a researcher at Harvard's Kennedy School, assisting the U.S. Ambassador to the United Nations, Samantha Power. She has published in journals such as *The Social Studies* and the *Journal of Global Citizenship and Equity Education.* Her current interests include inquiry-based teaching and learning, global citizenship, transformative learning, and cultivating learner agency.

MARLA J. SELL (msell@bethany.org) is the refugee site director for Bethany Christian Services. She has worked for over a decade in social services for refugees, previously supporting and leading efforts for Lutheran Child and Family Services and Catholic Charities. Sell is responsible for the vision and creation of the Refugee Community Center that recently opened in Allentown, PA, to provide services such as ESL classes and dinner gatherings to bring neighbors together over meals. Her work has been featured in a number of media outlets including *WFMZ-TV, The Morning Call,* and *The Express-Times.*

Learning From and With Community Organizations to Navigate the Tensions of Democratic Engagement

Brandon Whitney
ioby

Barbara Harrison

Patti H. Clayton
PHC Ventures, IUPUI, & University of North Carolina at Greensboro

Stacey Muse
University of Nevada, Reno

Kathleen E. Edwards
University of North Carolina at Greensboro & Interactive Resource Center

In his 2015 framing essay for the Service-Learning & Community Engagement Future Directions Project (SLCE-FDP), Edward Zlotkowski challenges the movement to think carefully about "where we locate the center of our efforts" (p. 84) and reconsiders whether the focus on academic legitimacy and institutional transformation he called for in his 1995 essay "Does Service-Learning Have a Future?" ought still to be the priority 20 years later. He also commends several of the 2015 SLCE-FDP thought pieces for calling attention to "voices often unrepresented or underrepresented" (p. 84). In this essay, we try to further deepen the role of community members and organizations in the movement's efforts to understand and address the opportunities and challenges of the present and future. Specifically, we call on our campus-based colleagues to seek out and learn from examples of community organizations that, in their day-to-day work, enact the principles of democratic engagement; and we call on our community-based colleagues to share and critique their own efforts. We envision the future of SLCE as bringing to life the commitments of democratic engagement and thereby nurturing shared responsibility for and shared power in nudging the world toward peace and justice. And we believe the SLCE movement as a whole can learn much from what may prove to be more democratic and cutting edge approaches in the broader community than are often found in the academy.

We have first-hand experience as leaders, staff, partners, and volunteers with community organizations that work diligently to achieve democratic ends through democratic means in social and cultural contexts that make doing so difficult. We find in candid examination of two of our organizations' efforts some illumination of the tensions associated with democratic engagement: asset-oriented norms and co-creation (as they occur within the Interactive Resource Center, described below by Kathleen) and place-based partnerships and a process orientation toward impact (as they occur within ioby, described below by Brandon). We offer these examples not as success stories full of lessons learned and words of wisdom but rather as demonstrations of both challenges and possibilities – attempting in this way to shine light on the complexities of democratic engagement as experienced in communities.

Interactive Resource Center

The Interactive Resource Center (IRC, http://gsodaycenter.org/) in Greensboro, North Carolina, is a daytime center for people experiencing homelessness. The IRC's mission is to "assist people who are homeless, recently homeless, or facing homelessness [in reconnecting] with their own lives and with the community at large." We offer practical services: laundry, showers, access to computers and Internet, case management, and referrals. We also partner with other nonprofits and grassroots organizations, sharing our space as an incubator for multiple services and activities (e.g., medical services, art therapy, gardening, transportation via refurbished bicycles, GED courses, and weekly community vegetarian dinners). The following analysis of the IRC's efforts to enact an asset-based orientation and co-creation is based on a snapshot of the organization from 2010–2014, a period that most honestly reflects the aspirations relevant to this thought piece.

At its inception, the people designing the IRC – many of whom were experiencing homelessness at the time – intentionally adopted an *asset orientation*: peer-based, strengths-focused, and collaborative. As we say every day in our morning meeting: "This is the Interactive Resource Center. Your best resource is each other." Our intention is for everyone affiliated with the organization to experience it as their community. The term "guest" displaces the term "client" – the common social service agency name for a person accessing services – because we believe it better establishes a respectful space and affirms non-hierarchical, multi-directional relationships. Guests' artwork hangs on the walls. Guests sweep the floors, take out the trash, and donate money for coffee. Former guests volunteer on weekends. Staff sit in the dayroom to catch up with people they have not seen in awhile. When everyone is viewed as having valuable knowledge and skills to contribute to the organization and to each other, artificial lines that can otherwise divide people begin to blur and the IRC transforms from an organization to a community.

Even with all of these investments in being asset-based, however, there are still challenges associated with the status quo understanding of homelessness (i.e., as the result of individuals' poor decisions). This is reflected in the ways some volunteers view guests from a deficit perspective: assuming individuals who frequent the IRC do not possess the skills, knowledge, or attitudes to be successful and must be "helped" by those who do have such attributes. Some staff push strongly for "accountability" among the guests, proposing, for example, that people should not be allowed to simply sit in the dayroom but rather should be expected to participate in job skills or computer training courses. Even guests sometimes try to make sure others (staff, volunteers, local community members) understand that they themselves are not "that type of homeless person" – meaning one who doesn't work hard, may use drugs or alcohol, may have an unmanaged mental illness, or doesn't really want to change or be a "contributing member of society." These attitudes clash with our commitment to being asset-based, creating disagreements among guests, staff, and volunteers. At the same time, these moments of friction give us opportunities to disrupt status quo assumptions, to educate ourselves and others, and to highlight the gifts that all IRC guests, staff, and volunteers bring to our community.

The IRC's commitment to *co-creation* is enacted in various ways: working toward transparency within organizational practices (e.g., guests participate in the hiring process for all new staff), creating space for discussion and shared decision-making amongst all IRC community members (e.g., changes in policies and practices are always brought to the morning meeting for discussion), and valuing and seeking out the knowledge of individuals based on their lived experiences (e.g., the floor plan for our new building was created with significant input by people experiencing homelessness because they knew best what to incorporate into the design of the building). As a result of these practices, which have been unfamiliar and even uncomfortable at times, there exists a "co-" ethos within the IRC. For people who have been part of the IRC for a while, "co-ness" is part of the culture: guests and volunteers know – and expect – they will be a part of decision-making and project development. Certain projects (e.g., *storyscapes*) and programs (e.g., the garden) were co-constructed by guests and volunteers, not initiated by staff, and a collaborative ethos persists through changes in their structure and membership.

There are numerous challenges to enacting co-creation, layered with issues of power, expectations, time, growth, and transiency of guests and volunteers. A stark shift in "co-" practices occurred when the IRC moved to its current location, nearer to downtown. Attendance exploded, from 75 guests on a busy day to 150 guests on a slow day. Several barriers to co-ness developed: the staff – which did not increase – quickly became overworked, more crisis situations emerged (e.g., need for emergency housing), and guests became more transient, sometimes present daily and at other times only once every six months. Since crisis situations rarely allow time for shared decision-making, staff found themselves making decisions independent of guest or volunteer input. This shift in operations had numerous effects: guests and volunteers feeling less engaged with what we thought of as *our* organization – including perceived lack of transparency and thus less trust in decisions – and staff feeling frustrated because of the increased number and pace of decisions to be made without time to discuss ideas with others. Very quickly there was a breakdown in "co-" practices, which led to disengagement and feelings of powerlessness. We haven't resolved all of these issues, but special interest groups have emerged within which co-creation is easier to implement: a creative writing group, the Artifacts Art Cooperative, the *Greensboro Voice* quarterly newspaper, and the Tiny Houses initiative (see Hicks, Seymour, & Puppo, 2015 for a discussion of co-relationships in Tiny Houses Greensboro). In these smaller groups, people share leadership roles and decision-making, and projects are redefined with the ebb and flow of people.

These tensions around being asset-based and co-creative always exist at the IRC, even as we gain more understanding of each other, in part because our community is always in transition. There are never two days alike at the IRC, including who is there volunteering or seeking services, which means we need to revisit these fundamental ideas regularly in morning meetings, staff meetings, and volunteer orientations. Trying to live them out means committing to a process that never ends: we are asset-oriented and co-creative and can always also be more deeply both of these.

ioby

ioby (www.ioby.org) is an online crowd-resourcing platform headquartered in Brooklyn, NY, and powered by a national network of leaders, donors, and volunteers who support citizen-led, neighbor-funded initiatives in urban areas around the United States. ioby's mission is to strengthen neighborhoods by supporting local leaders who want to make positive change through engaging their neighbors, one block at a time; We believe such individuals are among the most important assets in every community. The organization's name is derived from "in our backyards," the positive opposite of the disparaging acronym NIMBY ("not in my backyard"). Projects range from community gardens and neighborhood composting systems, to bike lanes and crosswalks, to tool-sharing libraries and small-scale solar power systems – with an average budget of about $4000 and an average donation of about $75. As of 2016, ioby has supported the leaders behind more than 675 projects who have raised almost $2.5 million through crowd-resourcing. Crowd-resourcing combines the concepts of crowd-funding (the ability to pool small donations made online to a specific cause or project) and resource organizing (a core tenet of community organizing that considers activists and advocates the best supporters to ensure success of a cause or project). It gives anyone and everyone the ability to organize all kinds of capital – cash, social capital, in kind donations, volunteer time, advocacy – from within the community to serve the community. Two interrelated dimensions of ioby's work – our place-based focus on projects in communities across the country and our commitment to impact that values process as much as product – are simultaneously strengths and sources of tension.

Place is central to ioby's work. It grounds the kinds of projects we support and gives rise to the community energy behind them. Every one of our projects is based in a neighborhood somewhere: that says it all. One of ioby's five core principles is that "local is best" – that "neighbors know best what their neighborhoods need . . . are best equipped to innovate, organize, and make positive change . . . are the best long-term stewards of solutions." Another is that "small is big" – that "small, neighborhood-scale actions have far-reaching and long-lasting impact on places and on people's lives . . . [and] taken together . . . make up a powerful movement of neighbor-led positive change that inspires hope and benefits us all." The grounding in place embodied by these principles reminds us that every interaction with citizen-leaders and their neighbors is significant. Place also provides a common language through which local leaders relate to one another across diverse project types, unique geographies, and particular challenges. And it has guided our growth into a national organization that supports citizen-led change in over 150 cities across the U.S. We have a physical presence in an ever-increasing number of cities – New York City, Memphis, Cleveland, Detroit, and Pittsburgh – where we hire local staff to work on the ground rather than remotely from our headquarters. This model helps build place-based partnerships and trust.

The tension here involves being place-based . . . everywhere. ioby is at once distributed and centralized, locally invested and outsider. Except in the aforementioned cities where we partner with respected local organizations and hire staff with deep community experience, we operate primarily out of the single city where we first developed our place-based model: New York City. We have deliberately expanded our connections with local leaders well beyond that community, however, because we believe that a national network of such leaders (with their donors and volunteers), each grounded in local work, can leverage collective resources, successes, challenges, diverse expertise, and varied passions and thus have a unique and powerful voice on the national stage. But scaling our organization to serve any leader, in any neighborhood, anywhere in the country means we cannot be present *ourselves* on the ground alongside them as that would take hundreds more staff than we will likely ever have. Further, because we are a national organization, we can easily come across as an outsider – perhaps worse, one from New York City – to potential local partners. Our team must confront our own outsider status when working with leaders by phone and email from our Brooklyn office and during visits to neighborhood project sites. We think about our work not in the dichotomous terms of local and national, but rather as a system that links the two – indeed, sees them as powerfully interdependent – through a network of relationships. However, this conceptual frame is constantly put to a practical test during conversations we have with individual leaders about local history, challenges, and opportunities – around which, no matter how well intentioned, our national office staff simply will never be able to interact with our leaders as a local resident might.

As with most nonprofits, ioby exists to make an *impact* – in our case, on the leaders we serve and their communities. We think about change agency in a way that is at once very concrete (the projects) and very diffuse (the networks), challenging the usual notions of innovation and change coming only from centralized "top-down" structures and focusing instead on distributed, grassroots, "bottom-up" approaches. Central to our approach are two convictions about change: (a) we believe local leaders bringing local ideas to life via relationships within and investment from the community is an effective way to support communities in reimagining what is possible, and (b) we believe building capacities of local leaders and organizations to marshal resources is effective as both short-term strategy and long-term investment. We use a coaching approach to training in crowd-resourcing as a method of fundraising, drawing from leading grassroots fundraising collaboratives and integrating the successful practices and techniques of the leaders in our network. We learn from them and assemble and share with others their knowledge on a wide variety of technical, tactical, and subject matter-specific issues – essentially, crowdsourcing the expertise we share. In some ways, then, the product of our work – in the form of successfully executed community projects, which we value highly – is less central to our conceptualization of the change we pursue than is the process by which it happens. Our way of thinking about impact is as much process- as product-oriented. For us, impact is about providing timely, right-sized capacity building around resource generation and organizing to leaders who are poised to catalyze change in their communities.

A key challenge in this take on impact is that few funders and investors support it (whether foundations, individuals, or agencies). For many, our focus on process is too slow, too uncertain, too diffuse, or too hard to measure. These are fair critiques on some level that represent very real challenges as we build our own capacity to pursue our mission in a world focused on quick wins, return on investment, and other product-oriented metrics. The onus is on us not only to meet these criticisms with thoughtful responses, but also to mount our own efforts to "prove" that our process-oriented approach provides effective and efficient solutions in the short term. This often puts us in the position of focusing simultaneously on the short game and the long game, and it is difficult not to allow one to overwhelm the other. The full impact of building social capital and increasing neighborhood involvement in civic work is notoriously difficult to measure and often takes time to manifest. So we often succumb to citing impacts such as number of trees planted, miles of bike lanes added, or number of children engaged in a project as short-term, product-based measures. In doing so, we run the risk of conflating – indeed, displacing – process-oriented values and impacts with product-oriented values and impacts, which can undermine the fundamental conversations and models of change we are trying to catalyze.

We do not expect these tensions around being place-based and process-oriented in our conception of impact to be resolved, but we do find that a systems perspective helps us understand them and hold them more creatively than we otherwise might. As we grow a national network of local citizen-leaders, we try to think of the unique characteristics that comprise their local contexts as a series of overlapping systems that contribute to the adaptability and resilience of the network overall and the social fabric of the U.S. more generally. These multiple systems interact to generate continuously emerging opportunities for connection, learning, and new understandings across the various local contexts. Similarly, we try to maintain a systems orientation to impact: not viewing it as a choice between process and product or short-term and long-term but considering all of these important dimensions simultaneously and in light of each other and trying to integrate them to generate synergistic alternatives.

More Community Stories Please

As we have surfaced in these two stories – likely no surprise to readers – democratic engagement is hard. Really hard. Individuals and organizations often face very real challenges in their efforts to enact democratic engagement, as illustrated here with four leading tensions: (a) adopting an asset-based orientation in a culture that tends to focus on needs and problems, (b) positioning everyone involved as co-creators despite deeply enshrined hierarchy, (c) engaging with the contexts of local places in work that is also of necessity and by design caught up in large scale (e.g., national) structures, and (d) valuing the dynamics of empowering processes in the face of pressures to focus almost exclusively on products. For the five of us as practitioner-scholars, it is just such tensions – more than contested purposes – that make SLCE so difficult to undertake effectively and with integrity, both on campuses and in communities.

A key takeaway here is that higher education is not and need not always be involved in, much less at the forefront of, community engagement work. Indeed, partnership with higher education institutions often exacerbates some of the tensions we have discussed here, especially when faculty, staff, and students bring a sense of themselves as experts relative to community members. As one example of the added challenge, ioby finds the tensions around conceptualizing impact in terms of process further intensified insofar as partnerships that involve the academy often require a distinct focus on learning outcomes and products. As one example of a response to the tensions of co-creation, a volunteer coordinator at the IRC engages with them directly by sharing with her academic partners a chapter written by community partner Amy Mondloch (2009) that speaks to the challenges and possibilities of positioning everyone involved in SLCE as "learners, teachers, and leaders" (p. 146).

All participants in SLCE – perhaps especially our colleagues in the academy – need to take seriously the experience of community members and organizations who have learned to navigate the tensions of democratic engagement. Ask them if you can visit and watch their day-to-day operations. Incorporate these two and other such stories into faculty and staff development activities. Insist that SLCE events on campus include community partners not merely as guests but as educators; and explicitly position yourself, whether student, faculty, or staff, as a learner in that setting. Invite community members not only to celebrate accomplishments but also to bring a critical perspective to their own and your work. Create ways to think and plan and write together; and please share what you learn with the rest of us!

Why do we believe so strongly that the SLCE movement must learn from the democratic engagement work of community members and organizations? When we look at examples of SLCE projects and partnerships, we see ourselves and others trying to live out deeply held commitments to reciprocity, power sharing, and sustainable and systemic change in contrary contexts of individualism, competition, and short-term reactivity. More generally, we see ourselves and others trying to be co-educators, co-learners, and co-generators of knowledge and practice while encountering deeply enshrined resistance in our society, our organizations, and ourselves. The result is often a discouraging disconnect between what we want to be and do and what we actually are and do – across all partner categories, roles, and identities in SLCE. We all can find encouragement and guidance in self-critical stories of on-the-ground efforts, happening day to day in communities, of persistence and resilience in the face of the very norms SLCE seeks to disrupt and replace with more hopeful and empowering alternatives. We believe the two examples shared here merely scratch the surface of an incredibly rich tapestry of democratic engagement work being done in civil society by non-higher education institutions. We invite our SLCE colleagues, on campuses and especially in communities, to inquire into and share your own such stories.

References

Hicks, T., Seymour, L., & Puppo, A. (2015). Democratic relationships in service-learning: Moving beyond traditional faculty, student, and community partner roles. *Michigan Journal of Community Service Learning, 22*(1), 105–108.

Interactive Resource Center. (n.d.). Retrieved from www.gsodaycenter.org

ioby. (n.d.). Retrieved from www.ioby.org

Mondloch, A. (2009). One director's voice. In R. Stoecker & E. Tryon (Eds.), *The unheard voices: Community organizations and service learning* (pp. 136–146). Philadelphia: Temple University Press.

Zlotkowski, E. (2015). Twenty years and counting: A framing essay. *Michigan Journal of Community Service Learning, 22*(1), 82–85.

Authors

BRANDON WHITNEY (brandon@ioby.org) lives in Brooklyn, New York, and is cofounder & COO of ioby.org, a crowd-resourcing platform powered by a national network of leaders, donors, and volunteers that support citizen-led, neighbor-funded initiatives in urban areas. He is an accidental techie interested in how blending technology and civic life can help us build healthier neighborhoods, more just communities, and more sustainable cities. An environmental anthropologist by training, Brandon is also an amateur chef, fair-weather runner, and urban gardener.

STACEY MUSE (staceymuse@gmail.com) is a doctoral candidate in the Higher Education program at the University of Denver. Having worked in the nonprofit sector for over a decade and holding an MA in nonprofit management, she is interested in the community voice/perspective and outcomes of community-university partnerships. She currently leads the Office of Service-Learning and Civic Engagement at the University of Nevada, Reno. When she's not working on her dissertation, Stacey enjoys sharing her love of music and "dancing" with her 1-year old daughter, laughing with her husband, and cuddling with her dog.

BARBARA HARRISON (barbara.a.harrison@gmail.com) is a community-based practitioner-scholar currently engaged in projects with NGOs responding to the refugee crisis in Greece. She was previously a research associate with the Community Engaged Scholarship Institute/Research Shop at the University of Guelph and a campus leader in an institution-wide service-learning initiative at Brock University, both in Ontario, Canada. Barbara is an avid vegetable gardener who has a great love of dogs and their shenanigans.

KATHLEEN E. EDWARDS (kathleen.e.edwards@gmail.com) volunteered at the Interactive Resource Center starting in 2010 and then accepted a full-time program director position from 2014–2016. Now she is focused on writing her dissertation, which challenges U.S.-based status quo frameworks for addressing homelessness. Additionally, she works part-time in the Institute for Community and Economic Engagement at the University of North Carolina at Greensboro where her multiple years of experience with both community and campus partner roles serve her well in supporting SLCE partnerships. Kathleen keeps a growing list of what she will do with her free time once she has finished her dissertation.

PATTI H. CLAYTON (patti.clayton@curricularengagement.com) is an independent consultant and SLCE practitioner-scholar (PHC Ventures) as well as a senior scholar with IUPUI and UNCG. Increasingly seeing democratic community engagement as co-inquiry among all partners, her current interests include critical reflection for civic learning; the integration of SLCE and relationships within the more-than-human world; and the power of such "little words" as *in*, *for*, *with*, and *of* to shape identities and ways of being with one another in SLCE. Not known for brevity, Patti is enjoying learning to co-author short essays and even blog posts with friends and colleagues old and new.

Winding Pathways to Engagement: Creating a Front Door

Lori E. Kniffin
University of North Carolina at Greensboro

Timothy J. Shaffer and Mary H. Tolar
Kansas State University

Service-learning and community engagement (SLCE) practitioner-scholars – meaning all who do the work of SLCE with a commitment to integrating practice and study – find avenues to this work in a variety of ways. Many of the thought leaders in this movement started as traditional scholars in their disciplines and, only in their later careers, focused on creating and enhancing SLCE on their own campuses and across the academy. Others first learned about SLCE as an epistemological framework and a pedagogy in graduate programs such as Curriculum and Instruction or Higher Education Leadership. Others came across it during their academic careers somewhat randomly in conversations with colleagues, at conferences, or in the literature. And still others began their journey to SLCE by working in the public sector (as did co-author Mary Tolar) with community organizations, as community organizers, or as social justice advocates. Members of a younger generation of practitioner-scholars have now experienced SLCE in undergraduate or graduate education and seek ways to integrate it into their academic or professional lives from the very beginning.

The edited volume *Publicly Engaged Scholars: Next Generation Engagement and the Future of Higher Education* (Post, Ward, Longo, & Saltmarsh, 2016) highlights the emergence of this "next generation" of SLCE practitioner-scholars. It offers an intriguing contrast to the question raised twenty years ago by Edward Zlotkowski (1995) of whether SLCE had a future and, if so, what it would need to flourish. Looking back to that moment twenty years ago in his 2015 framing essay for the Service-Learning and Community Engagement Future Directions Project (SLCE-FDP), Zlotkowski notes that it was "a good time to dream of a new era" (p. 82); and he ponders what the forces currently shaping the academy and democracy in the U.S. mean for the SLCE movement. *Publicly Engaged Scholars* strongly suggests there is currently considerable momentum and excitement around a reimagined future for SLCE. The narratives of 22 engaged scholars from both the academy and the broader community (including co-author Timothy Shaffer) make clear the progress of SLCE in recent decades. And yet, they also reveal dissatisfaction with where we are today and call for continued evolution of the movement.

The stories of these next generation practitioner-scholars, including their winding paths into SLCE, suggest to us the importance of supporting the ongoing development of the SLCE movement through more explicit, direct, formalized, and institutionalized points of entry into the work. Many of them went through the academy as graduate students and now work either on campuses or in communities across wide ranging professions. Indeed, graduate-level education is an increasingly common component of such journeys. It is not, however, an unambiguous point of entry to SLCE-related careers. Therefore, in this essay we call for increased attention to the potential of graduate education to serve as a doorway into SLCE. And we suggest the importance of designing graduate-level study with an eye to shaping how incoming SLCE practitioner-scholars understand and undertake the work (e.g., with an asset-based rather than a deficit-based orientation; as an integrated part of their lives rather than an add-on to other responsibilities).

Co-author Lori Kniffin's own journey provides an example of the presently common winding path into SLCE taken by members of the next generation of practitioner-scholars:

I experienced SLCE first as an undergraduate student in an introductory course in a leadership studies program. When I later joined the same department as a staff member and then as an instructor while completing my master's degree, I learned that the kind of SLCE I had experienced had a lot of room for improvement. I started participating in conversations to improve that course using best practices in the SLCE literature. I also dove into a community engagement experience through a leadership practicum I taught; its evolution over eight semesters – from simply meeting with community organizations that worked in the area of food security to listening to the experiences of individuals experiencing food insecurity and ultimately helping build a network to improve food security on campus – mirrored my own ever-deepening understanding of SLCE.

This rich mix of first-hand experiences with the challenges and possibilities of SLCE increased my desire to pursue a Ph.D. in a program that would allow me to immerse myself in SLCE and prepare me to be a community-engaged practitioner-scholar. Disappointed with the lack of opportunities for community engagement in my master's program, I began looking for a doctoral program that focused on SLCE both as a mode of teaching and learning and as the focus of scholarship. I had numerous conversations with SLCE colleagues, searched online, contacted many colleges and universities . . . and yet all of this yielded no clear answer as to my best options for a doctoral program.

So I did what I have since learned many graduate students do: I pulled together bits and pieces of an engaged graduate education into a whole that met most of my goals. I entered a fairly traditional academic unit that is oriented toward social justice and has flexible requirements, and I also became part of an innovative community engagement institute on campus through a graduate assistantship. And probably most importantly, I surrounded myself with other practitioner-scholars with whom I collaborate on a variety of SLCE-related projects. This combination of opportunities will, I hope, serve me well as I complete a Ph.D. and continue my career. But I still wonder why this patchwork approach seems to be the best avenue I could come up with and why I could not readily find a graduate program that could more explicitly and coherently support my interest in pursuing SLCE as an integral part of my scholarly development.

This story, although unique in its specifics, has similarities to other narratives of SLCE practitioner-scholars, including a good number of those assembled in *Publicly Engaged Scholars* and previously in *Collaborative Futures: Critical Reflections of Publicly Active Graduate Education* (Gilvin, Roberts, & Martin, 2012). Through custom-made pathways such as this, graduate students are forced to articulate and define their place in the academy, which can enhance voice, confidence, relationships, and identity exploration. Too often, however, students have to settle for a fairly traditional department as their primary academic home and seek out more innovative opportunities for learning and research elsewhere. When students enter a discipline-centered program, their studies must focus on deep understanding of and scholarly contributions within that discipline, often to the exclusion of study at the intersection of disciplines. Graduate students who want to self-define as SLCE practitioner-scholars thus experience identity fracturing, finding themselves needing to wear distinct "hats" as they move between disciplinary work in their departments and SLCE-related work in other arenas of their lives. Worse, students without a high level of persistence, the resources to devote significant time and attention to the search for a program, and/or strong connections in the field may never find these pathways – with the consequence that the SLCE movement may lose their participation and leadership. Further, the movement may disproportionately lose the voices of students who lack the privilege of access to the human, cultural, and economic capital needed to pursue such winding pathways toward SLCE.

We therefore believe that unclear, winding paths serve as a significant deterrent to growing the SLCE movement. The movement is more likely to flourish in the future if we create a "front door" to SLCE in the form of graduate education explicitly designed to integrate SLCE practice, study, work, and scholarship. Enhancing opportunities for doctoral education in particular as a point of entry could open up many new possibilities for more people – and for a greater diversity of people – and thereby grow the SLCE movement. Advanced graduate education is where many who choose an academic career or a research-oriented profession in the nonprofit sector develop their professional identities and internalize the habits, dispositions, and skills of scholarly work. Developing the perspectives and capacities associated with democratic engagement as part of this process would deeply influence the identities and practices of community-engaged practitioner-scholars.

We recognize there may always be a tension in doctoral education regarding employment opportunities for graduates with non-traditional degrees. However, we see signs that bode well for the career prospects opened up by doctoral programs that integrate SLCE: (a) the growing recognition of the complexities of challenges facing us, local to global, in the 21st century (see, for example, the United Nations Sustainable Development Goals); (b) the increasing demand in the public sector for advanced, interdisciplinary, community-engaged research to generate knowledge and inform policy; and (c) the increasing number of next generation practitioner-scholars who are undertaking such graduate work and successfully creating meaningful career paths for themselves on campuses and in communities (see Post, Ward, Longo, & Saltmarsh, 2016).

We share here an example of a "front door" we have been building to illustrate an approach to doctoral education that could support the holistic development of SLCE practitioner-scholars. At Kansas State University, we have recently created and are preparing to launch a new program that integrates community-engaged scholarship. This Ph.D. in Leadership Communication is a collaboration among three departments in three different colleges: Communication Studies (College of Arts and Sciences), the Staley School of Leadership Studies (College of Education), and Communications and Agricultural Education (College of Agriculture). The fourth unit involved is the Institute for Civic Discourse and Democracy, whose mission is to build community capacity for informed, engaged, civil deliberation.

The program is labeled in accordance with campus models as "interdisciplinary," but the faculty are still sorting through the appropriateness of "multi-," "inter-," and "trans-" disciplinary framings. The program will bring together students and faculty from multiple disciplines (some of which are themselves interdisciplinary), will nurture synthesis and integration among these disciplines, and will advance public problem-solving by transcending the boundaries of disciplinary or academic perspectives and incorporating community-based knowledge. Given the program's role as a front door into SLCE for graduate students coming from various backgrounds and its defining focus on cultivating civic leadership and collaborative change agency, we need to think carefully with students about the significance of "interdisciplinary" and "transdisciplinary" framings for community-engaged practitioner-scholarship and ensure that the program launches and grows accordingly.

Faculty and staff from the four units convened over the course of a year to co-create learning outcomes, courses and curriculum, and assessment strategies. The core curriculum developed by these units will be co-taught, with teaching responsibilities rotating amongst departments. Students will have the opportunity to choose major professors and dissertation committee members from the three academic units as well as from affiliate faculty across the university. Key to the program's function as a doorway into SLCE, then, is that students will have the freedom and flexibility to tap into the expertise of a range of faculty who support diverse approaches to SLCE and establish direct connections with community-engaged faculty.

Students will not only learn *how* to do community-engaged scholarship but will learn *by doing* community-engaged scholarship. Two of the core courses include theoretical foundations and application of community-engaged methods. The program requires students to develop community relationships, work with community organizations on public problems, and co-create scholarship with community members. We imagine dissertations that push the boundaries of traditional products to include artifacts accessible and useful to the general public and that demonstrate measurable progress being made with community partners on public issues. This model recognizes the disciplinary expertise students bring with them but focuses on how that is connected with other knowledge and leveraged for change through community-engaged scholarship. With an active, experiential learning orientation, throughout their engaged doctoral study and practice students will have the opportunity to develop and exercise the capacity to lead change in and with communities. They will, relatedly, work with one another, community members, faculty, and staff to develop innovative ways to assess progress achieved through collaborative change strategies – this being a major challenge both in the curriculum and in the work itself.

Although community engagement is at the center of this program, it is not a Ph.D. in engagement, and we do not advocate for SLCE as a siloed discipline but rather a cross-disciplinary approach to teaching, learning, and research (see Clayton, Edwards, & Brackmann, 2013 for discussion of next generation engagement perspectives on calls to frame SLCE as a discipline). Our aim is for graduates to be prepared for deeply collaborative work with communities as civic leaders and change agents, whether in higher education, government, nonprofits, or socially responsible businesses. They will need to understand SLCE from the very beginning as constrained neither by disciplinary lenses nor by academic orientations to knowledge and practice. Students will study and integrate multiple disciplines and combine this learning with knowledge and methods of community-engaged scholarship.

This doctoral program is just one example of what we think a front door could look like for graduate students. The important thing is that we find ways to cultivate interest in and access to community-engaged work instead of letting passionate people get lost or discouraged along the way. Beyond the need for such points of entry, per se, we have a lot of work to do to transform institutions of higher education so that they better support the work of SLCE (on the other side of the front door, as it were) and better organize to address complex issues in our world (for many, the reason for looking for a doorway to begin with). We believe these goals as well can be advanced through the design of graduate-level front doors.

As we create spaces for graduate students from many disciplines to collaborate with engagement as the central thread, we also create learning communities that connect faculty from many disciplines who share commitments to SLCE and who can, by coming together to deepen their engaged work, have greater influence over institutional change processes and priorities (see O'Donnchadha, 2015). For co-author Timothy Shaffer, as one example, such a network of faculty, students, and community members interested in community-engaged scholarship provides a place for collaboration and affirmation. Further, for many of his colleagues, a space such as the new doctoral program at Kansas State serves as their own front door into SLCE, providing a supportive environment for them, regardless of their home disciplines, to learn about and begin incorporating community-engaged teaching and research into their work. For both veteran and new SLCE practitioner-scholars, a graduate program such as this offers a community of colleagues who view such work as not only legitimate but also important. And that community, in turn, can have a strong voice in campus conversations about policy changes and other aspects of systems change that are key to any higher education institution's ongoing integration of community-campus engagement as central to its identity.

Community-engaged academic programs such as this one can at the same time help to organize and focus efforts that bring campuses and communities together to address public issues that transcend single disciplines or sectors. The United Nations' Sustainable Development Goals outline several such complex challenges the SLCE community can help address. Food security is one of these challenges, and advancing food security globally requires practitioner-scholars in the humanities, social sciences, and natural sciences to employ collaborative leadership and work in partnership with communities. The National Science Foundation's recognition that robust research can and must engage the public similarly provides an impetus to design graduate programs that work across disciplines and cultivate engaged learning communities oriented toward making progress on the complex global issues we face in this century.

There are many possibilities ahead for SLCE, especially as new generations of practitioner-scholars come into the movement. Individuals already working in SLCE have a responsibility to make the invitation into this work compelling and clear – to institutionalize, formalize, and broaden pathways toward engagement. Creating a front door for graduate students is one way to accomplish this, and we invite colleagues to make more visible their own examples of graduate programs that are being designed as alternatives to winding pathways. We also commit ourselves – and call on others – to create additional clear paths for SLCE practitioner-scholars to enter our community. As we see it, the SLCE-FDP itself serves as a front door: a space that will push the SLCE movement forward by convening and cultivating new voices, including both the next generation of practitioner-scholars and the many actual and potential participants who have valuable, if not yet heard, perspectives. We believe these front doors will broaden and strengthen the next generation of engaged scholars and empower them to advance the SLCE movement over the next twenty years and beyond.

References

Clayton, P. H., Edwards, K, E., & Brackmann, S. M. (2013). Disciplining service-learning and the next generation engaged campus. *Michigan Journal of Community Service-Learning, 19*(2), 80–88. http://hdl.handle.net/2027/spo.3239521.0019.207

Gilvin, A., Roberts, G. M., & Martin, C. (Eds.). (2012). *Collaborative futures: Critical reflections on publicly active graduate education.* Syracuse, NY: The Graduate School Press.

O' Donnchadha, B. (2015). Critically-reflective civically-engaged academics shaping the future of an academy striving for social justice. *Michigan Journal of Community Service Learning, 22*(1), 109–112.

Post, M. A., Ward, E., Longo, N. V., & Saltmarsh, J. (Eds.). (2016). *Publicly engaged scholars: Next generation engagement and the future of higher education.* Sterling, VA: Stylus.

United Nations Development Programme. (2015). 2030 agenda for sustainable development. New York. http://www.undp.org/content/undp/en/home/sustainable-development-goals.html.

Zlotkowski, E. (1995). Does service-learning have a future? *Michigan Journal of Community Service Learning, 2*(1), 123–133. Retrieved from http://hdl.handle.net/2027/spo.3239521.0002.112

Zlotkowski, E. (2015). Twenty years and counting: A framing essay. *Michigan Journal of Community Service Learning, 22*(1), 82–85.

Authors

LORI E. KNIFFIN (lekniffi@uncg.edu) is a doctoral student in Cultural Foundations of Education and a graduate assistant at the Institute for Community and Economic Engagement at the University of North Carolina at Greensboro. Her scholarly interests include food justice, community dialogue, and democratic classrooms. She is the 2016–2017 SLCE Future Directions Project Fellow and Chair of the International Association for Research on Service-Learning and Community Engagement (IARSLCE) Graduate Student Network.

TIMOTHY J. SHAFFER (tjshaffer@k-state.edu) is an assistant professor in the Department of Communication Studies and assistant director of the Institute for Civic Discourse and Democracy at Kansas State University. His research interests focus on the advancement of democratic engagement through deliberative democracy and citizen engagement in higher education and community settings. He is co-editor of *Deliberative Pedagogy: Teaching and Learning for Democratic Engagement* (2017) to be published by Michigan State University Press.

MARY H. TOLAR (mtolar@k-state.edu) is director of the Staley School of Leadership Studies at Kansas State University. She works with faculty and staff to provide learning experiences for more than 1000 students in an interdisciplinary leadership studies minor as well as for the wider campus community through the School's array of applied learning programs. Her research interests focus on the art and practice of civic leadership development, women's pathways to public service leadership, and undergraduate leadership development through applied learning.

Values-Engaged Assessment: Reimagining Assessment through the Lens of Democratic Engagement

Joe Bandy
Vanderbilt University

Patti H. Clayton
PHC Ventures, IUPUI, University of North Carolina at Greensboro & Kansas State University

Heather Mack
Heather Mack Consulting

Georgia Nigro
Bates College

Sarah Stanlick
Lehigh University

Ann Sims Bartel
Cornell University

Sylvia Gale
University of Richmond

Julia Metzker
Stetson University

Mary Price
Indiana University - Purdue University Indianapolis

What is one value that grounds you in your civic engagement work? How are you walking the talk of that value in your assessment work? Or, how might you? And, what both helps and gets in the way of your doing that? These questions were recently posed to service-learning and community engagement (SLCE) faculty and staff gathered for an assessment institute. Answering the first was easy. *Collaboration. Reciprocity. Vulnerability. Intentionality. Humility.* And on and on. But the second question was, at first, a dead weight in the room. Finally, one participant stood and spoke candidly:

> *I care about risk-taking. I am always encouraging my students to take risks and embrace the vulnerability that comes along with that. We have to be vulnerable in order to grow. But when I think about my assessment work, vulnerability is the last thing I want. I am not taking risks in that part of my work; I am looking for answers, usually in ways that keep everyone happy. That's not what I want my students to do, and I really have to look at that.*

We believe the SLCE movement as a whole also "really has to look at this": at the role SLCE values play in SLCE assessment practices.

Zlotkowski's 1995 essay on the future of SLCE called the movement to focus on achieving academic legitimacy. Since that time, academic legitimacy has become inextricably linked with academic assessment, which now, 20 years later, we need to critically examine and creatively reimagine. We are concerned that the ongoing quest for legitimacy, coupled with uncertainties about funding, often leads SLCE practitioner-scholars to a disempowered and inauthentic relationship with assessment – one in which we find ourselves conforming to the practices of the world around us rather than holding to the values that drew many of us to SLCE. We see this potential tension between our values and our assessment practices as a microcosm of the broader struggles SLCE as counter-normative work faces. It is challenging to live out commitments to democratic engagement in an academic culture and a society often characterized by technocratic tendencies to privilege academic expertise over broad community participation in knowledge creation (Saltmarsh, Hartley, & Clayton, 2009) and by neoliberal (market-driven) imperatives to frame SLCE merely in terms of charity, public relations, or revenue generation (Brackmann, 2015).

Assessment is always undergirded by values, but which values and who determines them? And do we default to them, let ourselves be pressured into alignment with them, or deliberately choose them? Our vision for SLCE is to "walk the talk" of democratic engagement (Clayton et al., 2014; Saltmarsh, Hartley, & Clayton, 2009). Democratic engagement focuses on relationships as much as results and on effectiveness as much as efficiency. It sees all participants in SLCE as co-inquirers and co-creators. It calls for transformative learning and change – in higher education, in communities, and in ourselves. How might we better walk the talk of the values of such engagement in our assessment work, navigating constraints while empowering all stakeholders through critical reflection on values? Realizing this vision, we believe, requires that we go beyond assessing community and campus outcomes by counting participants, hours, or dollars or by reporting levels of satisfaction; it invites us to inquire into qualities of relationships, the transformation of systems, and the empowerment of all partners over time. As we see it, democratic engagement invites us to reimagine assessment.

It is our conviction that the assessment work of SLCE practitioner-scholars can embody and nurture a set of relationships, practices, and modes of inquiry that is potentially transformative of technocratic and neoliberal tendencies in our institutions. To fulfill this potential, we call for what we have begun referring to as *"values-engaged assessment"* – by which we mean assessment that is explicitly grounded in, informed by, and in dialogue with the (contested) values of SLCE understood and enacted as democratic civic engagement.

We seek to build on promising thinking about assessment that invites focus on process as well as product, questions whose perspectives should be included and what metrics best give voice to them, and prioritizes relationships as much as – if not more than – outcomes. There have been many calls to broaden assessment beyond student learning (the focus of academic assessment) to arenas such as community impact, institutional change, faculty/staff/community learning, and partnership quality. Innovative approaches that attend to multiple stakeholder perspectives and ways of knowing are needed and, indeed, emerging. For example, Guijt (2007) advocates for reforming assessment so that it better supports efforts to build capacities and social movements, shift social norms, and strengthen citizenship and democracy. As another example, the Center for Whole Communities offers tools for impact assessment related to such values as equity, human rights, ecosystem health, and economic vitality.

We share here our experience trying to reimagine assessment in order to surface key possibilities, tensions, and questions. At the 2015 Imagining America (IA) conference, we raised the question of how the organization might think innovatively about assessment, specifically by examining assessment practices and dilemmas explicitly through the lens of values. IA's research group on "Assessing the Practices of Public Scholarship" (APPS) had earlier identified five core values to which assessment in SLCE ought to attend – *collaboration, reciprocity, generativity, rigor, and practicability* – and had begun exploring examples that express them. We wanted to advance and nuance this thinking with the broader membership of IA by thinking together about the possibilities and challenges of walking the talk of the values of democratic engagement in assessment practices, especially in contexts that may actively frustrate or contradict them. We share here four conversations from the event that we think help to reimagine assessment.

First, we considered with participants during the conference plenary the question of why we might think assessment needs reimagining. The answers we heard, sampled here, point to the frustrations that may arise when assessment goals and methods are defined for us in narrow ways:

- *I'm tired of accounting: counting hours, counting dollars, counting heads.*
- *I don't believe in mandates from above – I believe in inclusive processes that mandate from within, that help us identify and live into our mandates.*
- *I am not in the game only to document and justify my own existence. I am in this because I care about contributing to change.*
- *I don't need more boxes to check. I need more honest conversations that help us deepen the work itself.*

Second, building from these concerns, we explored how, concretely, we might reimagine assessment. We invited participants to articulate collaboratively the meanings of one of the five values that most readily come to mind in a technocratic or neoliberal paradigm and then to reimagine that same value through the lens of democratic engagement. Table 1 expresses the contrast generated around the value of "rigor."

Thus, it seems that while rigor may be taken to imply the expression of technocratic values – that is, prioritizing the knowledge creation of "experts," mandating quantitative analysis, assuming objectivity, and devaluing the messiness of dialogue with multiple knowledges – it can also enhance more democratic processes of questioning assumptions and seeking input from multiple perspectives in the pursuit of common goals. Since any one value may, it seems, invoke technocratic, neoliberal, *and* democratic paradigms, a necessary aspect of reimagining assessment is critically reflective examination of the potential meanings of the values themselves in all of their nuances.

Third, we brought to the discussion at the conference an insight we found very resonant with our

Table 1
Dominant and Reimagined Meanings of "Rigor" in Assessment as Generated during the IA Plenary

Rigor: Technocratic/Neoliberal	Rigor: Democratic
Rigor mortis	Includes multiple knowledges/diverse voices
Gatekeeping term/purpose to exclude	Being thorough
Static	Focuses concentration
Valuing only things you can count	Ethical
Includes some types of knowledge and omits others	Encourages ambition
	Questions assumptions
Code for not listening; devaluing relational knowledge	Holds you to purposes/objectives and helps ensure accountability
Used to impose meaning/expertise on others	Intentionality
Assumes a hierarchy of knowledge creation	Answers the skeptics
Expert vs. local knowledge	Conversation
Assumes objectivity	Keeps institutions honest/engaged
Assumes there is one right way	Can bring various stakeholders together
Doesn't always include reflection	Protection from detractors
Rigged! Someone else's framework (administrators, donors, public relations)	Does not assume limits

experience of being torn between the democratic values we want to enact and often technocratic, neoliberal norms we feel pressured to accommodate in assessment. Parker Palmer's latest book, *Healing the Heart of Democracy* (2011), explores how tensions between our values or aspirations and the realities of our everyday lives can become so frustrating that we can give up or shut down as a result. In this condition, we can fail to stand by our convictions and thus lose our voices. One of us shared a recent example of feeling disempowered in a conversation with an assessment specialist on campus. The specialist was resisting a proposal to involve faculty in examining artifacts from SLCE courses in order to begin identifying shared learning goals across disciplines. The specialist advised instead, "Don't ask them what to measure; tell them!" – contradicting the values of collaborative inquiry that fueled the proposal and that grounded the pedagogy. Palmer suggests we need to develop capacities to hold such tensions in creative ways and stay open to insights thereby generated. We discussed with conference participants the ways that engaging in critical reflection on our assessment practices in light of our values allows for co-creative processes whereby we are more likely to navigate these tensions effectively, be open to new generative insights, and resist tendencies to "shut down."

Fourth, we explored the possibility that values-engaged assessment might, in practice, begin to find its footing through the adaptation of existing rather than (only) the creation of new tools and instruments. We started with version II of the Transformational Relationship Scale (TRES; TRES I was published by Clayton, Bringle, Senor, Huq, & Morrison, 2010; TRES II is available upon request), which has several features that align with our five named values. With its purpose being to support inquiry into the transactional or transformational nature of relationships in SLCE partnerships and thus advance understanding and improving partnership dynamics, TRES is inherently focused on *collaboration*, *generativity*, and *reciprocity*. TRES demonstrates *practicability* through its structure as a short, 13-item scale as well as *rigor* (as conceived in the right-hand column of Table 1) in that it gathers desired partnership qualities along multiple dimensions and thereby supports focused, constructive dialogue among partners about changes they want to make moving forward. However, applying the values-engaged lens highlights the fact that this tool was developed by faculty drawing on the literature, not co-created with students and community members, and that to date it is not readily accessible by non-academics. The use of TRES, or any other practical approach to assessment, then, may well be complicated by a mix of "fit" and "mis-fit" with the values of democratic engagement; the extent of this is influenced by our choices in designing and undertaking it. Without reflecting intentionally and critically on the values it embodies – in its creation, its use, its products, its goals, and its adaptation – a democratic form of assessment is unlikely.

These conversations highlight a range of complexities in living out our values, and in the interest of transparency, we question whether "values-engaged assessment" is, in fact, the best term to express what we are after: Is it sufficiently explicit regarding democratic engagement as the focal point of our values? Is "justice-oriented," with its many complex and sometimes conflicting relationships with democratic principles, a better characterization of the reimagining we intend? More fundamentally, might we think of a values-engaged approach as applying more appropriately to *any* set of values – calling for intentionality and criticality in enacting them in assessment, whatever they may be?

Indeed, foundational to democratic engagement is the notion of *criticality*, or attentiveness to what is easily taken for granted as given, and a corresponding commitment to shine light on missing, often suppressed, alternatives. Rather than proposing a singular interpretation of any specific set of SLCE values, therefore, we are exploring here a deeply self-reflective and intentional *way of being* in assessment in which we maintain a critical, questioning, and open orientation toward our values and toward our own enactment of them. Our use of the word "engaged" in "values-engaged assessment" is intended to express our own particular focus on democratic engagement: Assessment as we are conceptualizing it here exists in mutually-formative relationship with such democratic values as co-creation, shared power, inclusivity, asset-orientation, common good, and justice.

The self-reflection and criticality that characterize a values-engaged approach to assessment demand that we acknowledge that the practice of democratic and transformational forms of assessment is not without its limitations and tensions. As an aid to refining this approach, therefore, we pose here four questions for further exploration with the broader community of SLCE practitioner-scholars.

Question 1: A values-engaged approach necessarily involves a critique of the values driving assessment. As our discussion of "rigor" revealed, our values, no matter how sacred, are always at risk of invoking concepts and practices that are counter to the transformative goals of democratic engagement and thus must be subject to continual re-examination and perhaps negotiation. *How might we best engage collaboratively in such ongoing critique?*

Question 2: The many values held dear within the SLCE movement may seem to contradict each other in practice. Valuing (and documenting) impact can be at odds with valuing humility and with attending as much to process as to product, for example. *How can we view these tensions as a generative mechanism by which new thinking and counter-normative approaches to assessment, or to SLCE, can be cultivated?*

Question 3: A values-engaged approach can be time-consuming, resource-intensive, and personally risky. The amount and intensity of critical reflection and candid communication associated with democratic engagement can pose significant logistical, resource, and interpersonal challenges – making clear the appeal of more traditional and perhaps more efficient approaches to assessment. We do not advocate abandoning the value of efficiency, but we also do not want to uncritically sacrifice other values to achieve it. And, when confronted with the time and effort demands of democratic engagement, we do not want to simply fall back on approaches that are expedient but demand less in the way of vulnerability and dialogue across difference without taking into account what might be compromised. *How might a values-engaged approach nurture generative collaborations among SLCE partners that are cost- and time-efficient and also help us learn to take interpersonal risks?*

Question 4: Values-engaged assessment offers no one method, no one-size-fits-all model of assessment. A values-engaged approach favors processes that are intentionally purpose-driven, collaborative, empowering, dynamic, and context-dependent. As a result, each assessment method will take shape based on the specifics of each project and the values embraced and negotiated by all partners involved. Nonetheless, we as practitioners crave methodological guidance that goes beyond general principles such as co-creative reflection and intellectual integrity, however important they may be. *What sorts of guidelines, structures for dialogue, models, and other forms of support might we fashion together in order to give clear aid in the challenging work of values-engaged assessment while not foreclosing generative processes for context-specific and inclusive engagement with values?*

Democratic engagement involves both co-creative processes among all partners – which underlie these questions – and public purposes, for example social justice. Values speak to and can be brought to life in both. We are eager to have a dialogue within the SLCE community about the ways our assessment approaches can critically and creatively examine and enact the values of democratic engagement. In issuing this invitation, we are reminded of a folklore story that periodically makes its way through the SLCE community (shared often, for example, by Russ Edgerton and Bob Bringle):

> Two medieval stonemasons are working at a construction site. One of them, upon being asked what he is doing, replies, "I am squaring a stone." The other answers "I am building a cathedral." Same task – two very different relationships with the work and perspectives on its purpose.

It is our hope and intention that the ongoing development of values-engaged assessment will proceed in the spirit of – and contribute to the flourishing of – "cathedral building."

It is essential for the future of the movement – indeed, possibly for high-impact educational practices, publicly engaged scholarship, and social change initiatives more generally – that the work of assessment self-consciously have a sense of purpose that is equally as significant and high stakes as that of the SLCE movement. Claiming and holding tightly to such a sense of purpose as part of deeply co-creative processes undertaken by the full range of participants in SLCE can, we believe, empower and embolden us – helping us to move beyond frustration with and alienation from assessment, to live out the values of democratic engagement in assessment, and to expand opportunities for democratic knowledge creation and inclusive dialogue. In this way, assessment can better support forms of SLCE that build a more democratic and just society.

Note

The authors are grateful to the participants in the preconference workshop and plenary session we facilitated at the 2015 Imagining America conference. Their ideas, questions, and concerns significantly shape our work. We are also especially thankful for the contributions of Imagining America's Assessing the Practices of Public Scholarship (APPS) team who have grounded much of our thinking and who contribute to ongoing efforts to reimagine assessment. We also are indebted to Susan Schoonmaker, APPS research assistant, for support of our collaborations.

References

Brackmann, S. (2015). Community engagement in a neoliberal paradigm. *Journal of Higher Education Outreach and Engagement, 19*(4), 115-146. Retrieved from http://openjournals.libs.uga.edu/index.php/jheoe/article/viewFile/1533/892

Center for Whole Communities. Whole measures. Retrieved from http://wholecommunities.org/practice/whole-measures/.

Clayton, P. H., Bringle, R. G., Senor, B., Huq, J., & Morrison, M. (2010). Differentiating and assessing relationship in service-learning and civic engagement: Exploitative, transactional, or transformational. *Michigan Journal of Community Service Learning, 16*(2), 5-22. Retrieved from http://hdl.handle.net/2027/spo.3239521.0016.201

Clayton, P. H., Hess, G., Hartman, E., Edwards, K. E., Shackford-Bradley, J., Harrison, B., McLaughlin, K. (2014). Educating for democracy by walking the talk in experiential learning. *Journal of Applied Learning in Higher Education, 6*, 3-36. Retrieved from https://www.missouriwestern.edu/appliedlearning/wp-content/uploads/sites/206/2015/02/JALHE14.pdf

Guijt, I. (2007). Assessing and learning for social change: A discussion paper. Brighton: Institute of Development Studies. Retrieved from http://www.ids.ac.uk/files/dmfile/ASClowresfinalversion.pdf

Saltmarsh, J., Hartley, M., & Clayton, P. H. (2009). Democratic engagement white paper. Boston: New England Resource Center for Higher Education. Retrieved from http://futureofengagement.files.wordpress.com/2009/02/democratic-engagement-white-paper-2_13_09.pdf

Zlotkowski, E. (1995). Does service-learning have a future? *Michigan Journal of Community Service Learning, 2*, 123-133. Retrieved from http://hdl.handle.net/2027/spo.3239521.0002.112

Authors

JOE BANDY (joe.bandy@vanderbilt.edu) is assistant director of the Center for Teaching and affiliated faculty in Sociology at Vanderbilt University, where he has worked since 2010. In his administrative roles, he supports instructional and professional development of faculty in Vanderbilt's many social science colleges, departments, and programs. He also supports pedagogical innovation and organizational development across the university in his specialty areas of SLCE, critical pedagogy, diversity and equity, and environmental education. As a sociologist, he has researched widely and taught on issues related to social movements, environmental justice, class relations, economic development, and community building.

ANN SIMS BARTEL (aws4@cornell.edu) serves as Cornell University's associate director for Community-Engaged Curricula and Practice in the Office of Engagement Initiatives (part of Engaged Cornell). Once described as "part activist, part administrator, and part academic," Anna earned her Ph.D. in Comparative Literature at Cornell. Anna's background includes faculty work, consulting, and public humanities initiatives as well the development of community-engagement centers at several higher education institutions in cold, white places (upstate New York, Maine, and Iowa). Her current research interests are broad and include civic poetry; the U.S. agrarian novel; and of course civic engagement. Her favorite publication ("Why Public Policy Needs the Humanities, and How") appeared in 2015 in the *Maine Policy Review*.

PATTI H. CLAYTON (patti.clayton@curricularengagement.com) is an independent consultant and SLCE practitioner-scholar (PHC Ventures) as well as a senior scholar with IUPUI and UNCG.

Her current interests include civic learning; the integration of SLCE and relationships within the more-than-human world; walking the talk of democratic engagement as co-inquiry among all partners; and the power of such "little words" as *in, for, with,* and *of* to shape identities and ways of being with one another in SLCE. Related to assessment per se, she supports integrated design of SLCE that aligns goals, strategies, and assessment (focused on learning, community impact, partnership quality, etc.); and she works with individuals, programs, and institutions to build capacity for authentic assessment.

SYLVIA GALE (sgale@richmond.edu) directs the Bonner Center for Civic Engagement (CCE) at the University of Richmond. She was the founding director of Imagining America's Publicly Active Graduate Education Initiative (PAGE) and since 2009 has co-chaired IA's initiative on "Assessing the Practices of Public Scholarship," (APPS) which explores and advances assessment practices aligned with the values that drive community-engaged work. She is committed to co-creating opportunities for transformative liberal arts learning far beyond traditional institutional boundaries and has published on innovative assessment, engaged graduate education, and the power of institutional intermediaries to effect change.

HEATHER MACK (impact@hmackconsulting.com) is a planning, tracking, and assessment consultant to higher education institutions, international and domestic NGOs, and philanthropic foundations. She can often be found facilitating the adaptation of highly effective practices to the unique contexts and values of SLCE and social change programs at work on the ground. Her current interests include promoting an SLCE assessment culture that uplifts and enhances SLCE endeavors rather than drains or diminishes them, and fostering SLCE practitioners-scholars' autonomy and agency to ensure the assessments of their work embody the fundamental standards of utility, propriety, accuracy, feasibility, and accountability.

JULIA METZKER (jkmetzker@gmail.com) joined Stetson University as executive director for the Brown Center for Faculty Innovation and Excellence in June, 2016 after serving as director of Community-based Engaged Learning and professor of Chemistry at Georgia College. She received a B.S. from The Evergreen State College (where she learned first-hand the value of a transformative liberal arts education) and a doctoral degree from the University of Arizona. She co-founded the Innovative Course-building Group (IC-bG), an inclusive collaboration of higher educators that provide professional development around issues of learning. Her interests include using civic issues to design learning experiences, developing of high-impact pedagogies, and advancing equity in higher education.

GEORGIA NIGRO (gnigro@bates.edu) is professor of psychology at Bates College where she teaches courses in community-based research methods and works closely with the college's Harward Center for Community Partnerships and regional Campus Compact offices. She joined the Bates faculty after receiving her Ph.D. at Cornell, where she worked with the Consortium for Longitudinal Studies to carry out some of the early evaluations of preschool programs that led to widespread support for Head Start. These early lessons in bridging the domains of research, practice, and policy serve her well today.

MARY F. PRICE (price6@iupui.edu) is an anthropologist and director of Faculty Development at the IUPUI Center for Service and Learning. Mary works with faculty, graduate students, and community members as a thought partner and critical friend to strengthen curricula through authentic partnership, facilitate the creation of actionable knowledge, and enact institutional change grounded in the principles of democratic engagement. Her scholarly interests include community-campus partnerships as craft, community-engaged learning environments, and the social relations of production in higher education.

SARAH E. STANLICK (ses409@lehigh.edu) is the founding director of Lehigh University's Center for Community Engagement and a professor of practice in Sociology and Anthropology. She previously taught at Centenary College of New Jersey and was a researcher at Harvard's Kennedy School, assisting the U.S. Ambassador to the United Nations, Samantha Power. She has published in journals such as *The Social Studies* and the *Journal of Global Citizenship and Equity Education*. Her current interests include inquiry-based teaching and learning, global citizenship, transformative learning, and cultivating learner agency.

Resisting the Siren Song:
Charting a Course for Justice

Joe Blosser
High Point University

Edward Zlotkowski's (1995) concern over 20 years ago was that without institutionalization in the academic structures of colleges and universities, service-learning and community engagement (SLCE) might fade away or be co-opted into "still another academic specialty" (p. 129). Fortunately, many heeded his call, and SLCE has become a central and defining feature of many higher education institutions. SLCE leaders on campuses worked hard to build coalitions of stakeholders in the past decades, but many of these stakeholders were enticed to support SLCE for their own ends: Public relations offices needed human relations stories for the media, business offices needed an easy way to ensure they met the 7% minimum threshold for federal work-study students serving in the community, student life offices wanted volunteer structures in place to make it easier to sentence students to community service for disciplinary violations, advancement offices wanted to lure donors based on the institution's service commitments, admissions offices wanted to tout volunteer opportunities, and so on. As an institutionalized movement, SLCE now must find a way to live and thrive within these neoliberal incentive structures that make its continued existence on campuses possible.

SLCE lives within the dominant neoliberal structure of American colleges and universities. Simply put, the neoliberal frameworks that infuse American life today strive to monetize all human interactions, turning institutions of higher education into sites of efficiency, productivity, revenue production, and customer service. More than just restricting the range of possible ends, neoliberalism produces within people a desire to conform and promote neoliberal ends. Some scholars are optimistic that SLCE can turn the tide on neoliberalism (Orphan & O'Meara, 2016), and others see SLCE as too wrapped up in a liberal agenda to be an adequate force for transformation (Simpson, 2014). I fall somewhere in the middle, believing that SLCE can create a powerful and transformative sub-culture through which students, faculty, and community members can create structures for justice within a neoliberal framework. But if we are not aware of the incentives driving our stakeholders, we may succumb to them. As Kliewer (2013) warns, "by maintaining a civic engagement movement that does not account for neoliberalism, we could potentially be undermining the very democratic sentiments and institutions that the movement attempts to revive" (p. 73). The future of the movement will depend on the ability of SLCE leaders to recognize and navigate the neoliberal incentives on our work, using them to further our objectives but resisting the urge to let the work be co-opted.

Influence of Incentives on SLCE

To see if my impressions of the movement were shared by other SLCE leaders, I spent the better part of my time at the North Carolina Campus Compact Pathways to Achieving Civic Engagement Conference and the Campus Compact 30th Anniversary Conference, both taking place in Spring 2016, soliciting attendees' stories about what incentivized their stakeholders to get behind SLCE. They told stories of campus public relations offices needing a "feel good" story of service to distract from bad press at the university. They told stories about faculty who wanted heart-warming service projects for their students in order to get good course evaluations. They told stories of students wanting to change the world by starting yet another campus mentoring program – without ever consulting any of the myriad of extant campus mentoring programs. And like good improvisational actors, the SLCE professionals and partners I spoke with responded to each of these situations with a, "yes, and . . ." They sought to encourage the energy, money, passion, and learning of these stakeholders but, in the process, nudge them away from their more neoliberal impulses and toward more sustainable, justice-oriented projects. Rather than promote neoliberal forms of service that depend on – and reinforce – the power gap between campus and community by emphasizing short-term, optics-oriented, results-driven service, many SLCE professionals want to push beyond "traditional" service-learning, charity models of service, and deficit-based mindsets to promote service that seeks deep social transformation by upending traditional power structures (Lupton, 2011; Mitchell, 2008). Engagement in such transformational work requires a deep understanding of the neoliberal incentives that can both facilitate and undermine our journey.

To be clear, I do not think any SLCE professional has "clean hands" – no one operates outside of entrenched – and sometimes damaged – systems. Nor do I think people using or offering neoliberal incentives are of questionable moral character. I am asking the pragmatic question, "How do we use the incentives that exist to move the work of justice forward?"

I start with the incentives mentioned by community partners. While many (maybe most) community partners come alongside practitioner-scholars seeking to help students learn and to improve the services provided to the community, all community partners also have additional pressures on them, which influence the shape of their involvement with institutions of higher education. They may seek a relationship with the campus to bolster their reputations, their fundraising, or their donor relations. They may know that solid campus partnerships sometimes open the door to financial resources. And, at some colleges and universities, community partners of distinction are invited to campus events and conferences, are eligible for awards, and so on. Given that nonprofits exist amidst similar neoliberal pressures as campuses, many are structured according to a deficit-based approach that perpetuates the neoliberal power structure of have and have-nots (Kretzmann & McKnight, 1993). Their boards are populated with philanthropists and well-meaning volunteers who see a problem in the community and want to fix it. Their desire can be to enlist students who want to volunteer to "solve" a problem. When SLCE practitioner-scholars try to engage in capacity building projects, asset-based approaches, or community-engaged research, some partners simply do not see the value or payoff. They need volunteers to sort clothes, organize the food pantry, and fix up the building. When students serve at such agencies, they may have positive experiences of feeling valued for the help they provide. Yet, they can also have experiences that reinforce their deficit mindsets, which can frustrate faculty who want to help students understand systemic social issues.

For their part, faculty tend to be driven by the incentive structures on our campuses. At 94% of schools studied by the American Association of University Professors (2016), much weight is given to student course evaluations – a nod to the power of the customer-service model of neoliberal higher education (Miller & Seldin, 2014). More than one professor has shared with me the need to design SLCE courses matched with well-staffed community partners who communicate quickly with the students, have flexible hours, and provide students with work that makes them feel like they made a difference (e.g., mentoring a child, filling food boxes, painting, delivering food). Deficit-based service can feel good and lead to solid course evaluations; it can even fulfill major community needs. But such "traditional service-learning" only reinforces power structures (Mitchell, 2008). It can be hard to get some faculty who are concerned about their course evaluations to take a risk on a community-engaged research project for the first time or work behind the scenes building an agency's capacity. Though I have seen amazing course evaluations come out of SLCE courses in which faculty and students adopt an asset-based orientation to their partnerships and projects, these professors often put in extra hours and frequently teach upper-level courses with smaller class sizes and more invested students.

At some institutions junior faculty have been told to wait until after attaining tenure to engage in SLCE. Community-engaged research is often seen as a lesser form of research, and faculty who spend extra hours developing community partnerships are seen as lightweights or wasting their time. With the rapid rise of contingent faculty that now make up 70% of all university faculty (AAUP, 2016), it is important to understand that incentives for engaging in SLCE differ depending on the institution. At some colleges and universities contingent faculty may shy away from SLCE because it is seen as too dangerous to risk a bad set of course evaluations due to forces beyond the instructor's control (such as staff turnover that leads to chaos at the community organization). But at other institutions, contingent faculty may seek out SLCE to demonstrate to their chairs and deans how seriously they are invested in their students' learning and the institution's commitment to the community.

Though most SLCE faculty I know have a heart for the work, even the most committed faculty feel the pressure to take on projects that are easier to manage. This can lead them toward deficit-based partnerships and projects in which students are plugged into service and faculty only have to drop-in from time-to-time to see how things are going. SLCE professionals who coordinate numerous SLCE experiences also know that these "plug-and-play" experiences are often easier to manage from an administrative standpoint. They demand fewer campus resources than asset-based projects, which often rely on teams of stakeholders, regular communication, and intensive relationship building. Deficit-based projects also typically result in more easily calculated service hours. In a community-engaged research project, for example, it can be hard to calculate how many research hours constitute community service hours versus course assignment time.

The societal shift toward a consumer model of higher education has, in some ways, given students (and their parents) substantial power to influence how SLCE looks on campus (Kreuter, 2014; Perry, 2014). Many students have a passion and longing to make a difference, to get involved. One of the pressures mentioned repeatedly by the SLCE faculty and program directors with whom I spoke was the desire of students to start something new, to be entrepreneurs, to follow their passions by creating a project. One SLCE professional attributed this to the "millennial start-up mentality." Instead of joining existing projects or long-term partnerships, students often want to pave their own trail. Our culture and our campuses emphasize being "job-makers," "leaders," and "entrepreneurs," so students often see SLCE as a place to test out their skills before they head to the job market.

There are also students who see SLCE as a way to bolster their resumes and popularity. A student once told me that, by winning service awards and being featured regularly in the campus news, she was achieving her goal of becoming known around campus – of being "college famous." While most of the students I work with are not so opportunistic about their SLCE involvement, the pressure to build resumes and job skills is high for many students. SLCE can easily become a laboratory for students who want to try new things, build their own programs, and leave their mark. These can be powerful motivators and positive traits if they are funneled in a positive right direction and are bolstered by regular reflection and solid community relationships.

The Effect of Institutionalization and Certification

With institutionalization comes the pressure to contribute to the mission of the campus as defined not by SLCE practitioner-scholars but by the neoliberal framework shaping most institutions of higher education. They may be asked by the public relations office for stories about how the campus has solved a community problem or improved the lives of community members. Stories about capacity building or relationship building often do not "sell" as well or have as vibrant a "visual appeal" because they often take years of relationship building and sustained effort in the community. Higher education institutions are also increasingly seeing the value of SLCE for student retention, alumni engagement, donor recruitment, and/or opportunities to feature the religious commitments of the school. These can be positive forces that more deeply embed SLCE into the cultural lifeblood of an institution, but they also come with pressure to produce de-politicized SLCE opportunities. In particular, there is pressure to avoid polarizing projects, like those involving activism, voter engagement, or community organizing around politically sensitive justice issues such as climate-change, marriage rights, or living-wage campaigns.

With the rise in national certifications, including the President's Honor Roll and the Carnegie Community Engagement Classification, campuses may see value in promoting SLCE in order to raise the institution's profile. These awards can be positive forces, but a higher education institution may also push to obtain the Carnegie Classification, for example, without developing the necessary infrastructure to produce sustainable, best-practice models of SLCE.

SLCE professionals who oversee curricular programs may feel institutional pressure to list a certain number of courses each semester, to ensure partners and projects have ongoing relationships with SLCE courses, and so on. As SLCE programs grow larger, they tend to need more logistical support to ensure campuses live up to their commitments. And if a minor or certificate program is offered, there is usually curricular pressure to offer courses on a reliable basis. These can be positive pressures, but they can also push faculty to continue teaching a course "beyond the lifespan of the project," as one professor recently remarked to me.

The Pressures of Assessment Culture on SLCE

Finally, in the list of incentives luring SLCE, I think there are pressures from the wider SLCE community. Numerous organizations and grant foundations support the work of SLCE and cultivate the spread of best practices. I have encountered two trends that trouble me related to this support: the epistemological takeover of assessment by the social sciences and the focus on student psycho-social well-being. With regard to assessment, the SLCE movement has fallen in line with the growing national assessment culture. Evaluating programs, partnerships, learning, and more can be positive; however, narrowing the framework for valid assessment to Bloom's Taxonomy or other traditional educational standards restricts our ability to value indigenous, relationship-based, non-western, and non-positivist ways of knowing. Human relationships are built on more than analytical forms of knowledge, and the reduction of a partnership to an assessment tool can diminish the partnership itself. Insertion of an assessment – especially one limited to positivist ways of knowing – to evaluate the quality of community partner relationships can even have a chilling effect on these relationships.

The Association of American Colleges and Universities, along with Bringing Theory to Practice, has recently promoted the idea – through publications and grant funds – that SLCE can and should have a positive influence on student psychosocial well-being. Checkoway (2011) defines psychosocial well-being, saying it "places emphasis on the conditions that enable people to flourish, rather than focusing on what is wrong with people, and tries to cure what ails them" (p. 7). It sounds like a worthy goal, but Bringing Theory To Practice interprets this to be about how service can reduce "substance abuse and depression on campus" (Swaner 2007, p. 16). The Robert Wood Johnson Foundation (1997) similarly supports the use of service to reduce substance abuse, saying campuses should require students to "undertake a certain number of hours of volunteer work to reduce their free time and to give their educational experience additional meaning" (p. 39).

Student life professionals and others who worry about student retention, substance abuse, and similar issues have different objectives in mind for service than many SLCE offices. Levine (2011) warns that "There is some risk that the default justification for civic engagement may become its psychological or developmental benefits for participants; resources will then be directed to non-controversial 'helping' and 'joining' activities, and youth engagement will become largely therapeutic" (p. 14). Student learning is quite different from student psychosocial well-being. Indeed, there are worthy civic engagement opportunities that may leave students depressed, anxious, and less sure of themselves and their place in the world – but through them students may grow, learn, and make a powerful impact on the world. Levine (2011) offers the Freedom Riders as just such an example of service that profoundly turned the world toward justice but left psychological scars on the participants.

Examining Motivations for SLCE

Quite often the incentives offered by our stakeholders urge us to travel in the direction of charity work: to hitch our wagons to easy, fun, assessable, visually-rich (for the media), and meaningful service opportunities that fit neatly into people's preconceived categories of "giver" and "recipient." But the further in this direction we travel, the harder it is for us to see the deeper injustices and policy failures that require such charity work to be done. There is most certainly a time and place for charity, for giving without question and offering help to those in need. But in our broken – in Christian terms, "sinful" – world, the pure gift, pure charity, pure love is impossible. It too often enables dependency and overlooks systemic injustice. As Reinhold Niebuhr (1979) reminds us, in such a broken world, justice is the closest thing we can obtain to true love. And the work of justice requires unearthing inequitable power structures; revealing sexism, racism, classism, and homophobia; and engaging in a struggle for genuine partnerships across communities. Many of the SLCE professionals with whom I talked at the conferences last spring want to engage in such justice work, but they also feel pressure from their stakeholders to engage in charity work to justify their SLCE programs. Charity work fits more cleanly into the neoliberal framework because it reinforces the often unspoken power inequalities between giver and recipient.

The hard part about justice work, which can (though does not always) include asset-based approaches, community-engaged research, capacity building, and policy work, is that to do it we may have to push back against the stakeholders we have spent years cultivating. Yet, we still need these stakeholders if we are to exist within higher education. It is difficult, though, to work toward justice without staking out particular moral and political positions – positions that may alienate key stakeholders. We must struggle head on with how to navigate these competing pressures. The danger I see for SLCE – having now become an institutionalized part of an increasingly neoliberal educational landscape – is that if we succumb to all these incentives, we will become nothing more than the "pressure release valve" of the academy, allowing faculty, students, and administrators to feel like we are helping "the community" as we place one bandage after another on a gushing wound.

Shaping Future Pathways Toward Justice

The future pathways of SLCE must navigate the tension between the neoliberal incentives that often support our work and the justice orientation shared by many in the field. We must become aware of and adept at navigating the incentives driving our stakeholders, but we cannot surrender to the neoliberal siren song. To be clear, this is not a moral critique of the character of individual stakeholders – the public relations staff, the advancement team, local philanthropists, eager students, or anyone else invested in charity models of service – nor do

I intend to suggest that SLCE practitioners are of higher moral character ourselves. This is an argument about systems and structures. To paraphrase Niebuhr (1932), it is about moral people in often immoral structures.

The future of SLCE is to educate students, faculty, and community members in the ways of justice, seeding a critical consciousness within the heart of our campuses and communities. It is about taking actions such as developing more qualitative and affirming modes of assessment, seeing "students as colleagues," co-teaching with community members as paid equals, and challenging everyone to recognize the neoliberal incentives luring our work and how to use these to move in a different direction – to move toward justice. I do not believe SLCE will overthrow the neoliberal frameworks that shape modern higher education, but we can be a refuge, a place to courageously explore and shape the pathways of justice that stretch out before us.

References

American Association of University Professors. (2016). Background facts on contingent faculty. Available at: http://www.aaup.org/issues/contingency/background-facts

Checkoway, B. (2011). New perspectives on civic engagement and psychosocial well-being. *Liberal Education, 97*(2), 6-11.

Kliewer, B. W. (2013). Why the civic engagement movement cannot achieve democratic and justice aims. *Michigan Journal of Community Service Learning, 19*(2), 72-79.

Kretzmann, J., & McKnight, J. (1993). Building communities from the inside out: A path toward finding and mobilizing a community's assets. Evanston, IL: Institute for Policy Research, Northwestern University.

Kreuter, N. (2014). Customer mentality. *Inside HigherEd*. Online. Retrieved from https://www.insidehighered.com/views/2014/02/27/essay-critiques-how-student-customer-idea-erodes-key-values-higher-education.

Levine, P. (2011). What do we know about civic engagement? *Liberal Education, 97*(2), 12-19.

Lupton, R. D. (2011). *Toxic charity: How churches and charities hurt those they help (and how to reverse it)*. New York: HarperCollins.

Miller, J. E., & Seldin, P. (2014). Changing practices in faculty evaluation. *Academe, 100*(3), 35-38.

Mitchell, T. (2008). Traditional vs. critical service-learning: Engaging the literature to differentiate two models. *Michigan Journal of Community Service Learning, 14*(2), 50-65.

Niebuhr, R. (1932). *Moral man and immoral society*. New York: Charles Scribner's Sons.

Niebuhr, R. (1979). *Interpretation of Christian ethics*. New York: Seabury Press.

Perry, D. (2014). Faculty members are not cashiers. *Chronicle of Higher Education*. Retrieved from http://chronicle.com/article/Faculty-Members-Are-Not/145363/.

Robert Wood Johnson Foundation. (1997). *Be vocal, be visible, be visionary: Recommendations for college and university presidents on alcohol and other drug prevention*. Princeton, NJ: Robert Wood Johnson Foundation, Fund for the Improvement of Postsecondary Education.

Simpson, J. S. (2014). *Longing for justice: Higher education and democracy's agenda*. Toronto: University of Toronto Press.

Swaner, L. E. (2007). Linking engaged learning, student mental health and well-being, and civic development: A review of the literature. *Liberal Education, 93*(1), 16-25.

Zlotkowski, E. (1995). Does service-learning have a future? *Michigan Journal of Community Service Learning, 2*(1), 123-133.

Author

REV. DR. JOE BLOSSER (jblosser@highpoint.edu) is the Robert G. Culp Jr. director of Service Learning and assistant professor of Religion and Philosophy at High Point University (HPU). He is the founding director of the HPU Service Learning Program and Bonner Leader Program, and he teaches courses in Business Ethics, Educational Ethics, and Modern and Contemporary Christian Theology. Dr. Blosser specializes in the ethical implications of economic theory and Christian theology. He has published articles in the *Michigan Journal of Community Service Learning, Research in the History of Economic Thought and Methodology, Journal of Religious Ethics, Journal of the Society of Christian Ethics, Journal of Cultural and Religious Theory, Encounter, Homiletic*, and *Religious Studies Review*.

Teach the Partnership: Critical University Studies and the Future of Service-Learning

David J. Fine
University of Dayton

Edward Zlotkowski's (1995) article "Does Service-Learning Have a Future?" challenges the academy to integrate community-engaged learning into the curriculum. As Zlotkowski suggests, students, staff, and faculty ought to engender a culture of civic action and ethical accountability enhanced by rigorous coursework, but this goal necessitates resources: administrators must invest in service-learning to reap its full benefits. Issues arise, however, when one considers this investment in light of the academy's corporatization. Nussbaum (2010) has noted, for instance, how colleges and universities increasingly emphasize vocational training and professional readiness at the expense of humanist inquiry and civic responsibility. The academy's corporatization, she argues, threatens to erode the skills at the heart of democratic citizenship. Williams (2012) likewise censures this market-driven academy "with research progressively governed more by corporations that fund and benefit from it, with faculty downsized and casualized, and with students reconstituted as consumers subject to escalating tuition and record levels of debt" (p. 25). He insists that students, staff, and faculty must engage critically with these unsettling trends in higher education – an appeal, I argue, service-learning educators in particular must heed.

As higher education, deeply influenced by neoliberalism's pressures to marketize, adopts the structure and value systems of big business, it risks placing private interest before public concern. This danger, even more acute twenty-one years after the publication of Zlotkowski's article, underscores the need for a reassessment of the institutional means by which service-learning happens. "Perhaps," Zlotkowski (2015) wonders in his framing essay for the Future Directions Project, "there is a fundamental mismatch at the heart of our work that we have not wanted to recognize" (p. 84). Higher education may not prove the best location, after all, from which to effect progressive democratic change. In what follows, I stay the course with this provocation and argue that service-learning and community engagement (SLCE) educators must teach their partnerships – the specific histories, missions, and stakeholders involved – and thereby contextualize SLCE within the often problematic forces at work within and upon higher education. I thus call on the movement to interrogate, pedagogically, the motivations behind institutional "commitments" to SLCE and to account, ethically, for the economic and social privilege animating this service.

Consider the Means

To look back on the past twenty years and forward to the next is to acknowledge higher education's rapid corporatization and internationalization. I recommend that SLCE educators engage with the academy's globalization – the process whereby higher education assumes a corporate mentality and expands its reach internationally – by designing instruction in the vein of critical university studies (CUS). CUS is an emerging field that examines higher education in light of its history and cultural context. CUS analyzes both historical shifts in conceptions of the academy and contemporary issues such as adjunct labor and student debt, thereby "examining the university as both a discursive and material reality" (Williams, 2012, para.10). CUS is interdisciplinary by nature and gives students the opportunity to analyze both higher education and specific institutions through a lens that is particularly relevant given the current trends toward corporatization and internationalization. Indeed, conversations about their school's history, governance, and endowment position students, staff, faculty, and, especially in the case of SLCE, community members to think about the ethical dimensions of the academy's presence and impact in broader publics.

While this sort of dialogue may well happen in SLCE classrooms around the world, the explicit inclusion of CUS in SLCE programming aims to make these conversations more intentional and concrete. Through guided reflection on experiences in and with communities, facilitators prompt critical conversation about the deep interconnection between the institution and its community, emphasizing their shared history, economy, and space. Such dialogue accepts Williams' (2007) invitation to "teach the university" (p. 25); according to Williams, careful examination of higher education "gives students a language to articulate some of the stakes in current policies and practices, to define its cultural images, and to discern steps in its evolution" (p. 32). Students then bring this knowledge of higher education's history to bear on their own institution. At its best, a teach-the-university approach "sets out terms upon which to judge and assess particular incarnations of the university" (p. 32). Within a CUS framework, SLCE educators not only approach colleges and universities as historical institutions – institutions that both shape and are shaped by the larger sweep of social and cultural forces – but also conceptualize SLCE as a distinct manifestation within that history. SLCE does not emerge in a vacuum. It participates in the adaptation and reinvention of institutions and is caught up in their missions, strategic plans, and promotional branding. CUS articulates these tensions and brings them to the table for ethical consideration.

Recognition of the academy as an evolving product of specific societal pressures is especially pressing as institutions globalize. Global engagement is, often enough, indicative of the profit-driven education that Keenan, SJ, decries (2015). For example, he cites how universities depend on the high tuition payments of international students to meet their budgets but fail to provide the support these students' academic and social flourishing requires. For reasons like these, Williams (2012) urges suspicion of "the globalization of higher education, which is promoted as altruistic but is often actually a profit-seeking endeavor through which American or European universities sell their brands and services" (para. 21). As institutions progressively incorporate the language of global citizenship into their mission statements, they articulate a fundamental ambivalence. A tension exists between the call for moral reflection on human interconnection, on the one hand, and the promotion of economic globalization, on the other. This strain, of course, is not unfamiliar to SLCE practitioners. It appears as well in local settings, where SLCE activities can, as Zlotkowski (1995) warns, repackage a "missionary mentality" (p.130). To avoid positioning SLCE as a means of "saving" others and to acknowledge both professional and geographical privilege, SLCE educators must wrestle with the moral and political questions about the globalizing academy that CUS raises.

Think the Process

What might it look like to engage such questions as part of SLCE? At this juncture, I share an example of how my colleagues and I integrated CUS into an SLCE activity. During a January 2015 intersession trip to Cambodia – as part of Lehigh University's Global Citizenship (GC) Program – Professor Sothy Eng, Graduate Assistant Whitney Szmodis, and I designed, in close collaboration with long-term community partners, a layered SLCE experience to provoke reflection on global service-learning in general and on Lehigh's partnership with Caring for Cambodia (CFC) in particular. Lehigh University's College of Education has worked closely with CFC, an NGO dedicated to improving children's education, for many years. Professor Eng's graduate students visit CFC schools twice each academic year, and during the summer he directs a CFC-centered internship program for undergraduate and graduate students. Lehigh's seasoned partnership with CFC provided the Global Citizenship Program with the opportunity to structure a multifaceted experience at CFC schools. Its aim was both to provoke critical reflection on global citizenship in theory and practice and to provide valuable feedback to CFC on its attempts to strengthen volunteer programming as a means of promoting local Cambodians' agency.

During the intersession trip to Cambodia, GC students visited NGOs, attended court at the Khmer Rouge Tribunal, toured historical monuments, and dialogued with local university students. In advance of a half-day session at CFC, my colleagues and I divided the twenty-three participating GC sophomores into three teams. Each group visited a different CFC school and performed a distinct type of service. The first team – which included various student leaders on Lehigh's campus – undertook traditional volunteer work. They painted stools and assembled hygiene packets. They did not collaborate with CFC students, staff, or faculty directly; in this sense, the unglamorous labor was practical but isolated. The second group – composed of bilingual students and English-language learners – observed an English class. The GC students met with the instructor after class and shared their own experiences learning English. Here, they reflected with the instructor on what they had seen and heard during the class and offered feedback from their own perspectives. The third team interacted with Cambodian high school students. The high schoolers showed the GC students some traditional gardening methods and invited them to assist in planting a small garden patch. This interaction provided the Cambodian students with a chance to practice spoken English and to share their cultural knowledge. Significantly, it prioritized local knowledge and put the GC visitors in the position of learners.

By design, the GC students did not become aware of the differences among their experiences until later in the day. We invited the CFC curriculum director to join our nightly reflection, and she asked the GC students questions relevant to CFC's programming for international volunteers. As they wrestled with these questions, the students realized they had engaged in very different activities during the day. Through dialogue that drew on distinct forms of service, they began to articulate the larger stakes of their dissimilar experiences, posing questions of privilege and equity. They wondered if their visit interfered with the school day. They asked how long one must stay in order to make a positive contribution to the community. They probed the white-savior complex and problematized the good feelings obtained through one-and-done service. Along the way, they thought carefully about their university's relationship with the East, for each approach to service imagined a distinct relationship between Western travelers and native Cambodians. The visit's design allowed for differences in perspective among students, teachers, and partners to emerge organically, and these disparities invited GC students to come to their own individual conclusions regarding service-learning and their university's global engagement.

This activity thus foregrounded Lehigh's partnership with CFC as itself an object of study and critique. It highlighted the partnership's evolution over time as it demonstrated how the partnership continues to develop through negotiation with local and international partners. While it might seem like some students participated in the "better" service – perhaps the one that prioritized Cambodian students' knowledge – conversation highlighted benefits and costs to all three experiences. That particular morning, CFC needed stools painted and hygiene packets assembled. GC students in the first group were able to accomplish concrete tasks, freeing up CFC staff for other work. They responded, in short, to a need articulated by the partner. In contrast, a lot of thought and planning on behalf of CFC staff members went into organizing the other two experiences, time that might have been better spent on Cambodian – rather than GC – students. Further, as one GC student pointed out, CFC's engagement with GC students had larger consequences for its own branding, since CFC wants to communicate to its volunteers and donors the importance it places on native voice and experience. Points like these confronted students with SLCE's moral murkiness and entangled them in its thicket.

Clearly, our visit to CFC was far too short for a high-quality service experience. The visit sought, instead, to engage GC students and community partners in a critical conversation about possible – and competing – models for international partnerships and future SLCE initiatives at CFC. These discussions continued in the Literature and Global Justice course that followed the two-week intersession trip. The GC students' experiences at CFC enriched their critical approach to literature and social justice as it grounded theoretical considerations in living partnerships and personal connections. In this way, our study of texts about colonial Indochina and from contemporary Southeast Asia – such as Graham Greene's *The Quiet American* and Vaddey Ratner's *In the Shadow of the Banyan* – remained in dialogue with the priorities of our home institution and the privilege lurking within abstract concepts like global citizenship. In their reflective writing and in classroom conversation, students situated their GC education in the concrete partnerships and privileges that made it possible in the first place.

Evaluate the Ends

This experience illuminates what I believe CUS offers to SLCE. While a CUS approach to SLCE reinforces SLCE's commitment to ongoing relationships, active reflection, and reciprocal exchange, it also underscores three benefits of teaching the partnership:

(a) A CUS approach grounds SLCE in the institutions that simultaneously support and thwart the movement's fruition. SLCE enhanced with a CUS framing sits with ambiguity and interrogates its own compromises, without sanitizing, idealizing, or infantilizing community members;

(b) CUS does not present higher education as an uncomplicated fount of truth from which good things inevitably flow, and it thus complicates SLCE educators' positions by defining them as embroiled in and sometimes in tension with systems larger than their individual research, teaching, and service (however progressive). Such candid recognition communicates to students the need for continued moral vigilance inside and outside the academy; and

(c) Finally, this method involves students directly in SLCE's thorny processes and thereby stimulates both critical reflection and judgment. It nudges learners beyond personal opinion to critical reflection and democratic interaction with peers, partners, and professionals as the learning community imagines situations from various perspectives and, given this diversity of viewpoints, judges a particular initiative's efficacy.

In other words, CUS strategically implicates both individuals and communities in the moral muddle that is SLCE's relation to the global, corporate academy.

Analysis of a specific institution's history, governance, and outreach builds a solid, ethical foundation for SLCE initiatives moving forward. As we move in this direction, students might shift from being the recipients of prepackaged SLCE experiences – wherein, as Zlotkowski (1995) notes, "reflection too often amounts to little more than student 'discovery' of a pre-determined, ideologically 'correct' interpretation of the service experience" (p. 125) – to co-creators, who plan, implement, and evaluate initiatives in collaboration with campus facilitators and community partners. Thus, students – indeed all participants – might engage with SLCE's ethical complications rather than assuming, in advance, that all SLCE efforts are inherently good. For higher education's globalization affects more than service-learning abroad: SLCE must interrogate, with honesty and precision, the academic structures and institutionalized benefits that buttress its efforts. The mere appeal to prosocial, civic virtues belies the privilege of students, staff, and faculty housed in the powerful, neoliberal institutions of U.S. higher education. Resources, however necessary, are not innocent. I hence call for the SLCE movement to adopt a CUS approach, one that critically assesses the academy's past, present, and future engagements.

Note

I would like to thank the editors for their generous and helpful feedback on previous drafts. I am especially grateful for Patti Clayton's attention to little words, because they make a big difference. I also wish to thank my dear friends, Jenna Lay and Emily Shreve, who both read this essay and offered comments. My most sincere gratitude belongs, however, to Whitney Szmodis, who first theorized and subsequently orchestrated GC's visit to CFC. This piece, while expressing my personal views on higher education and SLCE, has benefitted by Whitney's commitment to ethical and passionate engagement with others.

References

Keenan, J. F. (2015). *University ethics: How colleges can build and benefit from a culture of ethics.* Lanham, MD: Rowman & Littlefield.

Nussbaum, M. C. (2010). *Not for profit: Why democracy needs the humanities.* Princeton, NJ: Princeton University Press.

Williams, J. J. (2007). Teach the university. *Pedagogy: Critical Approaches to Teaching Literature, Language, Composition, and Culture, 8*(1), 25–42.

Williams, J. J. (2012, February 19). Deconstructing academe: The birth of critical university studies. *The Chronicle of Higher Education.* Retrieved from http://chronicle.com

Zlotkowski, E. (1995). Does service-learning have a future? *Michigan Journal of Community Service Learning, 2*(1), 123–133.

Zlotkowski, E. (2015). Twenty years and counting: A framing essay. *Michigan Journal of Community Service Learning, 22*(1), 82–85.

Author

DAVID J. FINE (dfine1@udayton.edu) is an assistant professor of English with specialization in literature, culture, and religion at the University of Dayton. Formerly, he served as the assistant director of Lehigh University's Global Citizenship Program. His research, teaching, and service explore the interface of literature, ethics, and community engagement.

Responses to the Call for a National Strategic Plan

Lori E. Kniffin
University of North Carolina at Greensboro

Jeffrey Howard
DePaul University

The Service-Learning and Community Engagement Future Directions Project (SLCE-FDP) was launched in 2015. Since then approximately 40 individuals from a wide range of perspectives have come together as contributors of thought pieces that issue bold calls to guide the future of SLCE. In an essay accompanying the ten thought pieces in Fall 2015, Howard and Stanlick (2015) called for the "development and implementation of a U.S. national SLCE strategic plan" (p. 128). Their essay provides one answer to the question of how all of the ideas about the future of SLCE being assembled by the SLCE-FDP – and also being articulated in other publications over the last few years – can become more than individual thoughts, questions, and actions. In this essay we review the highlights of the call for a national plan and then share some of the responses to it as a basis for ongoing engagement with the proposal.

Howard and Stanlick (2015) have in mind "an intentional organizing effort broadly developed by multiple stakeholders . . . [to] move us beyond the current prevalence of independent, individuals efforts . . . to a more coherent nationwide collective endeavor" (p. 128). Although the SLCE movement has made strides in the last twenty years, it has primarily occurred at the individual level: individual students, individual faculty and staff, individual courses, individual programs and centers, individual institutions, individual community organizations, individual disciplinary associations, individual regional and national organizations. Howard and Stanlick wonder "what collaborations might evolve if there were a platform to which many SLCE stakeholders and entities could contribute their voices," and they offer the metaphor of a compass that "not only guides individuals . . . but also synergizes across all levels of organizations . . . and all stakeholders . . . for more lasting civic engagement that has greater impact on social justice" (p. 129).

Their rationale for a national plan for SLCE includes the sheer growth of the movement within higher education, the recent calls among many thought leaders for new ways to think about and implement SLCE, the innovation and synergy that a national conversation can engender, and the value of greater clarity regarding our ultimate purposes as a movement and how best to advance them. Their sense is that a national planning process is needed to leverage the bold calls for enhancing SLCE being gathered by the SLCE-FDP, providing "the impetus, the structure, and the focus to bring each of them into conversation with other visions and strategies within and beyond this project" (p. 129). Their essay acknowledges several challenges: that the "very idea of a national strategic plan is likely to be contested," that inevitably some voices will not be at the table, and that reaching consensus on either general directions of or specific elements in a national plan will be difficult (p. 130). It asks: "What is the critical mass needed to move forward collectively and how do we best maintain open-ended dialogue around contested ideas?" (p. 131). And it proposes as a first step the identification or creation of a coordinating entity: Could the planning process be driven by a national organizational leader or by a group of representatives from several national organizations and a variety of other stakeholders? However it is coordinated, the authors note, there will need to be a way to engage stakeholders, identify funding, facilitate conversations, and develop and disseminate a product.

Howard and Stanlick summarize their call as follows:

> Intended to support the flourishing of the work and its purposes across a wide range of contexts, such a large-scale strategic plan would, of necessity, be grounded in a sense of our ultimate vision(s), emerge from a set of broad goals, be accompanied by illustrative strategies, and point to indicators of positive change – all dynamic and co-created by the SLCE community as a whole . . . . We envision a multitude of opportunities for co-creation and collaboration – from conversations to white papers to a finalized strategic planning process. We urge you to become involved and join us. (pp. 130–131)

Building on the invitation to share ideas regarding a potential national plan issued in Howard and

Stanlick's essay, the SLCE-FDP has worked over the last year in a variety of venues to solicit responses to and invite ongoing thinking about the call for such a plan. To investigate interest and investment in the idea of a national plan and to begin gathering suggestions for how a planning process might proceed and what a plan might include, we have hosted in-person conversations, assembled recommendations and concerns from hundreds of individuals at conferences, and solicited the perspectives of national SLCE organizations. In the remainder of this essay, we summarize what we have heard to date; a third essay on the topic of a national plan for SLCE, forthcoming in the Spring 2017 Special Section of *MJCSL* dedicated to the SLCE-FDP, will provide analysis of the conversation to that point and offer substantive recommendations for subsequent action.

Perspectives from National SLCE Organizations

We invited leaders of national SLCE organizations to read Howard and Stanlick's (2015) essay (as well as the Introduction and Framing Essay for the SLCE-FDP, also published in the *Michigan Journal of Community Service Learning*, Fall 2015) and to respond on behalf of their organizations to a set of questions we sent them. Our questions addressed six issues:

(a) their overall reactions to the Howard and Stanlick essay;
(b) their suggestion(s) regarding the content to be included in a national plan for SLCE;
(c) their suggestion(s) regarding the process of developing a national plan for SLCE;
(d) their organization's potential involvement in developing a national plan for SLCE;
(e) their reactions to the proposed coordinating entity for the development of a national plan for SLCE and their organization's potential role with such an entity; and
(f) their view of the goals for the SLCE movement in the next two decades.

Five[1] organizations participated: Community-Campus Partnerships for Health (CCPH), Campus Compact, Imagining America, the International Association for Research on Service-Learning and Community Engagement (IARSLCE), and the International Partnership for Service-Learning (IPSL). While they are by no means a comprehensive set of national organizations, their responses offer some key thought leader perspectives regarding the idea of a national plan to guide the future of SLCE. These responses are summarized below by question, not linked specifically to the respondent organization and in no particular order within each question.

Overall Reactions to the Essay

None of the five organizations objected to the idea of a national plan for SLCE, although they did raise some questions and cautions regarding the timing and the process through which it might move forward. They also wanted to ensure that such a plan would honor the autonomy of each organization to pursue its respective mission. One organization, in the midst of its own planning process, suggested that we should "get everything that can be got out of the current effort before focusing on something else." Another expressed support for "the spirit of creating a national strategic plan for SLCE and much of what it advocates" but was "skeptical about the specific approach suggested"; that organization proposed instead that "we could begin a process to first create a statement of strategic intent, or to craft a shared agenda" as a step toward "achieving a living, generative framework from which to articulate a general direction to pursue and a few basic principles for how to get there." One response emphasized the importance of identifying the best community engagement work and cultivating it through an organizing model. One indicated that developing such a plan "offers opportunity for important self-scrutiny." Another organization's leadership fully supported examining current practices and gathering "stakeholders and thought leaders around the table to discuss our collective future" and also asked "How does one gather the (many) disparate voices that now operate largely in silos?"

Content Ideas for a National Plan

The leaders of all five organizations offered suggestions for topics to be addressed in a national plan for SLCE. One proposed that the plan focus on the faculty reward system, explain social justice and how to measure movement toward it, and address "ways of enhancing the permeability of academic-community borders at multiple levels" (e.g., "entry points for community members to study, teach, engage in collaborative research"). Another similarly shared multiple suggestions: intertwining SLCE with diversity, inclusion, and equity; developing scholars' "epistemic orientation around community engagement"; and focusing on trans-disciplinary and asset-based approaches to SLCE. One response indicated that a "comprehensive vision for engagement" includes approaching engagement "in an integrated way across teaching, research, and functional areas of the institution such as purchasing, real estate, development, human resources, financial aid, and admissions" and "integrating institutions into community ecosystems in ways that promote a more just, equitable, and sustainable democracy." Another cautioned against creating a perception that the content of any national plan developed has been predetermined, suggested returning to the work begun by Zlotkowski's focus on SLCE in the disciplines, and called for new research on how two trends in higher education – the rise of adjunct faculty and neoliberalism – may affect SLCE's future. One organization wanted to ensure that any national plan developed would emphasize the ethical underpinnings of SLCE; its response also questioned whether the academy should be the "de facto delivery model for ethical service-learning practices."

Process Ideas for a National Plan

The leaders of all five organizations offered suggestions for how the process of developing a national plan for SLCE might best proceed. One response indicated that any process would need to "support existing organizations pursuing complementary objectives." Two organizations did not explicitly answer this question, but process suggestions were embedded in their responses to other questions. One of them suggested producing "a roadmap and suggested milestones for the journey . . . in order to ensure accountability, mark progress, and make appropriate adjustments along the course"; articulating a "problem statement"; and developing a "conceptual framework for what such a plan might address, as well as a vision for how that plan might be articulated, disseminated, implemented and ultimately evaluated." The other noted the difficulty and importance of "identifying the many actors in service-learning and in inviting them to participate in a way that serves not only the field, but the communities we purport to serve" and emphasized the importance of "open dialogue." One organization suggested that a national planning process be considered as "a collective, movement-building activity, not only a strategic plan but a 'theory of change' – this could focus attention on the long-term outcomes and how to achieve those outcomes." Another response supported the idea of a coordinating entity but not the notion that it be composed of and led by representatives of existing SLCE organizations, proposing instead locating leadership of the planning effort in a cross-cutting body (specifically, the Academy of Engaged Scholars (ACES) serving as a convener and secretariat).

Potential Organization Involvement in Developing a National Plan

Responses from four of the five organizations indicated readiness to be involved in developing a national plan for SLCE; the fifth indicated not knowing what their role might be until after their organization's planning process is completed. One organization expressed the desire to be represented on a coordinating entity and indicated that it could "help conceptualize and guide the steps needed to develop and advance the plan." One indicated wanting to "remain in dialogue with the process as it unfolds." Another proposed being a "core association involved in this endeavor." Another indicated willingness to "commit resources to an open dialogue" around content areas that fit their mission (e.g., ethical underpinnings of SLCE).

Reactions to a Coordinating Entity and Organizational Role Therein

The responses to the idea of a coordinating entity to guide the development of a national plan varied from suggestions for specific organizations to take on the role to important considerations for the formation of such group, including who should be involved. One, as mentioned above, proposed a crosscutting body such as ACES to serve in a coordinating role. One organization leader noted that any new structure would require resources that "existing organizations have no surplus of." Another indicated that a coordinating entity "as a coordinating GROUP is required" because "this is too large a task for one organization and there is tremendous value in getting broad buy in through contributing to plan development and feeling ownership . . . result[ing] in a stronger plan . . . more likely to be used as a guide to change." Another suggested strongly that community members must be involved with a coordinating entity to avoid the process of developing a national plan being an "'about them, without them' exercise." One pointed to Campus Compact's 30th anniversary gathering as an example of providing space for many organizations to showcase their work – noted as an essential step in movement building – and wanted to see more opportunities to work across organizations to build a movement.

Goals for the SLCE Movement

The set of responses about goals for the next two decades of the SLCE movement is multifaceted. One organization noted that its answers to the preceding questions reflected the goals of SLCE (e.g., equitable resource distribution, social justice). One response indicated: "We need higher education collectively to reclaim its public purposes by organizing all of its activities in ways that maximize public goods." Another suggested the purpose is social justice and specified that "the goals must include statements related to reducing/eliminating racism and discrimination, building community capacity for advancing community-defined social justice goals, and redistribution of power to promote equity." Another organization saw SLCE as "representing more of a struggle for the soul of higher education, its potential for racial and social justice, its promise of addressing social and economic inequality, and the explicit recognition that this is a political struggle – for the distribution of resources, for power and authority, for institutional policies and structures"; it proposed "an alliance between diversity, inclusion, and equity, and student success, and community engagement" and highlighted as a goal "the emergence of community engagement as an explicit and critical alternative to neoliberal logic – and an alternative future for higher education that emphasizes its public and democratic aspirations and purpose." Another organization was reluctant to specify goals, given concerns about traditional strategic planning processes, but noted "We are very concerned about the growing schism between (a) neoliberal values that have infiltrated the SLCE movement and (b) the democratic values that encourage education for education sake as a means to promote critical-thinking, justice-minded, responsible citizens who are engaged with their communities."

Perspectives from Individuals and Other Organizations

In addition to gathering responses from national organizations about the idea of a national strategic plan to guide the future of SLCE, the SLCE-FDP also collected ideas from other organizations and individuals throughout the past year, primarily (although not exclusively) at conferences. In these sessions, we asked for feedback from potential stakeholders on both the process of creating a national plan and the content of such a plan. These discussions proved to be fruitful, with contributors candidly sharing opportunities, concerns, and critical feedback on the prospect of creating such a plan. Here we share a few preliminary themes emerging in each of these three areas, some of which overlap with the responses from the national SLCE organization leaders.

Overall, the feedback from individuals and organizations supported the development of a shared plan. Comments noted that this kind of plan is "timely and urgently needed" and that "it is clear that acting in unison on this topic would be of great benefit to the SLCE movement as it would be for any national movement." There was a broad base of interest to participate in the process, provide feedback, and in some cases take on an organizing role. Those who did not express full support of a shared plan mostly cautioned regarding timing and potential duplication of work (e.g., with Campus Compact's Campus Action Plans).

When asked to provide thoughts on a process for a national plan, the majority of the respondents provided feedback on the coordinating entity and method of a plan and the stakeholders/participants to be included. The following ideas about the coordination of a planning process were suggested:

Grassroots organizing methods
Neutral convener/facilitator
SLCE organizations, consortiums, or regional partnerships
SLCE-FDP independently
Third-party organization not tied to SLCE
Communities of practice around content areas

Echoing the emphasis on including a diverse range of stakeholders from the national organization leaders, specific ideas regarding who should be involved in the development of a national plan converged around the following:

Government (local to national)
SLCE community partners and other practitioners of SLCE in communities (e.g., non-profit agencies, non-government organizations, faith-based organizations)
All types of educational institutions (4-year institutions, community colleges, K-12)
Students, administrators (including chancellors and presidents), faculty, staff
People from underrepresented cultures and backgrounds
Diversity of disciplines

Feedback cautioned against assuming that a single individual can speak for an entire stakeholder group and also urged the use of technology to include those who cannot travel to conferences or other convenings.

A wide range of topics were proposed as potential content for a national SLCE plan. Specific suggestions for what such a plan should speak to included, for example: faculty salaries and compensation for community partners, the ethics of responsible engagement, relationships between SLCE and other fields or movements (e.g., civic education in K-12, Black Lives Matter), deconstructing academic-community borders and power structures, assessment, intercultural understanding, and working both within and across disciplines. Broader ideas for how to determine the content of a national plan included, for example: dream big but be realistic, provide examples and case studies, name the role of neoliberalism in higher education, push for better practice, incorporate contested ideas and values, list overarching goals for the movement, use language that works for all stakeholders, focus on social justice, and speak to the full range of where campuses and communities are in their journeys with SLCE.

Two opportunities for thinking about the possibility of a national plan for SLCE were somewhat in-depth and, in addition to highlighting some of the same issues noted above, generated questions and tension points for further consideration, a few of which follow. There was general agreement that the SLCE movement should better articulate shared ends or purposes that transcend individuals, programs, organizations, institutions, and national associations; but there was less consensus on whether those ends are already established (e.g., social justice as the ultimate goal of SLCE) or should emerge organically through ongoing conversation about what we do and do not share in terms of our sense of purpose. Several participants in these discussions noted that how we think about a national plan and whether and how we proceed to develop one depends on whether SLCE is a "field," a "movement," both, or something else entirely. Relatedly, the question arose of whether we ought to be envisioning the future of SLCE (whether as a field or a movement) or of the world more generally. Echoing some of the thinking of the national organization leaders, one issue identified by several participants concerned the danger of losing SLCE's radical nature; one example was the question of how, assuming a plan will likely speak to civic skills, that be done through a broad-based national conversation in ways that maintain a critical edge? Some pointed to the range of barriers to having a voice in a planning process as a significant challenge to the development of a vision and strategies that are truly shared; the SLCE-FDP itself was discussed in these terms, with some individuals suggesting it is too academic to be truly inclusive. Use of the term "strategic plan" was also questioned as the most appropriate representation of what it might mean to generate and document a strong sense of direction for SLCE and guidance on how we might move forward together. And the distinction between developing a plan that is "strategic" and one that is "tactical" in orientation arose – the suggestion being to try to achieve shared understanding, purpose, principles, and goals but not to try to reach consensus on specific methods.

As with the national organization leaders' responses to our questions, we recognize these ideas from individuals and other organizations about a potential national SLCE plan are not comprehensive. Although hundreds of people have provided process and content suggestions, they are by and large faculty and staff who participated in the conference sessions we facilitated this past year. Many more perspectives, especially from community members and students, are needed, as are more opportunities for in-depth discussion. The input we have gathered to date does, however, begin to suggest the variety of visions our SLCE colleagues across the U.S. hold for a national planning process and document. At the very least, we are beginning to build out a set of issues that will require careful consideration as this conversation proceeds.

Now What?

We take this full set of input – preliminary as it is – as support from the SLCE community to continue the conversation about and move forward on a national plan for SLCE. Certainly this past year's conversations have helped bring into focus some of the central challenges associated with conceptualizing, developing, and using such a plan. Questions remain about process, including timeline, coordination, and participants. Yet it seems to us that beginning to move forward in accordance with a few of the process suggestions we have received may be in order. Specific ideas around distributed leadership for the next phase of this process have emerged, for example in the form of organizations that have expressed interest in convening SLCE colleagues around particular aspects of the plan. Even though it is unclear where the funding – that clearly will be needed to facilitate a broad-based and in-depth series of discussions – will come from, we are hopeful that the past year has nurtured a sense of commitment to and investment in the idea sufficient to bring forward the needed resources.

The SLCE-FDP leadership team makes four commitments at this time: (a) to following up with several individual and organizational participants in the conversation to date in the hope of formalizing their roles as supporters of an ongoing process; (b) to facilitating several additional conversations in the coming months that will be designed to yield substantive and diverse input regarding the future of SLCE and how we might best move forward together to advance a shared vision and strategies; (c) to collaborating with new and continuing contributors to publish more thought pieces that call attention to particularly important future directions for SLCE; and (d) to produce an analysis of the ideas gathered by the SLCE-FDP as of 2017, two years after our launch, as a basis for determining the future of the project overall and of the proposal it has generated for a national plan.

Equally if not more important, however, is the question of what thought piece contributors, readers, and other SLCE colleagues on campuses and in communities will commit to regarding the development of a movement-wide vision for SLCE. To that end, we ask you as a member of the SLCE movement to consider the following questions and how you might engage with the project in order to envision that future together.

- Will you be part of building on past work that has brought us to this place of readiness and need for a collective focus on our future? If so, how?
- Will you comment on this essay on the SLCE-FDP website?
- Will you participate in virtual gatherings to continue the conversation about the process and content of a national plan?
- Will you be part of analyzing the first rounds of thought pieces and thereby helping ensure the ideas developed there will be brought forward and built on at the movement-level?
- Will you offer to convene in-person gatherings to advance work on a plan? To fund them? To fund the SLCE-FDP more generally so that it can continue to hold open what seems to be a useful space for national and international idea sharing?
- Will you bring the SLCE-FDP to your campus, community organization, or association and thereby make explicit to your colleagues the invitation to contribute their questions, ideas, and concerns to the conversation about the future of our work generally and a potential guiding plan in particular?
- Will you develop your own thought piece or blog post for the SLCE-FDP website in response to the call for a national plan and the conversation around it to date?

This is an open call to anyone and everyone involved in SLCE to (paraphrasing Alice Walker) create in the present the future we wish to see. What are your thoughts on a national plan? This process needs your input. In the spirit of the original proposal for a national strategic plan, we must think beyond our own individual and organizational contexts and reach out through dialogue and action across the SLCE community to continue to advance our movement with enhanced intentionality, integrity, and impact. Please join the conversation on www.slce-fdp.org or email us at slce.fdp@gmail.com.

Note

[1] Two other national organizations were invited to participate but declined.

References

Howard, J., & Stanlick, S. (2015). A call for a national strategic plan. *Michigan Journal of Community Service Learning*, 22(1), 128–132.

Authors

LORI E. KNIFFIN (lekniffi@uncg.edu) is a doctoral student in Cultural Foundations of Education and a graduate assistant at the Institute for Community and Economic Engagement at the University of North Carolina at Greensboro. Her scholarly interests include food justice, community dialogue, and democratic classrooms. She is the 2016–2017 SLCE Future Directions Project Fellow and the chair of the International Association for Research on Service-Learning and Community Engagement (IARSLCE) Graduate Student Network.

JEFFREY HOWARD (jhowar15@depaul.edu) is director of faculty development at DePaul's Steans Center for Community-based Service Learning where he conducts faculty workshops and consults on service-learning courses and getting community-engaged scholarship published. He is the founder and editor of the *Michigan Journal of Community Service Learning*.

Review Essay

Scholarship Redefined

Dick Cone and Susan Harris
University of Southern California

Publicly Engaged Scholars: Next-Generation Engagement and the Future of Higher Education
Margaret A. Post, Elaine Ward, Nicholas V. Longo, & John Saltmarsh (Eds.)
Sterling, VA: Stylus Publishing. 2016

Publicly Engaged Scholars emerges from the Next Generation Engagement Project, a collaboration between the New England Resource Center for Higher Education (NERCHE), the American Association of State Colleges and Universities (AASCU), and Imagining America (IA), and is "led by a group of recognized scholars and practitioners to develop and implement civic engagement initiatives aimed at the next generation of students, faculty, and scholars in higher education" (New England Resource Center for Higher Education, n.d.). The book's contributors include scholars from a wide range of disciplines committed to co-created knowledge, the transformative power of narrative and dialogue, and "higher education as a vehicle to increase equality and justice in society" (p. xx).

This book arrives at an important moment in the history of service-learning and community engagement (SLCE) in higher education. In many ways, efforts to integrate community engagement into the academy have been tremendously successful, evidenced by the upsurge in SLCE research and practice across a wide range of academic disciplines, and by the expansion of institutional support through, for example, the creation of service-learning centers on campuses and the promotion of national agendas for SLCE in higher education by such influential organizations as the Carnegie Foundation for the Advancement of Teaching and the American Association of Colleges & Universities. However, most of the work to date has been inwardly focused, examining the positive impact of the pedagogy on college students and calling for changes within the academy to support engaged scholarship; less attention has been paid to the nature and potential of campus-community partnerships, particularly the role and experience of "the community" in those partnerships.

The growing support for service-learning and engaged scholarship across the academy has led to many creative approaches to this work in the U.S. and abroad. Yet the building enthusiasm for and the rapid, outward expansion of the practice leave it vulnerable to "growing pains" and a certain shallowness. Indeed, critics have lodged complaints against the field for lacking depth and an intellectual core (Butin, 2011; Stewart & Webster, 2011). This is the context in which *Publicly Engaged Scholars* emerges, and the context it reflects and attempts to address.

The book's editors note in the introduction:

> The central argument of this book is that a new generation of scholars, educators, and practitioners is committed to the public purposes of higher education, but not committed to perpetuating the existing policies, structures, and practices that have delegitimized their epistemological and ontological position. (p. 2)

The volume pays overdue and significant attention to the "public" in publicly engaged scholarship, making a strong case for renewing higher education's commitment to addressing community concerns, particularly in the wake of neoliberal policies and the devolution of public responsibility to the private sector and to individuals. It argues for expanding notions of what counts as "scholarship," acknowledging the important contributions that community partners can and do make in knowledge production, and identifying the need for substantial changes in the academy to support engagement practices that address issues of working between the two cultures (the academy and the community) and incorporate multiple points of view.

Yet the vast majority of the book's 32 contributors are from within the academy. While arriving via varied pathways and playing diverse roles, they nevertheless reflect the field's emphasis on university perspectives over community ones – even when the former underscores the significance of the latter. The nearly two dozen individual narratives recounted by "next generation" scholars in Part Two of the book are compelling but particularly inward looking. While embedded in the context of higher education and cognizant of the challenges facing engaged scholars in this context, the narratives are not well connected to the broader historical or conceptual contexts of SLCE – macro-level contexts detailed separately in other chapters, but without an explicit connection to these micro-level accounts. The incredible range of scholarship presented in the book is both a strength and a weakness, as well. It reflects the current breadth of the field while also contributing to an overall lack of clarity about what, exactly, is the work of publicly engaged scholars.

Despite these issues – or perhaps because of them – *Publicly Engaged Scholars* is a very timely book and a worthwhile read. It reflects the work of a current generation of scholars and the work that still remains to advance engaged scholarship's place in the academy.

In this review essay we present a brief overview of the contents of each chapter, followed by a critique of the book as a whole.

The Book's Chapters

In the opening chapter, the book's four editors identify a "Collaborative Engagement Paradigm" embraced by next-generation scholars as a means for "the reclaiming of higher education's public good" (p. 3). The paradigm embraces: (a) scholar-practitioners who connect higher education campuses with problem-solving taking place in communities; (b) increased participation by historically underrepresented groups; (c) a demand for "new modes of scholarship and teaching" (p. 4); (d) scholars who have emerged from undergraduate and graduate experiences in public scholarship and expect to continue in that vein; (e) an orientation to public engagement with respect for the expertise and experiences of all contributors, and (f) a desire to promote an inclusive, deliberative democracy.

In the second chapter, Saltmarsh and Hartley track the history of public scholarship as it was affected by "pure science," findings in cognitive studies, the relationship of the university and society, the period of civic disengagement, demands for social justice, and neoliberalism. It is an enormous undertaking in just nine pages. The chapter closes with a discussion of the "public engagement knowledge regime," in which it is considered to be "in the best interest of the campus's knowledge, learning, and democracy-building mission to be engaged deeply in the education, health, housing, employment, and overall well-being of the local community" (p. 29).

Chapter 3 continues with Hartley and Saltmarsh describing the history of civic engagement in American higher education with a focus on efforts to reclaim the civic mission in the 1980s, especially through a host of organizations (COOL, Campus Compact, ISAS, CNCS, COPC, etc.), national reports and conferences, funded projects, and publications. The clear focus of these efforts centers around service-learning. The chapter closes with a call for greater involvement of scholars who are personally involved in civic life.

Next, Longo and Gibson describe the landscape of teaching and learning in higher education, defining terms ("co-created knowledge," "deliberative pedagogy," "democratic education," "cognitive justice," etc.) and demonstrating their interplay in collaborative engagement. The chapter concludes by describing how this approach is critical to the future research and teaching missions of higher education in that the well-being of institutions are interwoven with the well-being of their communities.

In Chapter 5, Jacquez, Ward, and Goguen tackle the challenge of describing how engaged research is affecting institutional change, comparing the characteristics of "traditional academic research" and a "collaborative engagement paradigm." They present a useful table comparing the differences along with four narratives that demonstrate how different young scholars integrate traditional and collaborative research methods.

While Chapter 5 is full of hope and promise, Chapter 6 exposes challenges to the "legitimacy, agency and equality" (p. 97) of engaged scholarship and the cumulative, deleterious effects on the careers of engaged scholars. Author KerryAnn O'Meara examines the role of faculty hierarchies, publication priorities, tenure, promotion ladders, mentoring, and reward structures. She holds that there is an interplay between these factors and an over-representation of persons of color, women, and first-generation scholars engaged in public scholarship and, as a result, it is they who are most negatively affected by the current climate of the academy. The author closes the chapter with some possible steps forward in addressing the challenges, such as developing community-driven research priorities that emphasize democratic decision-making and the co-creation of knowledge.

Part Two of the book (Chapters 7–12) includes narratives by twenty-two "next generation" scholars describing the distinct pathways leading them to publicly engaged scholarship. Chapter 7 focuses on scholars' difficulty bringing their personal and professional lives into alignment. In this chapter, Janke, Miller, Post, and Ward discuss what it means to be a "boundary spanner" (scholar-administrator-community advocate for social justice), the disconnect between the categories of problems in the world and the way that higher education is organized by disciplines, the different "languages" used in communities and in academia, and the need for collaboration to understand and marshal against the existing academic culture and traditional conceptualizations of scholarship.

Chapter 8 details what is involved in developing a "community-engaged scholarly identity." Beck, Bush, Holguin, Morgan, and Orphan offer their individual as well as their collective struggles to identify and share pathways to engaged scholarship. They discuss the role of undergraduate experiences, community building, sharing stories, selecting graduate programs and mentors, and finding "pressure points and cracks" that offer a greater opportunity for a new paradigm of scholarship. A number of the authors discuss the added challenges inherent in being a first-generation scholar of color.

This theme continues in Chapter 9 as Green, Harrison, Jones, and Shaffer set forth their views about how their work and experiences challenge the "dominant narratives of higher education" that reinforce the belief that "scholarship" is to foster "basic research, intellectual tradition and education" and the "cult of the expert" (p. 142). They take pride in working across disciplines, within communities, and embracing both practitioner and scholar roles. They hold that an administrator within higher education can be legitimately considered a scholar and partner with members of the community in that scholarship. However, they admit that staff members (and non-tenured faculty) do not enjoy the academic freedom and contractual security of tenured faculty and call for "established criteria for evaluation specific to community-engaged scholar-practitioners" (p. 151).

In Chapter 10, Hartman, Sanchez, Shakya, and Whitney present four narratives describing how young scholars have attempted to navigate the difficult and challenging terrain of living in two worlds – campus and community – and how a focus on the research needs of the community can contribute to solutions to local issues. They describe how their work leads them to collaborative approaches that seek the expertise and knowledge of community partners, the need to be guided by a sense of justice rather than the norms of the academy, and to engage in a "collaborative, participatory . . . reflective process . . . reciprocal dialogue and mutual education" (p. 163). Their work has a democratic orientation with full participation, sharing of knowledge and expertise, and full and open access to results. Along the way, a sense of community develops. They hold that their approach presents a "moral imperative for faculty members and students" (p. 166).

The route to engaged scholarship as experienced by Anderson-Nathe, Jacquez, Kerns-Wetherington, and Mitchell in Chapter 11 is portrayed as a series of "fortunate accidents" and "winding pathways." The brief biographies of the four scholars describe their journeys toward "engaged scholarship," which were seldom well-planned but guided by a passion to follow their personal sense of justice and authenticity.

The final chapter in Part Two, Chapter 12 by Ward and Miller, attempts to summarize the themes emerging from the 22 narratives and provides a good overview for those eager to take away the lessons of Part Two, and include: (a) navigating the tensions, (b) spanning boundaries, (c) altering the legitimacy of expertise, (d) marginalization and validation, (e) implications for higher education, (f) implications for future community-engaged scholars, and (g) reclaiming higher education's larger public purpose.

The final section of the book, Part Three, looks ahead to the future of engagement, beginning with Chapter 13, which advocates for engaging students as colleagues (Longo, Keisa, & Battistoni). The authors describe the role of service-learning on students' civic engagement and weigh the negative and positive effects of institutionalizing service-learning. They document a new approach to student involvement in which students see their "work in communities . . . not as an alternative to politics but rather as 'alternative politics'" (p. 201).

The authors also discuss the need for students (and presumably engaged scholars) to work with community partners over considerable time to foster "civic knowledge, skills, and dispositions" (p. 203). Further, the commitment to community must be embedded in higher education institutions and be reflected in such structures as faculty recognition and rewards.

Perhaps most critical, the authors maintain that if institutions wish to promote civically engaged students, they must put students at the center of those efforts and honor student voice. Despite the fact that students are transient and community partnerships should be sustained, the authors suggest that students must play critical leadership roles.

Chapter 14, by Orphan and O'Meara, outlines the historic creep of neoliberalism on post-secondary campuses, shifting the financial burden for higher education from the public sphere to students. A preoccupation with the economic value of a college degree has led to the common perception that the institution exists to serve the individual and the economy rather than society and a learned citizenry. The authors suggest several steps that educational institutions could take that would make them more supportive of public engagement and create more obvious pathways for scholars to serve public needs. For example, they argue that academic departments should provide financial resources, mentoring, coursework, and "ideological support" to encourage engaged scholarship among graduate students.

In Chapter 15, White outlines efforts at Cleveland State University to fully embrace a public mission, presumably as a model for other institutions to emulate.

Critique

If you want to know what is right and wrong with *Publicly Engaged Scholars* – and with the field itself – read the Afterword. Peter Levine summarizes the strengths of the book with this passage:

> I concur with the brilliant historical chapters, which capture my personal memories of those times but put what I experienced and observed in a broader context. I find the personal narratives inspiring. And the strategies proposed in part three strike me as the right ones. (p. 249)

As individuals who have been deeply involved in attempting to foster high quality service-learning at a Research 1 campus for several decades, we too understand and appreciate the contributions of the Next Generation Engagement Project. *Publicly Engaged Scholars* offers a richly detailed account of the challenges scholars currently face in attempting to establish a new, more publicly-oriented research and teaching paradigm. We embrace their goal to engage in deliberative practices with students, community members, and colleagues, and salute their commitment to an engaging writing style that values personal narratives and lends itself to public consumption. And we can testify to all of the obstacles cited by the contributing authors, from altering the norms of the academy to affecting change in the educational/research paradigm that prevails on most post-secondary campuses.

We would have liked to have learned more about the actual scholarship of next-generation scholars. The narratives in Part Two focus more on describing the personal pathways to engagement, with less attention to current research questions, methodological approaches, and relevant findings. This may be intentional, given the title of the book, which suggests that it is more about the individual scholars themselves than the content of their scholarship.

It is unclear how the narratives truly mark a generational shift in the work being done across the country. They echo, yet do not acknowledge, the voices of earlier critics of higher education who have tried to make colleges and universities more responsive to public agendas. While Chapter 2 by Saltmarsh and Hartley offers an overview of the history of public scholarship and engagement, it focuses primarily on large convenings of stakeholders, declarations by national associations, and scholarly works that describe trends. However, the chapter overlooks the work of a number of grassroots "pioneers" who built upon the actions of students in the '60s and '70s (e.g., the civil rights, anti-war, and free speech movements) to link classroom education to problems in the world by creating service-learning programs and building bridges between campuses and local communities (Stanton, Giles, & Cruz, 1999). The chapter also might have included an historical overview of the civic mission of graduate education (Stanton & Wagner, 2006).

Without this history, the book neglects already-tested models and experiences, leaving next-generation scholars susceptible to repeating the same or similar mistakes while also depriving them of a fairly well-worn path. In addition, the book describes a compelling yet utopian vision of what the university "should" become without a clear set of strategies for achieving these goals.

Returning to the Afterward, Levine uses his few pages in the book to deftly explore the logical problems inherent in various approaches to thinking about the causes of and solutions to social problems – i.e., problems of discourse and collective action. These are thorny, theoretical problems that are, for the most part, unexplored in the volume, save Levine's contribution and a few key questions posed by Hartman. Levine's thoughtful and thought-provoking commentary serves less to summarize the text than to subtly point out its flaws – flaws that are, as he notes, pervasive in the field. He writes:

> This book has a generational focus and looks to younger scholars for new models and solutions. Those scholars will (and should) base many of their ideas on personal experience and identity. Their relatively diverse background and their relatively deep experience with engagement are assets. Yet I would also look to the next generation for groundbreaking theory, some of it highly abstract and challenging. The theories that are already embedded in their narratives must emerge; they may also need to develop new theoretical insights. We need theories not only about civic engagement but also about how society works and what causes it to

change for the better. Almost every successful social movement I can think of has developed new bodies of such theory. The theories of gender that accompanied second-wave feminism or the range of theological and political philosophies that emerged because of the civil rights movement are essential historical examples. I would expect nothing less from the next generation of engagement. (p. 256)

With this passage, Levine pinpoints a core problem in the text: the absence of a clear, underlying framework for understanding "public scholarship" that ties together the entire volume. Part of this conceptual challenge is related to language. Far too many terms are introduced and used almost interchangeably, including public engagement, public engagement knowledge regime, collaborative engagement, public scholar(ship), engaged scholarship, next generation scholarship/engagement, civic engagement, community engagement, and democratic engagement. Very likely this is due to the wide range of disciplines in which the contributors were trained. This is an editing challenge; the editors of the book could have done more to create a clear storyline that weaves through the various chapters. But it is also, as Levine suggests, a challenge facing the field. Although contributions to public scholarship, service-learning, and civic engagement have grown tremendously in the last 40+ years, the "movement" still lacks a unified core; the book – and the field – still needs to articulate a foundational disciplinary framework (Butin, 2011). *Publicly Engaged Scholars* offers many important insights about the pathways to public scholarship and the challenges such scholars face, but it fails to offer a clear, coherent strategy for the field moving forward.

The problem with not having a clear framework is perhaps most evident in the chapter describing Cleveland State University's successes in promoting publicly engaged scholarship at the institutional level. While the book provides a robust critique of the market-driven, neoliberal policies that are driving higher education, ironically it concludes by presenting a "model" university whose practices reflect exactly that: a top-down, administrator-led, corporate-structured initiative driven by market forces with minimal input from faculty and even less from students or the community. This is not meant to be a criticism of the work at Cleveland State University but rather a commentary on the disconnect between this chapter and most of the arguments that precede it. White's account demonstrates how universities can make significant, positive impacts even while conforming to the very things this book criticizes about higher education.

Perhaps, at this juncture, it makes sense to focus on what works – clear strategies implementable in the current climate and that can move the field, however incrementally, toward larger and truly transformative goals. Nevertheless, we need to do a better job of unearthing "the theories that are already embedded in [our] narratives" (p. 256).

Some might argue, appropriately so, that certain sectors of the field are overburdened by theory. In fact, the writing in some disciplines is highly abstract and theorized to the point of not being connected to the messiness of actual experience. We must think more carefully about how to theorize this work, building on the past without being shackled by it, and fundamentally connect theory to practices.

In short, while the book lacks an adequate theoretical and historical foundation, its overall argument about next-generation engagement and the future of higher education is a compelling and important one. The authors' inclusivity and demonstrated capacity to learn from one another, as well as the fresh, optimistic, "bring on the world" attitude that permeates the book, gives us hope. Indeed, the authors have tapped into a moral imperative that drives a deep commitment to publicly engaged scholarship that benefits communities and students; this next generation of engaged scholars may very well transform the culture of higher education.

The proverb, "We make the road by walking," inspired many of the experiential educators and service-learning practitioners who pioneered the current civic engagement movement (Bell, Gaventa, & Peters, 1990). May this motto provide a similarly fruitful path for the next generation of publicly engaged scholars.

References:

Bell, B., Gaventa, J., & Peters, J. (Eds.). 1990. We make the road by walking: Conversations on education and social change: Myles Horton and Paulo Freire. Philadelphia: Temple University Press.

Butin, D. 2011. Service-learning as an intellectual movement: The need for an "academic home" and critique for the community engagement movement. In T. Stewart & N. Webster (Eds.), Problematizing service-learning: Critical reflections for development and action (pp. 19–35). Charlotte, NC: Information Age Publishing.

New England Resource Center for Higher Education (NERCHE). (n.d.) Next Generation Engagement Project. Retrieved from http://nerche.org/index.php?option=com_content&view=article&id=355&Itemid=96

Stanton, T. K., Giles, D. E., & Cruz, N. I. (1999). Service-learning: A movement's pioneers reflect on its origins, practice, and future. San Francisco: Jossey-Bass.

Stanton, T. K., & Wagner, J. (2006/2010). Educating for democratic citizenship: Antecedents, prospects, and models for renewing the civic mission of graduate education at research universities. In H. E. Fitzgerald, C. Burack, & S. D. Seifer (Eds.), Handbook of engaged scholarship: Contemporary landscapes, future directions. (Vol. 1, pp. 411–436). East Lansing, MI: Michigan State University Press.

Stewart, T., & Webster, N. (Eds.) (2001). Problematizing service-learning: Critical reflections for development and action. Charlotte, NC: Information Age Publishing Inc.

Authors

DICK CONE (cone@usc.edu) is the retired director of the Joint Educational Project at the University of Southern California.

SUSAN C. HARRIS (scharris@usc.edu) is the associate director for Research and Academic Affairs at the Joint Educational Project at the University of Southern California.

Review Essay

The Confluence of Rivers

Lane Graves Perry, III
Western Carolina University

Service-Learning and Social Entrepreneurship: A Pedagogy of Social Change
Sandra Enos
New York: Palgrave Macmillan, 2015

Introducing the Rivers: Service-Learning and Social Entrepreneurship

Sandra Enos is a cartographer. Not in the practical sense of charting geological phenomena, topographies, or local transportation routes, but in the metaphorical sense. She seeks to create a map. Not necessarily with lines, colors, or scales, but with her words and a synthesis of the fields of service-learning and social entrepreneurship. The map she crafts in the book, *Service-Learning and Social Entrepreneurship: A Pedagogy of Social Change*, provides a historical context, a lay of the land, and an organizing theme for how we in higher education can "reconsider our [engagement] work on campus and to connect to broader and deeper purposes . . . [with] service-learning and social entrepreneurship" (p. 84). While these two are currently overlapping in practice (for example, see Ashoka U, DukeEngage, Ripple Effect Learning Community at Western Carolina University, etc.), empirical research into the relationship, or perhaps partnership, of service-learning and social entrepreneurship is limited. Enos notes that in 2013 a review of research focused on this relationship resulted in fewer than a dozen articles. Clearly there is much more to be known about and explored through the rich soil and fertile valley that lies between these two rivers.

In geography, two rivers meeting is a confluence. One particular conflux gaining recent attention has resulted from two rivers of work that seek to align an institution's mission and resources through community engagement (service-learning) and social innovation (social entrepreneurship). To not recognize the parallels of these rivers of work would be a missed opportunity to better understand the complementary frameworks currently used to navigate the engaged learning practices applied in these "social change spaces." Particularly relevant is Dee's (2001) conceptualization of social entrepreneurs as social sector change agents who develop a mission to create and sustain social value, pursue new opportunities to serve the mission, engage in a process of adaptation and learning, solve and think beyond resources, and exhibit high accountability to constituencies served and outcomes created. Core to Enos's argument is that despite their common spaces,

> there has been surprisingly little conversation, notice, or reflection on the work of the other from each field . . . [Enos] argues that these fields have much to offer to each other and that expanding definitions and ways of considering this work should characterize a next generation of community engagement. (p. 3)

She goes on to say, that "working together in a more collaborative, educational, and community[-focused] agenda holds great promise for community engagement that is deep, inclusive, and cares about impact on students, faculty, institutions, and community" (p. 1).

The book's primary goals are (a) to analyze the history and current status of service-learning and social entrepreneurship as both pedagogy and disciplines within higher education; (b) to identify the gap in empirical and conceptual research so as to better understand the relationship between service-learning and social entrepreneurship; (c) to offer numerous tributaries (in the form of research questions) to be explored; and (d) to propose strategies to advance an agenda that educates students deeply and broadly for active citizenship.

Charting the Rivers: Exploring each Chapter

The considerable thought and intentionality around the structure of the book directly addresses the context, key concerns, opportunities, and strategic practices associated with service-learning and social entrepreneurship. The four chapters that guide the reader through the author's thinking include: The Landscape of Social Change Education, Organizing for Engagement, Challenges for Service-Learning and Social Entrepreneurship, and Educating for Engagement: A Turning Point. Each chapter will be discussed in order to provide the reader with a sense of the written map Enos has charted.

Chapter 1, The Landscape of Social Change Education, frames the approaches of service-learning and social entrepreneurship within American higher education. This lay of the land chapter brings together and synthesizes a thorough review of social change and civic learning literature from relevant seminal works from the Carnegie Foundation for the Advancement of Teaching (Boyer, 1990; Colby, Beaumont, Ehrlich, & Corngold, 2007), the Association of American Colleges & Universities (AAC&U, 2012), and the National Civic Learning & Democratic Engagement Network (AAC&U, n.d.), which together serve as the compass guiding higher education to our true north – "greater engagement with the community by aligning [our] resources with community needs" (p. 2) and to "advance civic learning and democratic engagement as an essential cornerstone for each student . . . [and] to build a national agenda that will move civic learning from the periphery to the center of student learning" (p. 3).

A clear theme introduced in Chapter 1 and referenced in every chapter is the juxtaposition between the respective birthplaces and families into which social entrepreneurship and service-learning were born.

> They are like siblings, separated at birth, raised by two different sets of parents. You can see similarities in the source code and the ultimate purpose and goal of bettering humanity, but their respective environments shaped them in different ways. (Dostilio & Perry, in press)

Enos presents an important observation illuminated and discussed numerous times throughout the text. "Social entrepreneurship's roots are in the real world," (p. 53) and as it grew it matriculated into the university environment, whereas service-learning was born and developed in the academy, essentially on campus, and then migrated into the real world. Perhaps this is why an early service-learning book addressed the question, *Where's the Learning in Service-Learning?* (Eyler & Giles, 1999) and only after this question was asked and thoroughly answered, did researchers ask the question, *Where's the Community in Service-Learning Research?* (Cruz & Giles, 2000). This is not an inherent flaw of the service-learning field, but it is indicative of the field's early focus. Compare this to social entrepreneurship, which, over the years, has been primarily focused on impacts, results, and outcomes specifically within communities by addressing community challenges from the ground level. The Ashoka Fellows program is a prime example of this community practice focus. Since 1982 over 3,000 social entrepreneurs in 70 nations have been identified and supported as Ashoka Fellows – individuals identified locally, vetted locally, and tested locally to generate systemic local (and beyond) social change. Selection criteria for an Ashoka Fellow respect the individual and their history, the social change idea, and the positive social impact potential.

Chapter 1 ends with a comprehensively informative table comparing service-learning and social entrepreneurship on 18 different dimensions of practice, such as mission, language used, focus, central teaching goals, journals, and research organizations.

Chapter 2 offers the newest contribution to understanding the practical implications associated with the confluence of service-learning and social entrepreneurship. Giving insight into how ten current higher education examples of service-learning and social entrepreneurship are organized institutionally, Enos identifies, investigates, and offers transferable considerations for campuses navigating either or both spaces. An introduction into the process of institutionalization within higher education demonstrates the relationship that exists between service-learning and social entrepreneurship. Juxtaposing the growth of service-learning and institutionalization measures with the current status of institutionalizing social entrepreneurship education on these campuses illuminates a related pattern of cloth from which both have been cut. Salient here is the guidance that while "service-learning and civic engagement movements . . . play a critical role in helping advance social innovation education . . . it is essential that we distinguish the purpose, boundaries, and desired outcomes of each" (Ashoka U, 2014, p. 25).

Enos identifies "observable patterns in the organization of these programs . . . [the] disciplinary homes for service-learning and social entrepreneurship . . . how institutions frame engagement and how programs that offer service-learning and social entrepreneurship are related to each other" (p. 27). Enos researched the 10 institutions receiving both the Carnegie Community Engagement Classification and the Ashoka U designation. All 10 are members of state or regional Campus Compact organizations and also have received the Corporation on National and Community Service President's Higher Education Community Service Honor Roll. These 10 institutions are highly decorated, intensively engaged, and represent a range of institutional types and undergraduate populations.

Enos's findings derive from her analysis of semistructured interviews and campus artifacts (e.g., web page content, resources, etc.) from each of the 10 participant institutions. The eight key observations from the analysis primarily illuminated the "critical differences among the ten campuses" (p. 32), and ultimately what emerged were "individual profiles, tied to institutional size, history, culture, and leadership" (p. 33). The eight key observations include curricular and co-curricular engagement; institutionalization and program building; centralization and decentralization; size, complexity, and cohesion; centers for support and faculty ownership; language and definitions; centrality and marginality; and disciplines and schools. Considering the critical differences across the 10 institutions, perhaps the reader would have gained more insight into how service-learning and social entrepreneurship are organized on each campus through individual case studies on each institution. Enos pushes in this direction with a table that presents models of service-learning and social entrepreneurship education, but the reader may have been better informed about each of the eight key observations if they would have been used as a framework for crafting a robust case study of each institution. This would have been a large undertaking, but by doing so much more that could have been conveyed in this chapter. While a valuable extension and progression of knowledge was offered in this chapter, Enos acknowledges the limitations of the research. While the emergent themes (or observations) from unitized and categorized qualitative data are organic, emic, and therefore not considered *a priori*, the vehicle selected to articulate those findings is the choice of the researcher. In this, case studies would have provided a more robust and thorough articulation of the emergent themes.

Chapter 3, Challenges for Service-Learning and Social Entrepreneurship, discusses the unintended consequences associated with institutionalization, scalability, and the myriad definitions and articulations of service-learning and social entrepreneurship. Balancing the numerous definitions, interpretations, and applications with the goal to bring the proclaimed "pedagogy of social change" from the margins to the core of an institution, service-learning and social entrepreneurship must avoid the pitfall of becoming too focused on transactions and bean counting versus transformation and seed planting. This chapter focuses primarily on the complex arguments and critiques of service-learning and social entrepreneurship, suggesting that both pedagogies suffer from similar challenges, including the development of "better practices in community partnerships, assessing impact on students, faculty, institutions, and community, and extending definitions of engagement" (p. 43).

Enos illuminates and synthesizes four challenges with service-learning which are deeply rooted in a rich, but complex soil. First, she identifies service-learning's diverted history from being a tool of civic skills to a tool employed to teach disciplinary content (Saltmarsh, 2005), resulting in service-learning missing its civic gold standard. This seems to be associated with the perception that service-learning, as democratic engagement, is a Trojan horse of progressive politics and a liberal agenda. Second, she notes the tensions between those who serve and those who are being served that leads to sustained structural or systemic imbalances in power and privilege. Davis (2006) suggested that the reluctance to address these inequalities is a key reason why we do not talk about service and leads to an approach that perceives service is simple when in fact it is quite complex. Third, she describes a bend in the arc away from social justice or social change that is focused on transformative community building and a bend toward transaction-based nonprofit organization assistance. This is well articulated in the research of Korgen, White, and White (2011), Mitchell (2008), Lewis (2004), and Daigre (2000) through the juxtaposition between critical and traditional service-learning. And fourth, she suggests a too intensive focus on the goals of "transformation of the academy and changing the world" that has led to a failure to adopt the most traditional strengths of the academy (e.g., being a critical conscious producer and arbiter of knowledge). Enos echoes Jacoby's (2015) argument that to progress and maintain relevance, service-learning "must open itself up to constant and critical re-examination of the field's basic principles and practices. Failure to critically reflect on the aims, the claims, and the work of service-learning violates the core concepts of the field" (p. 53).

Similarly, social entrepreneurship and social entrepreneurship education are not without their own critics and critiques. The first comes with the two different codified approaches to social entrepreneurship: social enterprise and social innovation. Social enterprise is primarily concerned with supporting a socially infused mission through the generation of earned income (e.g., TOMS, BANGS, Warby Parker), while social innovation strives to develop new approaches to meet social needs (e.g., Modern Postal System, KIVA, Sistemas de Tecnologia Agro-electro). Many researchers call for a blurring of the lines or a bridging between these two approaches. The way to do this, according to Dees and Anderson (2006), is to be focused expressly on "social impact, using a combination of philanthropic and business perspectives" (cited in Enos, p. 54). This process, the blurring of boundaries between sectors, can lead to new ideas and educational opportunities vis-à-vis current community challenges.

Another divergent path comes with the critique comparing social entrepreneurship with other tools for change. Enos reviews Light's (2011) book (in the fall 2014 *Michigan Journal*) succinctly articulating the argument between social entrepreneurship, writ large, being *the model* of social change rather than *a component* of social change. Enos extends the idea that social entrepreneurship is *a* component of social change by discussing the complementary roles of social safekeepers, social explorers, and social advocates. Together, this cadre of social agents is in a position to tend the gardens of social change, development, and transformation. This extension and refinement of social entrepreneurship points to the assumption that "not every social problem requires a social entrepreneurial approach" (p. 58) and suggests that through the expertise of all four of these social change agents a broader, more impactful approach to social change can be developed.

Chapter 3 ends with a strong explication of the critiques of social entrepreneurship education and aligns the similar challenges associated with the teaching of service-learning and social entrepreneurship. Ultimately, this chapter frames and contextualizes a thick, complex challenge. Just when the reader is wondering where to go next, Enos suggests a modest proposal in Chapter 4.

Chapter 4, Educating for Engagement: A Turning Point, proposes four strategies to integrate service-learning and social entrepreneurship. These strategies are:

> ... organizing frames that fit campus culture and type and allow for a broader view of engagement while also incorporating frameworks to develop principles of engagement, the development of community engagement toolboxes, the exchange of best practices from both service-learning and social entrepreneurship, the development of learning goals that span several streams of community engagement. (p. 66)

The first strategy offers clearly defined frameworks to advance active citizenship, including a call to organize (a) around the public and civic purpose of higher education (e.g., *A Crucible Moment*, AAC&U), (b) for engaged learning (e.g., High Impact Practices, Kuh, 2008), and (c) around collective impact (Klein, 2011) and community focus (Cruz & Giles, 2000) . These frames serve as a resource for preparing the next generation of service-learners, social entrepreneurs, and social change agents to "translate careful thought into effective action" (Freeland, 2009, cited in Enos, p. 69). This particular proposition captures two imperatives of social change: first, a commitment to "careful thought," which includes the elements of civic learning identified in *A Crucible Moment* (knowledge, skills, values, and collective action), and second, an investment in "effective action," which includes approaches that center on collective community. The translation of careful thought into effective action is possible if college students are able to carefully and confidently work across borders, beliefs, communities, and systems to develop a common agenda, manage resources and teams responsibly, and manage and measure that agenda through to fruition.

The second strategy suggests a variety of tools that address social problems (e.g., Pathways to Public Service, Social Change Wheel, and the Community Engagement Toolbox). At their core, service-learning and social entrepreneurship are about empathic, reciprocal, and effective social change with an explicit emphasis on problem solving, and without effective problem solving, they are at best a hollow teaching approach and a failed venture, respectively. The third strategy, described in seven pages, represents a microcosm of the whole book. This strategy calls for an exchange of the best resources and perspectives from service-learning and social entrepreneurship in order to meet unmet social needs, positively contribute to communities, and add value to engaged partnerships, projects, and people. Finally, the fourth strategy reminds the reader that it is imperative that this work is organized around student learning goals. There is a sense of urgency that manifests in this brief section, and serves as a reminder that the work of higher education institutions is essential to develop a critical yet appreciative, civically yet civil, and personally-tuned yet community-focused democratic constituency.

Concluding Thoughts

Enos's book maps the spaces of social change pedagogies. Without her investigation and problematizing, as a field we could not come to collectively know it as well as we do now. In my opinion, few research books enable the reader to begin to strategically apply the contents while reading, as this book ably does. This text is for those who have been waiting to connect service-learning and social entrepreneurship. The urgency in this book is palpable, the timeliness is spot-on, and its applicability is quite literally at the reader's fingertips. Whether a person is entering into this space for the first time, has experience navigating these uncharted waters, is a practitioner looking to develop a better program, or a researcher investigating these pedagogies, this book will serve as the cornerstone for moving forward. The level of synthesis across the sections provides the breadth necessary of a primer and the depth demanded to serve as the clarion call to further explore the timely, complex, and provocative questions we in the service-learning and social entrepreneurship fields must address.

Without further investigation into and a strong application of these pedagogies of social change, the promise of bringing together service-learning and social entrepreneurship will remain unmet. But if these two rivers begin to join, the promise of which Enos has so capably helped us to see, we can harness the strengths of both to become a mighty force for community change and student learning.

References

Ashoka U (2014). *Trends in social innovation education.* Arlington, VA: Ashoka U.

Association of American Colleges & Universities (2012). *A crucible moment: College learning and democracy's future.* Washington, DC: AAC&U.

Association of American Colleges & Universities (n.d.). *Civic engagement value rubrics.* Washington, DC: AAC&U.

Boyer, E. L. (1990). *Scholarship reconsidered: Priorities of the professoriate.* Carnegie Foundation for the Advancement of Teaching.

Colby, A., Beaumont, E., Ehrlich, T., & Corngold, J. (2007). *Educating for democracy: Preparing undergraduates for responsible political engagement.* San Francisco: Jossey-Bass.

Cruz, N. I. & Giles, D. E. (2000). Where's the community in service-learning research? *Michigan Journal of Community Service Learning,* Special Issue (January), 28–24.

Davis, A. (2006). What we don't talk about when we don't talk about service. In E. Lynn & Davis A. (Eds.), *The civically engaged reader: A diverse collection of short provocative readings on civic activity* (pp. 148–154). Chicago: Great Books Foundation.

Dees, J. G. (2001). The meaning of "social entrepreneurship". Retrieved from https://centers.fuqua.duke.edu/case/wp-content/uploads/sites/7/2015/03/Article_Dees_MeaningofSocialEntrepreneurship_2001.pdf

Daigre, E. (2000). Toward a critical service-learning pedagogy: A Freirean approach to civic literacy. *Academic Exchange, 4*(4), 6–14.

Dostilio, L. D. & Perry, L. G. (*in press*). An explanation of community engagement professionals as professionals and leaders. In L.D. Dostilio (Ed.), *The community engagement professional in higher education: A competency model for an emerging field.* Virginia: Stylus.

Enos, S. (2014). What's all this I hear about social entrepreneurship? [Review of the book *Driving Social Change: How to solve the world's toughest problems*]. *Michigan Journal of Community Service Learning, 21*(1), 91–97.

Eyler, J. & Giles, D. E. (1999). *Where's the learning in service-learning?* San Francisco: Jossey-Bass.

Freeland, R. M. (2009). Liberal education and effective practice: The necessary revolution in undergraduate education. *Liberal Education, 95*(4), 6–13.

Jacoby, B. (2015). Facing the unsettled questions about service-learning. In J.R. Strait & M. Lima (Eds.), *The future of service-learning* (pp. 90–105). Sterling, VA: Stylus Publishing.

Korgen, K. O., White, J. M., & White, S. K. (2011). *Sociologists in action: Sociology, social change, and social justice.* Los Angeles: Sage.

Lewis, T. L. (2004). Service learning for social change? Lessons from a liberal arts college. *Teaching Sociology, 32*(1), 84–108. https://doi.org/10.1177/0092055X0403200109

Light, P. (2011). *Driving social change: How to solve the world's toughest problems.* Hoboken, NJ: John C. Wiley & Sons.

Mitchell, T. D. (2008). Traditional vs. critical service-learning: Engaging the literature to differentiate two models. *Michigan Journal of Community Service Learning, 14*(2), 50–65.

Saltmarsh, J. (2005). The civic promise of service learning. *Liberal Education, 91*(2), 50–55.

Author

LANE GRAVES PERRY, III (laneperry@wcu.edu) currently serves as the director of the Center for Service Learning and is an affiliated faculty member of the Human Services Department (College of Education) at Western Carolina University (WCU). Lane completed his Bachelors of Business Administration and Masters of Adult Education and Leadership at the University of Central Oklahoma and his Doctor of Philosophy in Higher Education degree at the University of Canterbury in Christchurch, New Zealand. Lane has presented and published extensively in the fields of community engagement, service-learning, global citizenship, and pedagogical approaches to disaster response. He served as a board member of the International Association for Research on Service Learning & Community Engagement (2013–2016), as well as a peer reviewer for seven journals and an editorial board member of one. Most recently he has been recognized as the 2015 North Carolina Campus Compact Civic Engagement Professional of the Year and the 2015 co-recipient of the John Saltmarsh Award for Emerging Leaders in Civic Engagement.

Reviewers – Volume 23

Nora Bacon	*University of Nebraska Omaha*
Rick Battistoni	*Providence College*
Robert Bringle	*Indiana University Purdue University at Indianpolis*
Susan Cashman	*University of Massachusetts*
Beth Catlett	*DePaul University*
Patti Clayton	*PHC Ventures*
David Cooper	*Michigan State University*
Thomas Deans	*University of Connecticut*
Lina Dostilio	*Duquesne University*
Michelle Dunlap	*Connecticut College*
Thomas Ehrlich	*Stanford University*
Sandra Enos	*Bryant University*
Joseph Erickson	*Augsburg College*
Janet Eyler	*Vanderbilt University*
Peter Felton	*Elon University*
Jessica Fogel	*University of Michigan*
Andy Furco	*University of Minnesota*
Sherril Gelmon	*Portland State University*
David Greene	*Colorado State University*
Thomas Hahn	*Indiana University Purdue University at Indianapolis*
Susan Harris	*University of Southern California*
Eric Hartman	*Kansas State University*
Julie Hatcher	*Indiana University Purdue University at Indianapolis*
Barbara Holland	*Independent Consultant*
Barbara Jacoby	*University of Maryland*
Rob Jagers	*University of Michigan*
Emily Janke	*University of North Carolina Greensboro*
Susan Jones	*The Ohio State University*
Cathy Jordan	*University of Minnesota*
Joseph Kahne	*Mills College*
Richard Kendrick	*SUNY - Cortland*
Cheryl Keen	*Walden University*
Arthur Keene	*University of Massachusetts Amherst*
Novella Keith	*Temple University*
Darcy Lear	*Independent Scholar*
Kelly Lockeman	*Virginia Commonwealth University*
Kathleen Maas Weigert	*Loyola University Chicago*
Clark Maddux	*Appalachian State University*
Sam Marullo	*Wesley Seminary*
Katerhine Mead	*Independent Scholar*
Ellen Middaugh	*San Jose State University*
A.T. Miller	*Cornell University*
Jerry Miller	*University of Michigan*
Tania Mitchell	*University of Minnesota*
Barbara Moely	*Tulane University*
David Moore	*New York University*
Keith Morton	*Providence College*
Kerry Ann O'Meara	*University of Maryland*
Andrew Pearl	*University of North Georgia*
Lane Perry	*Western Carolina University*
Kenneth Reardon	*Memphis University*
Roger Reeb	*University of Dayton*
Nora Pillard Reynolds	*Temple University*
John Saltmarsh	*University of Massachusetts Boston*
Lorilee Sandmann	*University of Georgia*
Rob Shumer	*University of Minnesota*
Timothy Stanton	*Stanford University*
Randy Stoecker	*University of Wisconsin*
Robert Swap	*University of Virginia*
Kelly Ward	*Washington State University*
Kathleen Maas Weigert	*Loyola University Chicago*
Edward Zlotkowski	*Bentley University*

Michigan Journal of Community Service Learning
VOLUME 24 – FALL 2017/SPRING 2018

CALL FOR PAPERS

Goals

To widen the community of community engagement educators and scholars

To sustain the intellectual vigor of those in this community

To encourage research and pedagogical scholarship on community engagement

To contribute to the academic legitimacy of service-learning and community-engaged scholarship

To increase the number of students and scholars who have a chance to experience the rich benefits that accrue from community engagement

Seeks

papers on research, theory, pedagogy, and other matters relevant to community engagement in higher education that:

- pertain to the development, implementation, and refinement of academic service-learning, campus-community partnerships, or engaged scholarship
- extend the knowledge base for community engagement
- support and increase the sophistication of practitioners' work
- go beyond description to critical analysis

MANUSCRIPT REVIEW PROCESS

1. A one-page abstract or précis is due by December 20, 2016 by e-mail, fax, or mail. Invitations to submit a complete paper will be e-mailed in January.
2. Complete papers are due the last Monday in March. To insure that we are able to return your paper when reviews are completed, please include in the cover letter your mail address and e-mail address for the months of June, July, and August.
3. Papers will be returned with peer reviewer comments in July/August.
4. Accepted papers needing additional author attention will be due back to the editor by mid-August to mid-September.
5. Authors of accepted papers will receive a complimentary copy of the Journal.

Jeffrey Howard, Editor
MJCSL • University of Michigan
1024 Hill Street • Ann Arbor, MI 48109-3310
jphoward@umich.edu

PAPER GUIDELINES

- Avoid the use of "volunteer" or "voluntary." "Community service," "service-learning," or "community service learning" are preferable.

- Manuscripts must be well written and of appropriate length for a journal article using Times New Roman 12 pt. font.

- Submit an electronic copy only (no hard copies) by the last Monday in March to the editor, Jeffrey Howard, at jphoward@umich.edu. Include a title page with author(s)' names and an end page with author bios so that we can easily separate these two pages for blinding purposes. Also, please replace any identifying information in the body of the article with XXX (e.g., XXX University, XXX City, etc.) to ensure a blind review process. That information will be inserted by authors upon article acceptance.

- Do not submit manuscripts under consideration by another publication.

- Use APA style, which is contained in *The Publication Manual of the American Psychological Association*, available from Order Department, APA, P.O. Box 2710, Hyattsville, MD 20784. **In particular, please follow APA reference style, both in the text and in the reference list, only include citations in the reference section that are cited in text, and place footnotes at the end of the paper under "Notes" rather than at the bottom of the pages.**

- Place each figure and/or table on a separate page at the end of the text of the paper, and include in the narrative of the manuscript where you would like to place the table or figure (e.g., PLACE FIGURE 1 HERE). Final placement may be influenced by page lay-out requirements.

- Use italics rather than underlines, both in the text and in the references section. We do not use underlines in the MJCSL.

- Where applicable, research data must be recent.

- Include an abstract that is a few sentences in length located between the title and the beginning of the text.

- For consistency throughout the Journal, use "service-learning" with a hyphen or "community service learning" without a hyphen.

- Follow the end of the paper with **Notes** (acknowledgements and/or footnotes which are identified by raised numbers), then **References**, and then **Author** (a few sentences of biographical sketch).

- Contact the Editor if you have any questions.